Dominic
1616 So. 24 ST.
Phila, Penna.

Saint Joseph's College
54th City Line Ave.
Overbrook Pa.

Do

DOMINIC SOPHOMORE

Do
D
T BRUNO

Dominic
Bruno

New
French Review Grammar
and Composition

New French Review Grammar and Composition

By

FRANCIS BROWN BARTON

and

EDWARD HINMAN SIRICH

University of Minnesota

⚜

1937

F. S. CROFTS & CO.

New York

COPYRIGHT, 1933, BY F. S. CROFTS & CO., INC.

First printing, January, 1933
Second printing, July, 1933
Third printing, September, 1933
Fourth printing, October, 1933
Fifth printing, September, 1934
Sixth printing, July, 1936
Seventh printing, September, 1937
Eighth printing, November, 1937

ALL RIGHTS RESERVED
NO PART OF THE MATERIAL COVERED BY THIS COPYRIGHT
MAY BE REPRODUCED IN ANY FORM WITHOUT PERMISSION
IN WRITING FROM THE PUBLISHER

MANUFACTURED IN THE UNITED STATES OF AMERICA
BY THE VAIL-BALLOU PRESS, INC., BINGHAMTON, N. Y.

To
B. H. B.
AND
M. W. S.

PREFACE

The New French Review Grammar and Composition is not merely a revision of the authors' earlier French Review Grammar and Composition although it may readily be used as an alternate text. The grammatical material in the present book has been considerably altered and the exercises are entirely new.

In this new text, the authors have attempted to provide:

1. a simple presentation of the grammar in all its essentials carefully avoiding unusual or exceptional usage; and in particular a more effective and practical statement of the uses and the avoidance of the subjunctive;

2. extensive and varied exercise material: connected composition largely in dialogue treating of a French milieu, conversational exercises, grammatical and replacement exercises, verb drills, etc. The exercises have been carefully graded and anticipatory material has been reduced to a minimum.

3. a practical vocabulary dealing in general with every day life and lending itself easily to conversational practice.

The authors wish to express their deep appreciation to Professors Edwin C. Byam of the University of Delaware and Paul H. Kennison of the Chauncy Hall School for their many valuable suggestions which are largely incorporated in the present text. Our thanks are also due to Mlle Marguerite Guinotte who has read the completed text in manuscript and has offered many helpful recommendations.

F. B. B.
E. H. S.

Minneapolis.

TABLE OF CONTENTS

PREFACE vii

LESSON I. Articles, forms, use, omission
Prepositions with names of countries and cities
Arrivée à Paris
Verbs: orthographic changes in verbs 3

LESSON II. The partitive construction
Dîner à l'hôtel
Verbs: avoir and être 10

LESSON III. Adjectives: feminine, plural, agreement and position
Anecdote historique
Verbs: aller and envoyer 17

LESSON IV. Adjectives: comparison. Interrogative word order
A la terrasse d'un café
Verbs: vouloir and ouvrir 24

LESSON V. The Present and Future Tenses. Plural of Nouns
Au théâtre
Verbs: croire and dire 31

LESSON VI. Avoir and être as auxiliary verbs
Agreement of past participle
Un nouveau arrive au lycée
Verbs: connaître and savoir 37

LESSON VII. Personal pronouns
Un nouveau arrive au lycée (suite)
Verbs: faire and idioms with 43

LESSON VIII. Negation. Ce and il as subjects of être
Un moment embarrassant
Verbs: mettre and prendre 50

LESSON IX. The Conditional Tenses. Conditional sentence
La Sorbonne
Uses of devoir 57

LESSON X. Past Tenses: imperfect, past definite, past indefinite, pluperfect, past anterior
Voltaire et Fréron
Verb: dormir 63

TABLE OF CONTENTS

LESSON XI. Uses of **falloir, pouvoir, savoir, faire**
Une visite 69

LESSON XII. Demonstrative adjectives and pronouns
Adverbs
A la recherche d'une pension
Verbs: **s'asseoir** and **voir** 75

LESSON XIII. Numerals and dates
Un emprunt
Verbs: **écrire** and **lire** 82

LESSON XIV. Possessive adjectives and pronouns
Expressions of time, dates, age
Une promenade
Verbs: **tenir** and **venir** 89

LESSON XV. Relative pronouns
Moyens de transport
Verbs: **recevoir** and **suivre** 96

LESSON XVI. Interrogative pronouns and adjectives
Le musée Carnavalet
Verbs: **mourir** and **naître** 102

LESSON XVII. Indefinite adjectives and pronouns
Un goûter
Verbs: **conduire** and **vivre** 107

LESSON XVIII. Subjunctive mood: significance, in noun clauses, sequence of tenses
Retour en Amérique
Verbs: **craindre** and **plaire** 114

LESSON XIX. Subjunctive in adjectival and adverbial clauses
Un pique-nique
Verbs: **fuir** and **rire** 121

LESSON XX. Subjunctive in principal clauses. Substitutes for the subjunctive. Present participle
Pasteur
Verbs: **cueillir** and **pleuvoir** 127

LESSON XXI. Infinitive after other verbs, after prepositions, as a noun
Les Martin s'en vont
Verbs: **acquérir** and **courir** 134

APPENDIX. The Verb 143
LIST OF IRREGULAR VERBS 169
VOCABULARY. French-English 173
             English-French 192
INDEX 213

New
French Review Grammar
and Composition

NEW FRENCH REVIEW GRAMMAR AND COMPOSITION

LESSON I

THE ARTICLES. PREPOSITIONS WITH NAMES OF COUNTRIES AND CITIES

THE ARTICLES

1. Forms of the definite and indefinite articles.

	Definite article		Indefinite article
	singular	plural	
Masc.	le, l'	les	un
Fem.	la, l'	les	une

1. **L'** is used before a vowel or **h** mute.
2. The definite article combines with **à** and **de** as follows: à + le = au; à + les = aux; de + le = du; de + les = des. There is no contraction of **à** and **de** with **la** or **l'**.

Le livre du garçon.	The boy's book.
Les amis des professeurs.	The professors' friends.
But: **De l'élève.**	Of the pupil.
A la ville.	To the city.

2. An article agrees in gender and number with the noun it modifies and is repeated before each noun.

Le père et la mère. The father and the mother.

3. The articles are used in general as in English.

4. The definite article is required in French, contrary to English usage:

1. with nouns used in a general sense and with abstract nouns;

L'amour de la patrie.	Love of country.
Les hommes sont mortels.	Men are mortal.

2. with titles preceding a proper name, except in direct address;

Le président Loubet.	President Loubet.
Docteur Martin, mon frère est souffrant aujourd'hui.	Dr. Martin, my brother is sick to-day.

a) The definite article is not required after **monsieur, madame, mademoiselle,** etc., unless they are followed by a title.

Monsieur Faure.	Mr. Faure.
Madame la comtesse de X.	The countess of X.
Monsieur le président.	Mr. President.

3. with names of countries and geographical divisions, except in certain cases after **de** and **en,** noted in §§ 5, 7, 8;

La France est un beau pays.	France is a beautiful country.
Avez-vous visité la Touraine?	Have you visited Touraine?

4. to translate the English *a* or *an* before nouns of weight or measure;

Deux sous la livre.	Two cents a pound.
Vingt francs le mètre.	Twenty francs a metre.

a) But English *a* or *an* before expressions of time are translated by **par.**

Il gagne quinze francs par jour.	He earns fifteen francs a day.

5. with the days of the week, to indicate repeated occurrence;

| Il vient le(s) lundi(s). | He comes Mondays. |
| But: Il vient lundi. | He is coming (next) Monday. |

6. with names of languages, except after **en**. It is usually omitted also after **parler**, immediately followed by the name of a language.

Nous étudions le français.	We are studying French.
Il parle français.	He speaks French.
But: Vous parlez bien le français.	You speak French well.

5. The definite article is generally omitted:

1. after **de** in adjectival phrases and after **en**;

En France. In France.	Une montre en or. A gold watch.
En avril. In April.	Les vins de France. French wines.
En ville. In town.	

2. generally, with nouns in apposition, used parenthetically.

| Paris, capitale de la France, est une ville intéressante. | Paris, the capital of France, is an interesting city. |
| But: Nous sommes à New-York, la plus grande ville des Etats-Unis. | We are in New York, the largest city in the United States. |

6. The indefinite article is omitted in French, contrary to English usage, before an unmodified predicate noun (i.e., être + a noun), indicating profession or nationality. The noun in this case has the force of an adjective.

Il est médecin.	He is a doctor.
Elle est Américaine.	She is an American.
But: C'est[1] un médecin excellent.	He is an excellent doctor.

[1] For the use of ce, cf. §§ 68–70.

Prepositions with Names of Countries and Cities

7. *To, in* and *into* before names of countries and geographical divisions are translated by:

1. **en** without the article before all feminine singular names;

En France.	In France.
En Amérique.	In America.

2. **à** with the definite article before feminine plural names and all masculine names;[1]

Au Canada.	In Canada.
Aux Etats-Unis.	In the United States.
Aux Antilles.	In the West Indies.

3. **dans** with the definite article before all names modified by an adjective or an adjectival phrase.

Dans l'Amérique du Sud.	In South America.
Dans la France méridionale.	In Southern France.

8. *From* before names of countries and geographical divisions is translated by **de** without the article before all feminine singular names; by **de** with the definite article in all other cases.

Il vient d'Amérique.	He comes from America.
Il vient du Mexique.	He comes from Mexico.

9. *To, at* and *in* before names of cities are translated by **à**; *from* is translated by **de**. The definite article is not expressed unless it is an integral part of the name.

Il est à Paris.	He is in Paris.
Elle vient de Londres.	She comes from London.
But: Le Havre, La Havane.	
Au Havre.	In Havre.
De la Havane.	From Havana.

---

[1] Names of countries ending in 'e' are feminine, except **le Mexique**. All others are masculine.

In the case of **le Danemark** and **le Portugal**, **en** without the definite article may also be used.

ARRIVÉE À PARIS

Le rapide venant du Havre vient d'arriver à la gare Saint-Lazare et les voyageurs commencent à descendre des voitures. Jean attend à la sortie des quais son ami Paul qui, parti des Etats-Unis le 12 juin, doit arriver à Paris ce soir-là. Le voilà enfin qui donne son billet au contrôleur. Les deux amis se serrent la main et Jean dit:

—Eh bien! Vous avez fait un bon voyage?

—Epatant! Nous avons eu une traversée superbe avec une escale à Plymouth qui m'a permis de voir la côte d'Angleterre. Mais je suis bien content de quitter ce rapide.

—Pourquoi? Les trains français sont bons et rapides.

—Justement. Celui-là était trop rapide. Nous avons fait du cent dix à l'heure entre Rouen et Paris et je préfère ne pas commencer mon séjour en France par un accident de chemin de fer. J'espère que je ne vous ai pas trop dérangé.

—Au contraire. Je suis toujours libre le lundi après-midi. Mais vous devez être fatigué. J'ai retenu une chambre pour vous à l'Hôtel du Pas-de-Calais où vous trouverez le Docteur Martin et sa fille Agnès. Nous ferions bien d'y aller tout de suite.

On donne les valises à un porteur. Les deux amis traversent le hall de la gare et descendent dans la rue où Jean paye le porteur et appelle un taxi.

—59, rue des Saints-Pères, dit Jean au chauffeur.

—Bien, Monsieur, dit le chauffeur. Et le taxi démarre.

CONVERSATION

1. Qui est-ce que Jean attend? 2. Par quel train arrive-t-il? 3. D'où vient-il? 4. A-t-il fait un bon voyage? 5. A quelle ville le paquebot a-t-il fait escale? 6. Pourquoi Paul est-il content de quitter le rapide? 7. Les rapides français marchent-ils vite? 8. Quel jour de la semaine est-ce que Jean est libre? 9. Où a-t-il retenu une chambre pour Paul? 10. Est-ce que Paul a des amis à Paris? 11. A qui donne-t-on les valises? 12. Qui paye le facteur? 13. Comment est-on allé à l'hôtel?

COMPOSITION

Doctor Martin and I were waiting in the St. Lazare station for the arrival of the express from Havre. We were hoping that our friend Paul, who had left the United States [on] the ninth [1] of June, would arrive by that train. Paul is a Canadian. He lives in Toronto but he always takes the boat at New York because the service between Canada and France is not very good.

"There's the train!" said the Doctor suddenly. The travelers were already beginning to get out of the coaches and we looked eagerly for Paul in the immense crowd of tourists from America who were coming [to] spend the summer in Europe.

"I see him. He has just given his ticket to the gateman. Well, Paul, how goes it? Did you have a pleasant crossing?"

"Excellent, except the two days that [2] I was seasick. How do you do, Doctor Martin? I hope that I have not inconvenienced you. Our train is very late because of an accident at Rouen."

"Oh, not at all. We are always free Friday afternoons. Give your valises to the porter and John will call a taxi. Agnes is waiting for us at the hotel."

"I met a friend of Agnes on the boat, a girl from New England who has just spent a year in South America. She hopes to see Agnes here in Paris."

"I'll pay the porter," said John. "Chauffeur, you will drive us to number 65 rue des Saints-Pères."

DRILL EXERCISE

1. They speak French very well. 2. Do you understand German? 3. They arrived this morning from Canada. 4. Doctor Martin used to earn a hundred francs a day. 5. We are using this book in the French class. 6. Many of our friends land at Havre. 7. His father gave him a gold watch for his birthday. 8. What lessons are we beginning today? 9. French is spoken in Canada. 10. In Switzerland, French and German are spoken. 11. One of my brothers is a doctor; the other is a lawyer. 12. Their parents are now in London. 13. We

---

[1] Cf. § 106.
[2] où.

shall see them in France. 14. Have you ever been in South America? 15. He arrives from Mexico (the) next week. 16. She comes from the United States. 17. I see him in town Mondays. 18. Marshal Foch was an excellent general. 19. She is a French woman; her brother is a superb actor. 20. We pay six cents a pound [for] it. 21. Germany is now a republic.

GRAMMATICAL EXERCISE

Translate into French the words in parentheses:

1. Il vient (from Paris; London; the United States). 2. (In Spain) on parle espagnol. 3. Quand êtes-vous arrivé (in Havre)? 4. Avez-vous jamais visité (Switzerland)? 5. Il a passé ses vacances (in Mexico). 6. (France) est un pays très intéressant. 7. Il vient (Tuesday mornings). 8. Nous lisons très facilement (French). 9. (French wines) ne sont pas très chers. 10. Comprenez-vous (Spanish)? 11. (Doctor Martin) est un très bon médecin. 12. Ils vont arriver (Monday).

VERB REVIEW

Orthographic peculiarities of the first conjugation. Cf. §§ 179–182.

commencer, to commence	jeter, to throw (away)
manger, to eat	appeler, to call
céder, to yield, give up	geler, to freeze
espérer, to hope	payer, to pay, pay for
préférer, to prefer	essayer, to try
acheter, to buy	nettoyer, to clean

1. Marie is cleaning the rooms. 2. I hope that you will pay the porter. 3. Let's begin to translate the sentences. 4. Where were they eating? 5. What is her name? 6. How much does one pay [for] a first-class ticket? 7. They are buying some gifts. 8. John is getting up now. 9. I shall throw this newspaper [away]. 10. It is freezing this morning. 11. I am trying to discover them. 12. We shall call John now. 13. The passengers were beginning to get out of the coaches. 14. What were you buying? 15. She prefers to stay here.

LESSON II

THE PARTITIVE CONSTRUCTION

The Partitive as an Adjective

10. Nouns may be used in two ways: 1) in a general sense, applying to all members of the class named; and 2) in a partitive sense, applying to an indefinite quantity or an indefinite number of the members of the class named.

When a noun is used in a general sense in English, *all, every, each* or *the* is expressed or understood before the noun.

When a noun is used in a partitive sense in English, *some* or *any* (in an affirmative sentence) or *no* or *not any* (in a negative sentence) is expressed or understood before the noun.

(All) automobiles are (The automobile is) a modern convenience.
He has (some) friends everywhere.

11. In the general sense, nouns in French are preceded by the definite article.

Les automobiles ne sont pas très chères.	Automobiles are not very expensive.

12. The partitive as an adjective (i. e., *some* or *any,* expressed or understood, before a noun) is regularly expressed in French by:

1. **de** + the definite article;

Avez-vous des amis à Paris?	Have you (any) friends in Paris?
Il y a de la viande et du pain sur la table.	There is (some) meat and (some) bread on the table.

2. **de** without the definite article:

a) after a general negation;[1]

Nous n'avons pas d'argent.	We have no money.

b) before a noun preceded by an adjective;[2]

Nous avons de bons amis.	We have (some) good friends.
But: Il a des livres français.	He has (some) French books.

c) after nouns and adverbs of quantity, except **bien**, *many*, and **la plupart**, *most*, which are followed by **de** + the definite article.

Une livre de sucre.	A pound of sugar.
Beaucoup d'amis.	Many friends.
But: Bien des amis.	Many friends.
La plupart des élèves.	Most of the pupils.

1) The commonest adverbs of quantity are:

assez, enough	peu, little, few
autant, as much, as many	plus, more
beaucoup, much, many, a lot	tant, so much, so many
combien, how much, how many	trop, too much, too many
moins, less, fewer	un peu, a little

3. by the noun alone:[3]

a) after **ni . . . ni;**

Il n'avait ni amis ni argent.	He had neither friends nor money.

---

[1] **Ne . . . que** (*only*) is followed by **de** + the definite article. **Je n'ai que des livres anglais.** I have only English books.

[2] The use of the definite article in this case is not considered incorrect.

[3] In long enumerations, the use of the article is optional:

Vous trouverez sur ma table (des) crayons, (des) livres, (des) plumes, (de l') encre et (du) papier-buvard.	You will find on my table pencils, books, pens, ink and blotting paper.

b) after **avec** in adverbial phrases and after **sans**;

| J'accepte avec plaisir. | I accept with pleasure (gladly). |
| Un homme sans expérience. | A man without experience. |

c) after verbal expressions and certain adjectival expressions followed by **de**.

Une bourse pleine de monnaie.	A purse full of change.
Il a besoin d'argent.	He needs money.
La terre est couverte de neige.	The ground is covered with snow.

THE PARTITIVE AS A PRONOUN

13. The partitive as a pronoun (i. e., *some* or *any*) is expressed in French by **en**.[1]

Il a de l'argent. Je n'en ai pas.	He has money. I haven't any.
En avez-vous?	Have you any?
J'en ai déjà donné à Jean.	I have already given some to John.

14. *Of it, of them* must be expressed in French by **en** with numerals, adverbs of quantity and nouns of quantity.

Nous en avons six.	We have six (of them).
En avez-vous beaucoup?	Have you many (of them)?
Donnez-m'en une livre.	Give me a pound (of it).

DÎNER À L'HÔTEL

Jean est assis dans le salon de l'hôtel où il feuillette des journaux sans grand intérêt. Paul, qui est monté à sa chambre avec le porteur, a besoin de faire un bout de toilette avant le dîner mais il ne tarde pas à descendre.

—Vous avez raison, dit-il en entrant dans le salon. Cet hôtel est très bien. Il y a l'eau courante dans ma chambre et une salle de bains à côté. Le seul inconvénient, c'est qu'il y a trop d'étages à monter. J'en ai compté quatre.

—C'est vrai. La plupart des petits hôtels du quartier ont un ascen-

---

[1] For the position of **en**, cf. § 54.

seur mais celui-ci n'en a pas. Tant pis. Cela vous donnera de l'appétit.

—J'ai déjà faim, c'est vrai.

—Dans ce cas, allons dîner. A cette heure-ci nous trouverons une table sans difficulté. Mettons-nous là-bas près de la fenêtre et voyons la carte. Vous prendrez un potage sans doute.

—Non, merci. Je n'aime pas le potage. Je choisirai plutôt des hors-d'œuvre.

—Et après? interrompt le garçon. Je vous recommande ce gigot ou bien une côtelette de veau aux épinards. Le rôti de porc est excellent aussi.

—Je ne désire ni mouton ni veau, dit Paul. Vous m'apporterez un entrecôte aux pommes frites et une salade de laitue. N'oubliez pas une bouteille de vin blanc, parce que j'ai bien soif.

—Deux entrecôtes, alors, dit Jean. Et comme dessert, du Brie et des fruits.

Les services se succèdent sans hâte: hors-d'œuvre, grillade, légumes, dessert; et tout en mangeant, les deux jeunes gens font avec enthousiasme des projets pour le séjour de Paul à Paris.

CONVERSATION 3

1. Que fait Jean dans le salon de l'hôtel? 2. Où est Paul? 3. Pourquoi est-il content de sa chambre? 4. Quel est le seul inconvénient de cet hôtel? 5. Y a-t-il beaucoup de monde dans la salle à manger? 6. Où les jeunes gens se sont-ils assis? 7. Ont-ils commandé un potage? 8. Quel plat le garçon leur a-t-il recommandé? 9. Qu'est-ce qu'ils ont commandé comme boisson? 10. Qu'ont-ils pris comme dessert? 11. Qu'est-ce qu'ils ont discuté pendant le repas?

COMPOSITION 4

"Are you hungry, Paul?"

"No. I breakfasted very late. Generally I take only toast and coffee but this morning everything was so good that I ate too much."

"What did you eat?"

"Eggs, toast, marmalade and some excellent coffee. If I lunched now, I should be sleepy all the afternoon. I should like to write some letters first. You can read the newspapers. You will find enough of them in the salon without doubt."

Paul found writing paper and envelopes on the desk in the salon but there was neither pen nor ink.

"Will you lend me your fountain-pen," he said to John. "I left mine in my room. There is no elevator in this hotel and I do not want to climb four floors to get (**chercher**) it. I have so many letters to [1] write that I am almost afraid to begin."

However he wrote four. Then he looked at his watch. It was half past one.

"Let's go into the dining-room now. I am tired and hot. This work has given me an (some) appetite and I need something to eat."

They sit down near a window and look at the bill of fare.

"You don't want any soup, do you?"

"No, I shall take some hors-d'œuvre; then, some leg of lamb, vegetables and perhaps a salad. And you?"

"I don't like lamb. I shall take a steak with fried potatoes."

With their meal, they order red wine as they are very thirsty. Instead of a dessert, they order cheese. While eating, they discuss with enthusiasm plans for their stay in Paris.

DRILL EXERCISE 3.

1. Meals in this hotel are very good, aren't they? 2. Most hotels have elevators. 3. How many days shall you spend here? 4. I hope to spend at least six. 5. He would have needed a lot of time. 6. Do you like to begin dinner with (**par**) hors-d'œuvre? 7. No, I never take either soup or hors-d'œuvre. 8. There was neither bread nor butter on the table. 9. John and Paul have good friends in Paris. 10. What do you wish? I wish cheese and coffee. 11. The waiter has already given John some. 12. With money one can do almost anything. 13. There are too many tourists in Paris in summer. 14. Have you enough time? Yes, I have even too much. 15. Many Americans come to Paris in August. 16. I shall take some meat but I do not want any vegetables. 17. Do you need any money? No, I have some. 18. They have as much as I. 19. Without patience, one can do nothing. 20. He had his pockets full of candy.

[1] Cf. § 162.

GRAMMATICAL EXERCISE

I. Where necessary, replace the dash by the proper form of the definite article or the partitive as adjective:

1. Nous n'avons pas — amis ici. 2. Aimez-vous — bons livres? 3. Il prend toujours — œufs pour le petit déjeuner. 4. Il n'a ni — plumes ni — crayons. 5. Jean a besoin — argent. 6. Je n'aime pas — viande. 7. Il y a — bonne viande sur la table. 8. Beaucoup — touristes viennent à Paris. 9. Il a commandé — pain et — beurre. 10. Je ne prends pas — légumes. 11. Jean a — livres intéressants chez lui. 12. Je ne bois jamais — vin; je ne bois que — lait. 13. Sans — argent, on ne peut rien faire. 14. Très peu — Américains parlent bien le français. 15. Bien — élèves n'étudient pas assez.

II. Insert **en** in the proper place and translate into English:

1. Il a autant que moi. 2. Nous avons six; Jean a huit. 3. Je n'ai pas; Marie a beaucoup. 4. Combien avez-vous? 5. Il n'y avait pas sur la table. 6. Donnez-lui six. 7. Je lui ai déjà envoyé. 8. Ne nous donnez pas trop. 9. Il a plus que vous. 10. Elle n'a pas tant.

VERB REVIEW

être, to be. Cf. § 175
avoir, to have. Cf. § 174
   avoir chaud,[1] to be warm
   avoir froid, to be cold
   avoir faim, to be hungry
   avoir soif, to be thirsty

avoir sommeil, to be sleepy
avoir raison (de), to be right
avoir tort (de), to be wrong
avoir peur (de), to be afraid
avoir honte (de), to be ashamed
avoir besoin de, to have need of

1. He is ashamed to see us again. 2. What do you need? 3. You were wrong to do that. 4. Marie will be afraid to go out alone. 5. You are always right. 6. It is late and I am sleepy. 7. When I am thirsty, I always drink water. 8. He will be very[1] hungry, I am sure of it. 9. They were very cold in that room. 10. I shall be warm in front of the fireplace. 11. I think that he will be afraid to do that.

[1] With these idioms, translate *very* by **bien** (or, for first four, **très**).

12. If I were in (à) your place, I should be ashamed. 13. I do not want you to be afraid of it. 14. He needed (*p. def.*) money last year. 15. We do not wish them to be here. 16. They were (*p. def.*) very sick last year. 17. Let us have patience. 18. If they were not tired, they would not be sleepy. 19. I was cold in the salon. 20. Were you hungry this morning?

LESSON III

ADJECTIVES: FORMATION OF THE FEMININE AND OF THE PLURAL. AGREEMENT. POSITION

FORMATION OF THE FEMININE OF ADJECTIVES

15. The feminine of adjectives is regularly formed by adding -e to the masculine singular. Adjectives ending in -e remain unchanged.

Petit, petite, little
charmé, charmée, delighted

facile, facile, easy

16. Irregular formation of the feminine.

1. Final **-f** becomes **-v**, **-x** becomes **-s**, **-c** becomes **-ch** or **-que** and **-g** becomes **-gu** before the feminine ending **-e** is added.

actif, active, active
heureux, heureuse, happy
blanc, blanche, white

neuf, neuve, (brand) new
public, publique, public
long, longue, long

2. Final **-el, -eil, -ien, -on** and usually **-s** and **-t** double the final consonant before the feminine ending **-e** is added.

cruel, cruelle, cruel
pareil, pareille, like, such
ancien, ancienne, old, former
bon, bonne, good
bas, basse, low

gros, grosse, big
épais, épaisse, thick
sot, sotte, stupid
coquet, coquette, dainty

3. Many adjectives in **-eur** have a feminine in **-euse**. **Meilleur** and adjectives ending in **-érieur** form their feminine regularly.

17

causeur, causeuse, talkative
flatteur, flatteuse, flattering

supérieur, supérieure, superior

4. Five adjectives have a double form in the masculine singular. The form ending in -l is used only before a masculine singular noun beginning with a vowel or **h** mute.

beau, bel, belle, beautiful, fine
nouveau, nouvel, nouvelle, new
vieux, vieil, vieille, old

mou, mol, molle, soft
fou, fol, folle, mad

5. The following adjectives have irregular feminine forms:

cher, chère, dear
complet, complète, complete
doux, douce, sweet
faux, fausse, false

favori, favorite, favorite
frais, fraîche, cool, fresh
sec, sèche, dry

Formation of the Plural of Adjectives

17. The plural of adjectives is regularly formed by adding -s to the singular.

18. Adjectives ending in -s or -x remain unchanged in the plural; those ending in -eau, add -x; those ending in -al, drop this ending and add -aux.

grand (e), grand(e)s, tall, large
beau, beaux, beautiful

heureux, heureux, happy
égal, égaux, equal

Agreement of Adjectives

19. Adjectives agree in number and gender with the noun they modify.

20. An adjective modifying two or more nouns is masculine plural, unless all of the nouns are feminine, in which case it is feminine plural.

Des poésies et des romans intéressants.	Some interesting poems and novels.
Les femmes et les jeunes filles françaises.	The French women and girls.
La petite fille est très jolie.	The little girl is very pretty.

Position of Adjectives

21. There is no invariable rule for the position of adjectives in French. In general, adjectives used in a literal sense, to define or to emphasize, follow their noun; but, when used figuratively or to point out an inherent characteristic, they usually precede.

Une église fameuse.	A famous church.
La fameuse cathédrale de Notre Dame.	The famous cathedral of Notre Dame.
Une porte étroite.	A narrow door.
Une étroite amitié.	A close friendship.

22. The following very common adjectives usually precede the noun they modify:

beau	gros	long	moindre	vilain
bon	jeune	mauvais	petit	
grand	joli	meilleur	vieux	

23. Adjectives indicating nationality, shape, and color and participles used as adjectives generally follow the noun they modify.

Une table carrée.	A square table.
Un livre français.	A French book.
De la craie blanche.	Some white chalk.
But: **Mon meilleur ami.**	My best friend.

24. Two or more adjectives modifying the same noun follow the above rules, unless they are connected by **et,** in which case they both usually follow the noun.

Une jolie petite fille.	A pretty little girl.
Une grande maison verte.	A big green house.
Un jeune homme grand et beau.	A tall and handsome young man.

25. Certain adjectives vary in meaning according to position.

Mon cher ami.	My dear friend.
Un livre cher.	An expensive book.
Un brave homme.	A good man.
Un homme brave.	A brave man.
Un ancien voisin.	A former neighbor.
L'histoire ancienne.	Ancient history.
Un nouveau livre.	A new (another) book.
Un livre nouveau.	A new (recently published) book.
Le pauvre homme.	The poor (wretched) man.
Un homme pauvre.	A poor (indigent) man.

26. Note the position of a predicate adjective in exclamations.

Comme } Que } Marie est jolie!	How pretty Mary is!

ANECDOTE HISTORIQUE

C'était une vieille petite dame aux cheveux blancs, à la voix douce. Elle était française et baronne, mais elle était bonne et elle n'était pas fière. Elle parlait rarement du passé, n'étant pas causeuse; mais ce soir-là, renversée dans sa bergère tapissée de velours ancien, elle évoqua pour nous une scène qu'on ne trouve pas dans les livres d'histoire.

—Nous étions en 1867, l'année de l'Exposition Universelle de Paris. Jeune, élégante et jolie, j'étais allée avec mon mari au bal que Napoléon III donnait en l'honneur des représentants des gouvernements étrangers à Paris. Il se faisait déjà tard et j'étais sur le point de partir, quand ma charmante petite nièce est accourue riante et heureuse. O ma tante, s'est-elle écriée, je me suis tellement divertie ce soir; j'ai dansé avec un si beau cavalier. Et il aime tant la France. "Mademoiselle, m'a-t-il dit, vous avez un grand pays, un beau pays, un pays riche et heureux. J'espère que votre France restera toujours aussi belle, aussi riche, aussi heureuse qu'elle l'est aujourd'hui."

—Et votre beau cavalier qui aime tant la France, comment s'appelle-t-il?

La voix fraîche articula alors ce nom que toute l'Europe devait bientôt connaître:

"Le Prince de Bismarck."

CONVERSATION

1. Qui a raconté cette histoire? 2. A quelle classe de la société appartenait-elle? 3. Où était-elle assise? 4. En quelle année l'Exposition Universelle a-t-elle eu lieu? 5. Qui a donné un bal à cette occasion? 6. Qui a-t-on invité à ce bal? 7. Avec qui la baronne y est-elle allée? 8. A quel moment y a-t-elle vu sa nièce? 9. Pourquoi sa nièce s'était-elle beaucoup amusée? 10. Comment savait-elle que son cavalier aimait la France? 11. Comment s'appelait ce monsieur? 12. De quel pays était-il? 13. Comment s'est-il distingué plus tard?

COMPOSITION

Among the guests at a ball given by Napoleon III during the World's Exposition of 1867 was the representative of a German state. He was a prince who was to become, in the short space of four years, one of the great men of Europe, but who was then neither well-known nor famous. He was, however, an elegant dancer and an interesting talker and the charming young French girl with whom he danced many times was delighted with her handsome partner. The prince, too, enjoyed himself very much and at the end of a long evening he said:

"Mademoiselle, I am carrying away with me a very pleasant memory of you and of your country. France is a great and beautiful country, where everyone is happy. I sincerely hope that it will always remain great and rich and happy as it is (it) today."

"Ah Monsieur, you are very kind. But may I ask you to tell me your name? I cannot remember the names of all the distinguished foreigners whom I have met this evening. You who love our France, you will pardon me, will you not?"

"Certainly, Mademoiselle. I am the Prince of Bismarck."

DRILL EXERCISE

1. Your cousin is an amusing little girl. 2. Mary is my favorite friend. 3. Two old gentlemen were seated in the park. 4. My dear friend Doctor Martin is an excellent doctor. 5. Give me some white chalk and I shall write the French words. 6. A tall and handsome foreigner entered the room. 7. The teacher was standing behind a large round table. 8. An active life is always interesting. 9. One always listens with interest [to] flattering words. 10. We saw there some charming paintings and art objects. 11. He did not offer the slightest excuse. 12. Everyone visits the famous church of St. Denis. 13. How interesting is the study of French! 14. We had a short and dry summer. 15. An ugly old woman entered the park. 16. The letters he writes are brief but interesting.

GRAMMATICAL EXERCISE

Translate the adjectives given in English and place them in proper position with respect to the noun opposite. Insert the conjunction **et** if necessary.

1. **Les femmes**	charming, talkative
2. **Les feuilles**	dry, dead
3. **Une histoire**	brief, complete
4. **Une table**	long, square
5. **Une amie**	small, pretty
6. **Une dame**	French, charming
7. **Une jeune fille**	beautiful, intelligent
8. **Les enfants**	pretty, young
9. **Les peintures**	new, German
10. **Les yeux**	beautiful, brown
11. **Un chapeau**	old, gray
12. **Mes voisins**	former, French
13. **Mes amies**	best, American
14. **Un complet**	blue, good-looking
15. **Un arbre**	green, beautiful

VERB REVIEW

aller, to go. Cf. § 183.
  s'en aller, to go away
envoyer, to send. Cf. § 184.
  envoyer chercher, to send for

1. Where are you going? 2. Who sent for us? 3. They were going to the theatre. 4. He will send you some. 5. He wants us to go away. 6. I would go with you, if you sent for me. 7. Don't go away yet. 8. Send for them. 9. We are sending them seven. 10. We shall go with you tomorrow. 11. He went away (*p. def.*). 12. He sent her flowers every day. 13. He would send them, if he had them. 14. They do not want us to send for them. 15. We sent (*p. def.*) the book to him.

LESSON IV

THE COMPARISON OF ADJECTIVES. INTERROGATIVE WORD ORDER

The Comparison of Adjectives

27. The comparative of an adjective is regularly formed by placing **plus,** *more;* **moins,** *less;* **aussi,** *so, as,* before the adjective and **que,** *than, as,* after the adjective.[1]

Il est plus (moins, aussi) grand que moi.	He is taller than (not so tall, just as tall as) I am.
Il est plus riche que je ne [2] le pensais.	He is richer than I thought.

1. **Si** usually replaces **aussi** after a negative.

Jean n'est pas si fort en français que sa sœur.	John is not so good in French as his sister.

28. The superlative of an adjective is regularly formed by placing the proper form of the definite article before the comparative form. If the adjective follows the noun, as it commonly does when modified by **plus,** the definite article as a sign of the superlative must not be omitted.

La pièce la plus intéressante de l'année.	The most interesting play of the year.
La plus belle ville du monde.	The most beautiful city in the world.

---

[1] Before an infinitive, *than* is usually translated by **que de:**

Il est plus facile de lire le français que de le parler.	It is easier to read French than to speak it.

[2] For this use of **ne,** cf. § 67. For the translation of *more than* + a numeral, cf. § 96.

1. After a possessive adjective, the article is omitted, if the adjective precedes its noun.

Mes plus chers amis.	My dearest friends.
But: Mes livres les plus chers.	My most precious books.

2. *In* after a superlative is usually translated by **de**.

Le meilleur élève de la classe.	The best student in the class.

29. The following adjectives are irregularly compared:

bon, good	meilleur, better	le meilleur, best
mauvais, bad	plus mauvais, pire, } worse	le plus mauvais, le pire, } worst
petit, small	plus petit, smaller	le plus petit, smallest
	moindre, less	le moindre, least

Note: **pire** is generally stronger than **plus mauvais** and may mean *harmful* or *evil*.

Le plus mauvais élève de la classe.	The poorest student in the class.
Un criminel de la pire espèce.	A criminal of the worst sort.
De deux maux, choisissons le moindre.	Of two evils, let us choose the lesser.
Marie est plus petite que vous.	Mary is smaller than you are.

Interrogative Word Order

30. Subject pronouns (also **ce** and **on**) follow the verb, as in English, and are joined to it by a hyphen.

Sait-il votre adresse?	Does he know your address?

31. Subject nouns (or possessive, demonstrative or indefinite pronouns) stand before the verb and are repeated after it by the suitable conjunctive pronouns.

Vos parents demeurent-ils ici?	Do your parents live here?
Cela est-il vrai?	Is that true?

32. After certain interrogative expressions such as **qui, que, quel, combien, comment, où,** etc., noun subjects frequently follow the verb, except in compound tenses, when the position before the verb is preferable.

Où sont vos livres ?	Where are your books ?
Comment s'appelle ce monsieur ?	What is that gentleman's name ?
Comment ce monsieur s'appelle-t-il ?	
Quand Molière a-t-il écrit l'Avare ?	When did Molière write l'Avare ?

33. Est-ce que, *is it that;* **n'est-ce pas que,** *is it not that,* placed before or **n'est-ce pas,** *is it not so,* placed after any declarative sentence form a question without changing the word order. **Est-ce que** followed by the declarative word order may also be used after the interrogative expressions **qui, combien, où,** etc.

Est-ce que Joseph les lui a donnés ?	Did Joseph give them to him ?
Joseph les lui a donnés, n'est-ce pas ?	Joseph gave them to him, didn't he ?
N'est-ce pas que Joseph les lui a donnés ?	Didn't Joseph give them to him ?
Combien est-ce que vous avez payé ces livres ?	How much did you pay for these books ?

34. The interrogative order is also used in explanatory statements after direct quotations and frequently after the adverbs **aussi,** *so, therefore;* **peut-être** and **à peine.**

—Prenons un autobus, dit Marie.	"Let's take a bus," said Mary.
Peut-être a-t-il oublié son billet.	Perhaps he has forgotten his ticket.
But: Il a peut-être oublié son billet.	He has perhaps forgotten his ticket.

A LA TERRASSE D'UN CAFÉ

Après le dîner, les jeunes gens entrèrent dans le salon de l'hôtel pour jeter un coup d'œil sur les journaux du soir. Ils y découvrirent M. Martin et sa fille qui avaient passé la journée à Chantilly, où se trouve un des plus beaux châteaux de la région parisienne. M. Martin proposa tout de suite d'aller prendre le café à la terrasse d'un grand café.

—Ce sera plus intéressant, dit-il, que de rester ici et vous verrez un des endroits les plus caractéristiques de Paris. Il y a une station du Métro à deux pas d'ici.

—Prenons plutôt un autobus, dit Agnès. En été le Métro est le pire des moyens de transport. La chaleur y est insupportable.

—Je veux bien, répondit M. Martin. Agnès m'en veut déjà parce que je n'ai pas voulu prendre un taxi pour revenir de la gare cette après-midi.

On trouva facilement un autobus qui n'était pas complet et un quart d'heure plus tard, on descendit devant le café de la Régence.

—Eh bien, qu'est-ce qu'on prend? demanda M. Martin, quand tout le monde fut installé à la terrasse. C'est moi qui offre les consommations.

—Trouve-t-on de bonnes glaces à Paris? demanda Agnès. Je suis très difficile, vous savez.

—Les meilleures du monde, répondit Jean. On a tous les parfums mais les portions ne sont pas si généreuses que chez nous.

—Une glace au chocolat alors pour Mademoiselle, dit le garçon. Et pour ces messieurs?

—Un bock brune[1] pour moi, dit Jean. Et pour vous, Paul?

—Un demi blonde.

M. Martin commanda un sirop de groseille avec de la glace.

—Deux bières, une glace et un sirop, observa Paul en souriant. Voilà une façon bien américaine de prendre le café.

CONVERSATION

1. Où est-ce que les jeunes gens ont découvert les Martin? 2. Où les Martin avaient-ils passé la journée? 3. Qu'est-ce que c'est que

---

[1] i. e., **un bock de bière brune.**

Chantilly? 4. Où a-t-on décidé de passer la soirée? 5. Comment y est-on allé? 6. Pourquoi n'a-t-on pas pris le Métro? 7. A quel café est-on allé? 8. Qu'est-ce que c'est que la terrasse d'un café? 9. Qui a offert de payer les consommations? 10. Qu'est-ce qu'Agnès a commandé? 11. Est-ce que les glaces sont bonnes à Paris? 12. Lequel des messieurs a commandé du café?

COMPOSITION

John, Paul and Mr. Martin are seated on the terrace of a café after having dined at the hotel. Mr. Martin has invited the two young people to have coffee with him and he has chosen one of the most characteristic of Parisian cafés where you have one of the best views of the Avenue de l'Opéra.

Paul: It is very nice here. We can hear the orchestra inside and watch the people strolling in the street and looking in the shop windows. Street life is as interesting for me as the theatre.

John: Yes, I like this café better than the noisier cafés of the boulevards.

Mr. Martin: Waiter!

Waiter: Yes, sir. What do the (**ces**) gentlemen wish?

Mr. Martin: What are you going to take, Paul? And you, John?

Paul: I'll take coffee. Do they have ice cream (*pl.*) here?

Mr. Martin: All flavors. You won't find better ice cream in Paris. John, do you wish (an) ice cream too?

John: No thank you. And I hope you will not be put out with me, if I do not take coffee either. Coffee prevents me from sleeping, if I take it [in] the evening. I'll take some beer.

Mr. Martin: Beer is really better for the health than coffee. I recommend the dark beer here. Paul, won't you change your mind? I don't know whether you like our black coffee.

Paul: I haven't the slightest desire to drink beer now and I have drunk coffee much worse than French coffee.

Mr. Martin: Very well. As for me, I shall take a currant syrup with charged water. Don't laugh. That drink is not as bad as you think (it).

Waiter: Good. A coffee, an ice cream, a dark beer and a currant syrup.

DRILL EXERCISE I

1. John is more intelligent than you think. 2. Here is the most interesting story of Maupassant. 3. My dearest friend and my favorite cousin (*f.*) will be here. 4. Mary is not so small as Jane. 5. Your least desires are for him commands. 6. I would rather keep it than to give it to John. 7. I am always put out with flatterers. 8. He has perhaps forgotten the most amusing details. 9. Paul did not lend them his most expensive books. 10. John and Mary are the best students in the class.

DRILL EXERCISE II

1. Where did John find this good-looking cravat? 2. Have you ever made a worse crossing? 3. How much did she pay for them? 4. Are not the taxis more expensive here than in Paris? 5. What better aperitive will you offer us? 6. What was that gentleman's name? 7. Are these flowers fresher? 8. When did John and Mary arrive? 9. You gave them to John, didn't you? 10. Where do you find better ice cream than here?

GRAMMATICAL EXERCISE

Translate the English word or words and place in proper position with respect to the French phrase:

1. Les jeunes filles	best looking
2. Mes cousines	youngest
3. Les cadeaux	most expensive
4. Les détails	least
5. Mon frère	smaller
6. Le livre	more interesting
7. L'histoire	most complete
8. Le dîner	best
9. La vue	finest
10. Ma cravate	oldest
11. Mes amies	dearest
12. Les petites filles	happiest

VERB REVIEW

vouloir, to wish. Cf. § 229.
    en vouloir à, to be angry with, have a grudge against, be put out with
    vouloir bien, to be willing to, to be kind enough to
ouvrir, to open. Cf. § 192.
    couvrir, to cover
    découvrir, to discover
    offrir, to offer
    souffrir, to suffer

1. What did he offer you? 2. He opened (*p. def.*) the door. 3. I hope that you are not put out with me. 4. He did not want to stay here. 5. Will you be kind enough to give this book to John? 6. The ground was covered with leaves. 7. Columbus discovered (*p. def.*) America in 1492. 8. He was suffering a great deal yesterday. 9. I opened the window. 10. I should like very much to go with you. 11. I did not want to do it. 12. They want us to offer you this present. 13. We are afraid that he does not wish any. 14. What did he want? 15. If you should offer him that, he would be put out with you.

LESSON V

THE PRESENT AND FUTURE TENSES. THE PLURAL OF NOUNS

The Present Tense

35. The present tense is used in general as in English. It translates all three forms of the English present tense.

| Il travaille. | He works (does work) (is working). |

36. The present tense is used in French with **depuis, depuis quand, depuis que** and **il y a ... que**,[1] to denote an act or a state that began in the past and is still going on. English usage here requires the present perfect.

Depuis quand êtes-vous ici?	How long have you been here?
Il y a trois jours qu'il est ici. } Il est ici depuis trois jours. }	He has been here for three days.
Depuis que je suis ici, je n'ai vu personne.	Since I have been here, I have seen no one.

The Future and Future Perfect Tenses

37. The future and future perfect tenses are used in general as in English.

38. The future and future perfect tenses are used, however, in French to translate the English present and perfect tenses after such conjunctions as **lorsque**, *when,* **quand**, *when,* **aussitôt que**, *as soon as* and **dès que**, *as soon as,* when futurity is implied.

---
[1] **voici ... que** and **voilà ... que** may be used in place of **il y a ... que**. For use in negative sentences see § 66, 2.

Je le lui donnerai, quand je le verrai.
I shall give it to him, when I see him.
Quand je l'aurai acheté, je vous l'enverrai.
When I have bought it, I will send it to you.
Dites-lui de venir me voir, aussitôt que vous le trouverez.
Tell him to come and see me, as soon as you find him.

Note: When futurity is implied, the verb in the main clause of the English sentence is in the future tense or is an imperative. *When* in the sense of *whenever* does not imply futurity but refers to an habitual act. In such clauses, **lorsque** and **quand** are used in French with the present tense.

Je le vois tous les jours quand je suis à l'université.
I see him every day, when (ever) I am at the university.

39. *Will* denoting volition and not futurity, that is, when it implies willingness or unwillingness, is rendered in French by the proper tense of **vouloir**.

Il ne veut pas venir.	He will not (does not want to) come.
Il ne voudra pas venir.	He will not (be willing to, wish to) come.

The Plural of Nouns

40. The plural of nouns is regularly formed by adding **s** to the singular.

41. Irregular plurals.

1. Nouns in **s, x** and **z** remain unchanged in the plural.

   le bras, les bras, the arm(s)
   la voix, les voix, the voice(s)
   le nez, les nez, the nose(s)

2. Nouns in **au, eu** and certain nouns in **ou,** add **x** to form the plural.

    le château, les châteaux, the castle(s)
    le jeu, les ieux, the game(s)
    le bijou, les bijoux, the jewel(s)
    But: le sou, les sous, the cent(s)

3. Most nouns in **al** change **al** to **au** and add **x**.

    le cheval, les chevaux, the horse(s)
    le journal, les journaux, the newspaper(s)
    But: le bal, les bals, the dance(s)

4. Certain nouns in **ail** have a plural in **aux**.

    le travail, les travaux, the work(s)
    le vitrail, les vitraux, the stained glass window(s)

5. Note the following irregular plurals:

    le ciel, les cieux, the sky (skies)
    l'œil, les yeux, the eye(s)
    l'aïeul, the grandfather, les aïeux, the ancestors, les aïeuls, the grandfathers

42. The plural of compound nouns.

Unhyphenated compound nouns are treated as a single noun. In the case of hyphenated compound nouns, usage varies according to their formation. The following common nouns should be noted.

    la grand'mère, les grand'mères, the grandmother(s)
    le grand-père, les grands-pères, the grandfather(s)
    le chef-d'œuvre, les chefs-d'œuvre, the masterpiece(s)
    le (les) cure-dents, the toothpick(s)
    le (les) tête-à-tête, the private interview(s)

43. Plural of proper names.

Names of persons and families are generally not pluralized.

    Les Duval, the Duvals.

AU THÉÂTRE

—Voilà huit jours que je suis à Paris et je ne suis pas encore allé au théâtre. Quand pourrons-nous y aller?

—Quand vous voudrez. On donne justement ce soir à l'Odéon une pièce dont les journaux disent beaucoup de bien. Quand je vais au théâtre, j'aime à m'amuser et je crois que cette comédie sera tordante. D'ordinaire, je prends mes places en location mais je veux bien faire la queue cette fois-ci. Peut-être que les Martin voudront nous accompagner.

—Je ne le crois pas. Ils sont sortis tous les soirs depuis dimanche et ils vont se coucher de bonne heure. Attendez-moi un petit moment. Aussitôt que j'aurai pris mon chapeau, je vous retrouverai ici.

—Nous avons le temps. Il n'y aura pas beaucoup de monde en cette saison et nous aurons facilement de bonnes places.

En effet, Jean put prendre deux fauteuils au troisième rang de l'orchestre. Il présenta les billets au contrôleur qui lui en rendit les talons. Ils entrèrent alors dans la salle, après avoir laissé leurs chapeaux et leurs pardessus au vestiaire. Une ouvreuse leur montra leurs places et leur offrit un programme. Jean paya le programme deux francs cinquante et donna un franc de pourboire à l'ouvreuse. Le rideau se leva aussitôt.

Pendant les entr'actes, des vendeuses circulèrent dans la salle offrant des bonbons et des "Esquimaux," mais la plupart des spectateurs se rendirent au foyer où ils se promenèrent avec des amis ou bien ils allèrent dans le buffet prendre une consommation.

Le spectacle se termina à minuit moins cinq et nos deux amis regagnèrent leur hôtel, en suivant à pied les vieilles rues du Quartier Latin.

CONVERSATION

1. Depuis quand êtes-vous à Paris? 2. Qu'est-ce qu'on donne ce soir à l'Odéon? 3. Où prenez-vous des places ordinairement? 4. Croyez-vous que les Martin vous accompagneront? 5. Quelles places avez-vous prises? 6. Où laisse-t-on les chapeaux et les pardessus? 7. Qu'est-ce que c'est qu'une ouvreuse? 8. Que fait-on pendant les entr'actes? 9. A quelle heure se termine le spectacle? 10. Quelle route ont-ils suivie pour regagner l'hôtel?

COMPOSITION

"Hello, John. I have been looking for you since this morning. I want to ask you for some information about the theatres. I am going to the Opera tomorrow evening to hear 'Faust,' one of Gounod's masterpieces. I know that you will not want to go (to it), for you don't like music and I shall invite Agnes to accompany me. But where do I get tickets?"

"Well! I'll tell you (it). You must get your tickets at the Opera. When you enter the lobby, you will see a ticket window marked 'Location.' It is there that you can get reserved seats. I advise you to get orchestra seats. You will hear better and see more people. When you enter the theatre tomorrow evening, you will go to the cloak-room where you will leave Agnes' wrap and your coat and hat. Then an usher will conduct you to your seats."

"Shall I give the usher a tip?"

"Yes. You will give her a franc. You will also buy your programs from (à) the usher. During the intermissions almost everyone goes to the lobby. There you will see Parisian society (**le beau monde**) and also a lot of Americans. When you hear a bell ring,[1] you will know that the curtain is going to rise for the next act. Next week, if you wish, we shall go together to the Théâtre Français."

"That will interest me immensely. I have been in Paris for two weeks and I haven't gone to the theatre yet. Au revoir and thank [you] for the information."

"Not at all.[2] I hope that the performance will please you."

DRILL EXERCISE

1. How long have you had those horses? 2. We shall tell him that, when we see him. 3. I have been very busy since the arrival of the Martins. 4. Corneille wrote many masterpieces. 5. Tell him to come to see me, as soon as you have seen him. 6. I see John every day, when I am in town. 7. Her eyes are very beautiful. 8. The châteaux of Touraine are famous. 9. We have been in Paris for a week. 10. My two grandmothers live with us. 11. I shall believe it,

---

[1] entendre la sonnerie.
[2] Il n'y a pas de quoi.

when I see it. 12. Our ancestors came from Germany. 13. I invited him to accompany us but he will not come. 14. Since the weather has been cold, I stay at home. 15. He has been standing in line for an hour.

GRAMMATICAL EXERCISE

Replace the words in parentheses by the proper French word or words:

1. Je l'ai vue quand je (*arriver*). 2. Aussitôt qu'il nous (*voir*), il partira. 3. Depuis quand est-ce que Jean (*étudier*) le français? 4. Les (*horses*) font les (*work*) de la ferme. 5. Les (*newspapers*) de cette ville sont très mauvais. 6. Après trois (*private interviews*), ils se sont séparés. 7. Avez-vous vu les (*stained glass windows*) de Notre Dame? 8. Dès que Marie (*partir*), je vous dirai ce qu'elle a dit. 9. Il y a trois semaines que nous (*être*) à Paris. 10. Faites-le entrer quand il (*arriver*).

VERB REVIEW

croire, to believe, think. Cf. § 204.
dire, to say, tell. Cf. § 205.

1. I do not wish you to tell him that. 2. Do you believe it? 3. If you said that to John, he would not believe it. 4. We shall tell you what he says. 5. Shall I believe him? 6. Don't believe that. 7. Tell him that I desire it. 8. He is afraid that you may believe us. 9. We did not tell him that you did not believe him. 10. I used to believe everything. 11. I would tell him (it), if I were in (à) your place. 12. He believed (*p. def.*) what they said to him. 13. He used to say that he believed what he saw in the newspapers.

LESSON VI

AVOIR AND ETRE AS AUXILIARY VERBS. REFLEXIVES. THE AGREEMENT OF PAST PARTICIPLES

Avoir AND Etre AS AUXILIARY VERBS

44. Avoir is used to form the compound tenses of all transitive verbs and most intransitive verbs.

45. Etre is used as the auxiliary with 1) the passive, as in English; 2) all reflexive verbs, and 3) some intransitive verbs.

46. The most common intransitive verbs conjugated with être are:

1. mourir, to die
   naître, to be born
   rester, to remain

2. The following intransitive verbs indicating a change of condition or motion, but not stating the kind of motion:[1]

aller, to go
descendre, to descend
devenir, to become
entrer, to enter
monter, to go up
partir, to go away

rentrer, to reënter, go home
retourner, to return, go back
revenir, to come back
sortir, to go out
tomber, to fall
venir, to come

But: The transitive verbs **monter**, *to carry up;* **descendre**, *to carry down;* **entrer**, *to carry in* and **sortir**, *to take out* are conjugated with **avoir**.

[1] Intransitive verbs which state the *kind of motion* such as **courir, marcher, voler**, etc., are conjugated with **avoir**. **Monter** and **descendre** are also conjugated with **avoir** in such sentences as: **Elle a descendu la rue** and **Il a monté l'escalier**.

Napoléon est mort à Ste Hélène.	Napoleon died at St. Helena.
Elles sont arrivées il y a une heure	They arrived an hour ago.
Elle est montée à sa chambre.	She went up to her room.
But: Le concierge a monté les malles.	The janitor carried up the trunks.

Reflexive Verbs

47. Reflexive verbs are verbs in which the object pronoun of the verb (whether direct or indirect) refers to the same person or thing as the subject. All transitive verbs may become reflexive, in which case they are conjugated with **être**.

Elle a bien amusé les enfants.	She amused the children well.
Elle s'est bien amusée.	She had a good time.
Elles ne s'étaient rien dit.	They had not said anything to each other.
Nous nous sommes parlé un instant.	We spoke to each other a moment.

48. The passive voice is formed in French, as in English, with **être** + the past participle of a transitive verb. The agent is usually denoted by **par,** in the case of a specific act; by **de,** when the action is habitual or when it represents a condition or an emotion.

Jean a été accompagné par son ami.	John was accompanied by his friend.
Elle est toujours accompagnée de sa mère.	She is always accompanied by her mother.
Il est aimé de tout le monde.	He is liked by everyone.

49. The passive voice is used less frequently in French than in English. When the agent is not expressed, the passive is often replaced by:

1. an active verb with the indefinite pronoun **on;**

On vend des timbres ici.	Stamps are sold here.
On m'a volé.	I have been robbed.

2. a reflexive construction.

Cela se dit souvent.	That is often said.
La sténographie s'apprend facilement.	Stenography is easily learned.

The Agreement of Past Participles

50. Past participles of intransitive verbs conjugated with **être** and of verbs in the passive voice agree with the subject in gender and number. Past participles of intransitive verbs conjugated with **avoir** are invariable.

Marie est sortie à trois heures.	Mary went out at three o'clock.
Ces cravates ont été choisies avec soin.	These neckties were chosen with care.
But: Nous avons marché très vite.	We walked very fast.

51. Past participles of all reflexive verbs (auxiliary, **être**) and of all transitive verbs (auxiliary, **avoir**) agree in gender and number with a preceding direct object. If there is no preceding direct object, the past participle is invariable. The past participle never agrees with **en**, whatever the antecedent of **en** may be.

Voici les fleurs que nous avons achetées.	Here are the flowers we bought.
Elle s' (*direct object*) est blessée sérieusement	She injured herself seriously.
Elle s' (*indirect object*) est fait mal.	She hurt herself.
Je vous ai rendu votre argent.	I gave you back your money.
Il en a acheté.	He bought some.

UN NOUVEAU ARRIVE AU LYCÉE

Nous étions dans la classe de latin quand le proviseur est entré suivi par un nouveau. Ceux qui dormaient se sont réveillés et tous se sont levés. Le proviseur nous a fait signe de nous rasseoir, puis se tournant vers le professeur, il lui a présenté un garçon d'une quinzaine d'années qui tenait à la main une casquette démodée et ridicule. Le proviseur est sorti et le nouveau, qui avait l'air très embarrassé, s'est assis sur un banc tenant sa casquette sur ses genoux.

—Levez-vous, lui a dit le professeur.

Le nouveau s'est levé, sa casquette est tombée. Toute la classe s'est mise à rire.

Il s'est baissé pour la reprendre mais un voisin l'a fait tomber de nouveau.

—Débarrassez-vous donc de votre casquette, a dit le professeur.

Un éclat de rire a déconcentané le pauvre garçon. Il ne savait pas s'il devait garder sa casquette à la main, la laisser par terre ou la mettre sur sa tête. Il s'est rassis et l'a posée sur ses genoux.

—Levez-vous, a répété le professeur, et dites-moi votre nom.

Le nouveau a articulé un nom inintelligible.

—Répétez.

On a entendu les mêmes syllabes, couvertes tout de suite par les huées de la classe.

—Plus haut, a crié le professeur.

Le nouveau a ouvert alors une bouche énorme et a crié comme pour appeler quelqu'un, ce mot: Charbovari.

CONVERSATION

1. Pourquoi le proviseur est-il entré dans la salle de classe? 2. Qu'est-ce que les élèves ont fait en le voyant? 3. Quel âge avait le nouvel élève? 4. Que tenait-il à la main? 5. Est-il resté debout longtemps? 6. Que lui a dit le professeur? 7. Pourquoi la classe s'est-elle mise à rire? 8. Combien de fois sa casquette est-elle tombée? 9. Comment s'est-il débarrassé de sa casquette? 10. Puis, que lui a demandé le professeur? 11. Pourquoi le professeur l'a-t-il prié de répéter son nom? 12. Quel est le mot qu'il a articulé enfin? 13. Comment a-t-il crié ce nom?

COMPOSITION

In the girls' lycée, the English class had already begun, when the principal entered, accompanied by a new student. There was a vacant seat in the front row and Mary Berget sat down there. She was very late, having stopped on the way to chat with some friends and was much embarrassed by the disorder that her entrance into the classroom had caused. She felt that all (the) eyes were fixed upon her. Even the most bored of the girls had awakened and were looking at her. Suddenly, a gust of wind, entering by the open window carried away the light scarf that she had laid upon her lap and dropped it on the professor's desk.

"Oh, my scarf!" she exclaimed, trying to seize it.

The class burst out laughing. The professor, amused rather than angry, arose and turned towards the abashed girl.

"This bit of finery (**chiffon,** *m.*) belongs to you, Mademoiselle?"

Mary remained silent. The professor came down from the platform and placed herself in front of her.

"What is your name?"

Mary did not answer. The professor repeated the question. Finally, making an immense effort, Mary opened her [1] mouth and cried out:

"Mary Scarf."

DRILL EXERCISE

1. All the guests got up immediately. 2. They came to see me last night. 3. John and Paul stayed until midnight; Mary left at ten o'clock. 4. Our friends have returned to France. 5. Did she have a good time? 6. By whom was she accompanied? 7. At what time did John go out? 8. They have gone to see their friends. 9. The neckties I bought are very pretty. 10. The girl we saw is the youngest of my cousins. 11. We gave them back to John. 12. Suddenly the laughter of the students was heard. 13. The janitor carried down my trunk. 14. They got rid of their overcoats. 15. What did they say to each other? 16. She entered the room and sat down. 17. Mary arose and turned toward the professor. 18. Where was she born? 19. The gifts which she made me are very expensive. 20. Mary and Jeanne spoke to each other a moment. 21. We hurried to wash ourselves. 22. They went up the stairs (in) running. 23. His cap which he had put on his lap fell on the floor (**par terre**). 24. The paintings which he bought are very interesting. 25. Lycées are found in every large city.

[1] Cf. § 113.

GRAMMATICAL EXERCISE

Replace the infinitive by the proper form of the past participle:

1. Nous sommes (*rentrer*) de bonne heure. 2. Les fleurs que je lui ai (*envoyer*). 3. Marie et Jeanne se sont bien (*amuser*) hier soir. 4. Marie Antoinette est (*mourir*) à Paris. 5. Il lui a (*envoyer*) des cadeaux. 6. Qu'est-ce qu'elles se sont (*dire*)? 7. Elle a (*travailler*) toute la matinée. 8. Jean nous a (*accompagner*) chez nous. 9. Quand sont-ils (*arriver*)? 10. Les feuilles mortes sont (*tomber*). 11. Est-ce qu'elles sont (*revenir*)? 12. Votre sœur, qu'est-ce qu'elle est (*devenir*)? 13. Elle s'est (*laver*) les mains. 14. Le concierge a (*monter*) les malles. 15. On les a (*expédier*) par colis postal.

VERB REVIEW

connaître, to know, be acquainted with. Cf. § 201.
   reconnaître, to recognize
   paraître, to appear, seem
savoir, to know, know how. Cf. § 226.

1. I used to know him a few years ago but I no longer know where he lives. 2. He is sorry that we do not know the Martins. 3. He knows Paris very well. 4. Did you ever know where he lived? 5. If we knew where he is, we would find him. 6. He will know when I arrive. 7. We should know all that, if we had been with you. 8. John would recognize me, I am sure of it. 9. As soon as I have seen him, I shall know him. 10. Although I know what you want, I cannot help you. 11. We knew (*p. def.*) that he had come. 12. If I have ever known them, I have forgotten them now. 13. Do you know this novel of Victor Hugo's? 14. Two years ago, I knew him very well. 15. It appears that you did not recognize me.

LESSON VII

PERSONAL PRONOUNS

52. Table of the conjunctive and disjunctive personal pronouns.

	Conjunctives			
Subject	Direct object	Indirect object	Reflexives	Disjunctives
je	me	me	me	moi
tu	te	te	te	toi
il, elle	le, la	lui	se	lui, elle
nous	nous	nous	nous	nous
vous	vous	vous	vous	vous
ils, elles	les	leur	se	eux, elles

53. The conjunctive forms of the personal pronouns are those forms used as the subjects or objects of verbs.

The disjunctive forms of the personal pronouns are those forms not used as the subjects or objects of verbs.[1]

Conjunctive Pronouns

54. Position of conjunctive pronouns.

1. All conjunctive object pronouns, and also **en** and **y**, precede the verb, or the auxiliary in a compound tense, except in the imperative affirmative, when they follow the verb.
2. The order of conjunctive pronouns before a verb, or before an auxiliary in a compound tense, is:

[1] For exceptions cf. § **55**, 4, 5, 6.

me		le				
te		la		lui		
se	before		before		before y	before en
nous		les		leur		
vous						

Il nous les donne. — He gives them to us.
Je le lui ai donné. — I gave it to him.
Ne leur en donnez pas. — Don't give them any.
Vous l'a-t-il donné? — Did he give it to you?

3. The order of object pronouns after the imperative affirmative is: verb—direct object—indirect object—**y**—**en**.

   a) In the imperative affirmative, **moi** and **toi** replace **me** and **te**, except before **en** and **y**.

Donnez-le-moi. — Give it to me.
Donnez-nous-en. — Give us some.
But: Donnez-m'en. — Give me some.

4. When the direct object of a verb is **me** (**moi** in the imperative affirmative), **te** (**toi** in the imperative affirmative), **se**, **nous** or **vous**, the indirect object is translated by a disjunctive pronoun preceded by **à** and is placed after the verb.

Il s'est présenté à moi. — He introduced himself to me.
Présentez-moi à elle. — Introduce me to her.
But: Présentez-la-moi. — Introduce her to me.

Disjunctive Pronouns

55. Disjunctive pronouns are used:

   1. absolutely, without a verb;

Qui vous a dit cela? Lui. — Who told you that? He (did).

2. after ce + être;

| C'est lui, elle, moi, etc. | It is he, she, I, etc. |

3. after all prepositions;

| Avec moi; sans eux. | With me; without them. |

4. in compound subjects or objects when one or both of them are pronouns;

| Jean et moi (nous) sommes allés en ville. | John and I went down town. |
| Je les ai vus, lui et elle. | I saw him and her. |

5. in place of a conjunctive subject pronoun, if the subject is separated from the verb by any word except **ne**, pronoun objects, **y** or **en**;

| Lui seul va avec nous. | He alone is going with us. |

6. for emphasis, with or without **même**.

Il a fini le travail lui-même.	He finished the work himself.
Moi, j'ai fini le travail.	*I* finished the work.
Lui jouait du piano, eux travaillaient.	*He* was playing the piano, *they* were working.

On Soi

56. The indefinite pronoun, *one, they, people, we,* is rendered in French by **on,** followed by a verb in the third person singular. The disjunctive form of **on** is **soi**.

| Il faut qu'on pense à soi. | One must think of himself. |

En and Y

57. En is equivalent to **de** (= *of, from, with,* etc.) + *it* (*them*). When used partitively as a pronoun to translate *some, some of it* (*them*), *any of it* (*them*), etc. (cf. §§ 13–14), it may refer either to persons or to things. Otherwise it refers to things only.

Avez-vous des amis ici? Oui, j'en ai.	Have you any friends here? Yes, I have (some).
Il en parle tout le temps.	He is always talking about it.
But: **Il parle toujours d'elle.**	He is always talking about her.
J'en suis très content.	I am very glad of it.
But: **Je suis très content de lui.**	I am well satisfied with him.

58. **Y** is equivalent to **à** (= *to, at, in, etc.*) + *it* (*them*) and refers only to things. As an adverb, **y** translates the English *there,* and when so used, refers to a place previously mentioned.

Voici la liste. Que faut-il y ajouter?	Here is the list. What must be added to it?
Est-il à l'université? Oui, il y va tous les jours.	Is he at the university? Yes, he goes there every day.

UN NOUVEAU ARRIVE AU LYCÉE (*suite*)

Jamais on n'avait entendu dans la classe un vacarme pareil. On hurlait, on répétait: Charbovari! Charbovari! Un moment le professeur est resté indécis à sa place, puis il est descendu au milieu du tumulte. L'ordre s'est rétabli peu à peu. Les élèves se sont courbés sur leurs cahiers. Le nouveau est resté debout, les yeux baissés, regardant ses gros souliers mal cirés.

Le professeur est remonté dans sa chaire. Il y a fait venir le pauvre garçon et s'est adressé à lui:

—Epelez-moi votre nom; dictez-le-moi.

Le nouveau le lui a épelé, puis il le lui a dicté.

Le professeur a réussi ainsi à saisir le nom de Charles Bovary.

—Vous vous appelez Charles Bovary, alors? Etes-vous par hasard le fils du Docteur Bovary?

—Oui, c'est moi.

—J'en suis désolé. Votre père ne doit pas être très content de vous. Et il a commandé au pauvre diable d'aller s'asseoir sur le banc de paresse devant la chaire. Le nouveau a hésité.

—Que cherchez-vous? a demandé le professeur.

—Ma casquette, a répondu timidement le nouveau, lançant autour de lui des regards inquiets.

Les rires ont éclaté de nouveau.

—Cinq cents vers à toute la classe, s'est écrié le professeur d'une voix furieuse. Les rires ont cessé.

—Restez donc tranquilles, vous autres, a-t-il continué, en s'essuyant le front[1] avec son mouchoir. Quant à vous, le nouveau, vous me copierez vingt fois le verbe *ridiculus sum*.

Puis, d'une voix plus douce:

—Eh, vous la retrouverez, votre casquette; on ne vous l'a pas volée.

d'après Flaubert.

CONVERSATION

1. Qu'est-ce que c'est qu'un vacarme? 2. Qu'est-ce que le professeur a fait pendant le vacarme? 3. Comment a-t-il rétabli l'ordre? 4. Qu'est-ce que le nouveau a fait pendant tout ce temps? 5. Où le professeur l'a-t-il fait venir? 6. Que lui a-t-il demandé? 7. Comment a-t-il réussi enfin à saisir son nom? 8. De qui Charles était-il le fils? 9. Où le professeur a-t-il commandé à Charles de s'asseoir? 10. Pourquoi Charles n'y est-il pas allé tout de suite? 11. Comment le professeur a-t-il arrêté un nouvel éclat de rire? 12. Comment savez-vous que le professeur avait chaud? 13. Quelle punition a-t-il infligée à la classe? 14. Comment a-t-il puni Charles?

COMPOSITION

The uproar broke out anew. On all sides were heard exclamations of surprise: "Mary Scarf! What a funny name! Why! She is making fun of us." The professor cast a furious glance at the class and the tumult subsided. Then, turning towards the miserable girl who remained seated [with] lowered eyes,[2] she said to her:

"I do not need to introduce you to the students. You have already told them your name and they will remember it, I am sure of it. As for your scarf, I'll return it to you now, if you wish it. Here it is."

[1] Cf. § 113.
[2] Cf. § 113 and French passage on p. 46.

"Thank you, Mademoiselle," said Mary (in) taking it. Then, looking timidly about her, she added: "But my name is not Scarf. My name is Berget."

"Berget? How is it written?"

Mary wrote her name on a piece of paper and gave it to her.

"Ah, your name is Mary Berget? Why didn't you tell me so (it) in the first place?"

"I was so embarrassed. I was thinking of my scarf and . . ."

"But why didn't you tell me it, when you entered the room?"

"You didn't ask me (it). Besides, I didn't think of it."

"A new student must always introduce herself to me before taking her seat in the classroom."

"But my aunt told me not to disturb you."

"Your aunt? Who is your aunt? It is I who am the mistress here."

"Why, you know her very well, Mademoiselle. She is the principal."

DRILL EXERCISE

1. They will introduce us to them. 2. Who told you that? He. 3. I did not give them any of it. 4. Give us some but do not give us too much. 5. You will find them there. 6. I shall not send him any. 7. John and I did not see them last night. 8. It is I, we, you, they. 9. Without them, we can do nothing. 10. He alone of all their friends helped them. 11. What must we add to it? 12. John is always thinking of her. 13. He introduced me to him. 14. Why didn't you give them to me? 15. He did all that himself. 16. Let's not go away. 17. Without saying anything to her, they left. 18. We were glad of it. 19. As for them, they will doubtless stay. 20. Let's not send them to her, she has enough already.

GRAMMATICAL EXERCISE

Insert in proper position the French equivalents of the words in parentheses:

1. On présentera (*him to her; you to them; us to you; them to him*). 2. Je n'ai pas donné (*any to him; it to them*). 3. N'envoyons pas (*it to her; any to him*). 4. Donnez (*some to me; them to her; it to him*). 5. Il ne veut pas dire (*it to her; it to us*). 6. Vous

trouverez (*them there; some there*). 7. Expédiez (*it to me; them to us; some to her*). 8. Il faut penser (*of oneself; of them; of her; of it*). 9. Qui a envoyé (*them some; it to him; any to her; them there*)?

VERB REVIEW

faire, to do, make, have (done), order, etc. Cf. § 83 and 207.
faire froid (chaud, frais, beau, mauvais, etc.), to be cold (hot, cool, fair, stormy, etc.)
se faire tard, to be getting late
se faire à, to get used to
faire venir, to send for

1. It is very cold here. 2. When we left, it was getting late. 3. I shall do it. 4. She never got used to it. 5. They sent for (*p. def.*) John immediately. 6. I am sorry that you are doing that. 7. The weather will be fine tomorrow. 8. It was cool when we arrived. 9. He would have had me come, I am sure of it. 10. Do what you want. 11. We should do it, if we were in your place. 12. I shall get used to it. 13. They want you to have him come. 14. Let's call on Mr. Martin. 15. We are visiting some friends in town.

LESSON VIII

NEGATION. CE AND IL AS SUBJECTS OF ETRE

Negation

59. The most common negatives used with verbs are:

ne . . . pas, not	ne . . . personne,[2] no one, nobody
ne . . . point, not	
ne . . . jamais,[1] never	ne . . . aucun,[3] none, no one, no
ne . . . guère, scarcely	ne . . . rien, nothing, not anything
ne . . . plus, no more, no longer	
ne . . . que, only	ne . . . ni . . . ni, neither . . . nor

60. Ne always precedes the verb and any pronoun objects.

61. Pas, point, jamais, plus, guère and **rien** stand immediately after the verb in simple tenses and immediately after the auxiliary in compound tenses. They usually stand together before an infinitive.

Je ne l'ai pas vu.	I have not seen him.
N'a-t-il rien fait?	Has he done nothing?
Elle n'y va plus.	She does not go there any more.
Etre ou ne pas être?	To be or not to be?
J'ai envie de ne pas le faire.	I have a mind not to do it.

---

[1] **Jamais** used without **ne** means *ever;* used without a verb and without **ne**, it means *never.* **Avez-vous jamais été en France? Jamais.** Have you ever been in France? Never.

[2] **Personne** in the sense of *nobody* is masculine but in the sense of a *person* or *individual,* is feminine. **Personne n'est venu.** No one has come. But: **Quelques personnes sont déjà arrivées.** A few people have already arrived.

[3] For uses of **aucun** as an indefinite, cf. § **138.**

62. Personne usually stands after a past participle or an infinitive.

| Je n'y ai rencontré personne. | I met no one there. |

63. Ni, the **que** of **ne . . . que** and the negative adjective **aucun,** stand directly before the words they modify.

Il n'y a que deux livres sur la table.	There are only two books on the table.
Je n'ai aucune envie de voyager.	I have no desire to travel.
Il n'a trouvé ni amis ni connaissances à Paris.	He found neither friends nor acquaintances in Paris.

64. Aucun, rien[1] and **personne** may be used as subjects of a verb. **Ne** must be used before the verb.

| Personne n'est arrivé. | No one has come. |
| Aucune de ses amies ne lui a écrit. | None of her friends has written to her. |

65. If the verb is omitted, **ne** is also omitted, the complementary negative retaining full negative force. **Pas,** however, must be supported by some other word.

| Qu'avez-vous vu? Rien. | What did you see? Nothing. |
| Est-ce que le président est arrivé? Pas encore. | Has the president arrived? Not yet. |

66. Ne used without **pas.**

1. **Ne** may be used without **pas** with the verbs **cesser, oser, pouvoir** and **savoir.**

| Il ne cesse (pas) de raconter ses ennuis. | He is always telling his troubles. |

2. **Ne** is used without **pas** with compound tenses after **il y a . . . que, voilà . . . que** and **depuis que.**

---
[1] For use of **rien** + adjec., cf. § 144.

Il y a deux ans que je ne l'ai vu.	It is two years since I have seen him.
But: Je ne l'ai pas vu depuis deux ans.	I have not seen him for (since) two years.

67. Redundant **ne.**[1] A redundant **ne** is generally used with the verb in the second member of a comparison.

Il est plus riche que je ne le croyais.	He is richer than I thought.

Ce and Il as Subjects of Etre

68. *He, she* and *they* are translated by **il, ils, elle, elles,** when the verb **être** is followed by an adjective or an unmodified noun.

Il est pauvre.	He is poor.
Ils sont amis.	They are friends.
Elle est Française.	She is French.

69. *It, this, that* are usually translated by **ce,** when the verb **être** is followed by an adjective or an adverb. In the case of an adjective, **il** or **elle** may replace **ce,** when referring to a specific noun or pronoun. With **il** or **elle,** the adjective agrees; with **ce,** the adjective is invariable.

C'est très bien.	It is very well.
Vous avez fait cela? C'est très beau.	Did you make that? It is very beautiful.
Comment trouvez-vous cette comédie? C'est très intéressant. (or: Elle est très intéressante.)	How do you like that comedy? It is very interesting.

70. *It, this, that, these, those, he, she, they* are translated by **ce** in all other cases, that is, when **être** is followed by 1) a modified noun, 2) a pronoun, 3) a proper name, or 4) a superlative.

[1] For other uses of redundant **ne**, cf. §§ 151, 3, 4 and 155, 3.

1. Ce sont des amis de mon frère. — Those (they) are friends of my brother.
   C'est une Française. — She is a French girl.
2. C'est moi, vous, elle; ce sont (c'est) eux. — It is I, you, she; it is they.
3. Ce sont les Chamard. — It is the Chamards.
4. C'est le plus beau de ses romans. — That / It is the finest of his novels.

UN MOMENT EMBARRASSANT

Mon cher Georges:

Il y a longtemps que je n'ai reçu de vos nouvelles et je commence à vous en vouloir sérieusement. Depuis que je suis en France, personne ne m'a écrit. Je n'ai reçu d'Amérique ni lettre ni carte postale. Si vous ne répondez pas tout de suite à cette lettre, je ne vous dirai rien des incidents de mon séjour en France.

Hier après-midi, n'ayant pu trouver aucun de mes amis, je suis sorti faire une promenade tout seul. En passant devant la mairie de notre arrondissement, j'ai vu une affiche annonçant un cours de diction fait par un acteur connu. Evidemment je ne pouvais pas perdre une aussi belle occasion d'apprendre un peu de français. Me voilà donc assis dans une salle de conférences tout près de l'estrade. Juste devant moi, je remarque un gros monsieur qui regarde avec intérêt le public déjà nombreux. Soudain, il se retourne vers moi. "Etes-vous sérieux, Monsieur?" C'est bien à moi qu'il parle, mais je suis trop déconcerté pour répondre. "Etes-vous venu pour travailler? Savez-vous quelque chose?" Je ne sais rien mais je n'ose pas le lui dire et bêtement je réponds: "Oui, Monsieur." "Montez sur l'estrade." Vous devinez le reste. Je monte sur l'estrade et avec mon affreux accent américain je déclame une fable de La Fontaine qui semble amuser énormément mon auditoire. Quant à moi, jamais je n'ai été aussi embarrassé. C'est la première fois que j'ai parlé devant un public français et je n'ai guère besoin de vous dire que ce sera la dernière.

Bien à vous,
Paul

CONVERSATION

1. Est-ce que Paul a reçu beaucoup de lettres des Etats-Unis? 2. Pourquoi est-il sorti faire une promenade tout seul? 3. Qu'est-ce qu'il a vu à la mairie? 4. Pourquoi est-il entré dans la salle de conférences? 5. Qui a-t-il remarqué dans la salle? 6. Qu'est-ce que ce monsieur lui a demandé? 7. Que lui a répondu Paul? 8. Qu'est-ce que Paul a fait alors? 9. Parlait-il bien le français? 10. Aimait-il à parler devant un public français?

COMPOSITION

Dear George:

I hardly need to tell you how glad I was to receive your letter and to learn that neither you nor Helen have forgotten me. I know that I have written you only once but I promise not to forget you in the future.

As you know, I have never been in France before and I have had lots of difficulty in (à) orienting myself. It is harder to speak French than I thought. I haven't read a word of French for five years and naturally I understand almost nothing. As I have no desire to leave France without having learned to speak French, I am taking some lessons with M. Bourget whose address the Martins gave me. He is an excellent teacher. I shall never forget the first time I saw him. Entering a small room where a dozen people were awaiting, apparently, the arrival of the professor, I sat down quietly in order not to disturb anyone. Suddenly a gentleman seated near me turned toward me an open book in his (à la) hand. I did not know what he was saying to me but as he offered me the book, there was only one thing to do. I took the book and read with my terrible American accent a fable of La Fontaine. No one said anything, no one laughed, no one smiled; but M. Bourget, for it was he, did not ask me to read a second fable. He realized that I did not know French well enough to [1] follow a course in (de) diction. And so did I.[2] Write me soon and tell me what you are doing.

Sincerely yours,
Paul

[1] Cf. § 166, 3.
[2] **Et moi aussi.**

DRILL EXERCISE

1. It is a month since I saw Dr. Martin. 2. Didn't you see anyone in the salon? 3. It is a pity that no one knows him. 4. John wrote me neither letters nor postal cards. 5. Never had I heard such an accent. 6. I hardly have the time to do that. 7. She is an American and she is very rich. 8. It is the finest of his paintings. 9. They are friends of my sister. 10. It is very fine what you have done. 11. None of his friends has seen him. 12. We have not any more of them; we had only four. 13. He has never given me anything. 14. Have you ever been in France? Never. 15. Nothing has happened. 16. It was an amusing comedy that we saw. Yes, it was very amusing. 17. Don't give him any more. 18. There were only six in the room. 19. Nothing is simpler than to stay here. 20. It is probable that no one will come.

GRAMMATICAL EXERCISE

Replace the dash by *il, ils, elle, elles,* or *ce:*

1. — sont amis. 2. — est une Anglaise. 3. — est pauvre mais content. 4. — est très bien habillée. 5. — sont eux qui nous l'ont dit. 6. — est très jolie. 7. — est médecin. 8. — est un avocat fameux. 9. — était le plus intéressant de tous ces romans. 10. — est Français. 11. — sont très gentilles.

VERB REVIEW

mettre, to put, put on. Cf. § 209.
  remettre, to put back, postpone
  permettre, to permit
  promettre, to promise
  se mettre à, to begin
prendre, to take. Cf. § 212.
  apprendre, to learn
  comprendre, to understand
  aller (venir) prendre, to go (come) and get, call for (a person)

1. What did he promise you? 2. Where are you putting my hat? 3. I shall take my breakfast here. 4. He would learn a great deal, if he should begin to study. 5. I am sorry that he does not understand.

6. They will permit me to do that. 7. In your place, I should put them here. 8. He postponed (*p. def.*) his trip until the month of July. 9. Take this and put it on the table. 10. I took nothing from (**sur**) your desk. 11. What do you have (**prendre**) for your lunch? 12. He took (*p. def.*) the book and put (*p. def.*) it in my room. 13. He had taken my coat and was putting it on, when I saw him. 14. He is glad that they will allow it.

LESSON IX

THE CONDITIONAL TENSES. THE USES OF **DEVOIR**

The Conditional and Conditional Perfect Tenses

71. The conditional and conditional perfect tenses are used in main clauses of conditional sentences.

J'irais avec vous, si j'avais le temps.	I should go with you, if I had the time.
Nous serions allés au théâtre, si nous avions eu le temps.	We should have gone to the theatre, if we had had time.

72. *Should* and *would* do not always indicate the conditional in English. Distinguish carefully between the following:

1. *Should* (= *ought*), implying duty, is rendered in French by the conditional or conditional perfect of **devoir**.

Vous devriez étudier davantage.	You should study more.
Vous auriez dû venir plus tôt.	You should have come sooner.

2. *Would,* implying volition, is rendered in French by the appropriate tense of **vouloir**.[1]

Il ne voulait pas me donner son adresse.	He did not want to (was unwilling to) give me his address.
Il n'a pas voulu le faire.	He would not (refused to) do it.

[1] Cf. § 39.

3. *Would* indicating an habitual action in the past is translated by an imperfect tense.[1]

| En été, je le voyais tous les jours. | In summer, I would see him every day. |

Conditional Sentences

73. Conditional sentences follow the same tense sequence as in English, except that, unlike the English, **si** meaning *if* may never be followed by a conditional or future tense. For the English future in an *if* clause, use the present indicative in French. For the English conditional in an *if* clause, use the imperfect indicative in French.

Je le ferai, si j'ai le temps.	I shall do it, if I (shall) have the time.
Je le ferais, si j'avais le temps.	I should do it, if I had (should have) the time.
Je l'aurais fait, si j'avais eu le temps	I should have done it, if I had had the time.

1. **Si** meaning *whether* is followed by the same tense as in English.

| Il ne sait pas s'il pourra venir. | He does not know whether he will be able to come. |
| Il ne savait pas s'il pourrait venir. | He did not know whether he would be able to come. |

Uses of Devoir

74. Devoir (cf. § 221) *must, be supposed to, be to, have to, ought,* etc.

Devoir expresses primarily a sense of duty, the obligation coming from the speaker himself and not from external circumstances.

[1] Cf. § 75.

Pres. indic. **je dois:** must, am to, am supposed to, am expected to, have to, etc.

Je dois être à la gare à trois heures. — I must (am expected to) be at the station at three o'clock.

Impf. indic. **je devais:** was to, was expected to, had to, etc.

Il devait venir me trouver chez moi. — He was to (was supposed to, etc.) meet me at my house.

Past def. **je dus** (literary): was to (*and did*), had to (*and did*).

Il dut le faire. — He had to do it. (*moral obligation, no external coercion*).

Past indef. **j'ai dû:**

1) conversational past with same meaning as past def.

Il a dû le faire. — He had to do it.

2) probability in past time. Must have + past part.

Je ne le vois pas. Il a dû partir. — I do not see him. He must have gone. (He has probably gone.)

Fut. **je devrai:** must, shall be expected to, shall have to, etc. (same use as the present and frequently replaced by it).

Je devrai le faire demain. — I must (shall have to) do it tomorrow.

Condl. **je devrais:** ought to, should

Je devrais travailler ce soir. — I ought to work this evening.

Condl. perf. **j'aurais dû:**   ought to have, should have
                                   + past participle.

Il aurait dû m'attendre.   He ought to have (should have)
                                   waited for me.

LA SORBONNE

—Je viens d'assister à une conférence à la Sorbonne, dit Jean. Je suis inscrit pour les cours de vacances et je dois passer un examen à la fin de juillet.

—Si je savais le français aussi bien que vous, je suivrais les cours aussi, répondit Paul.

—Vous devriez le faire quand même. Si on veut apprendre une langue, on doit profiter de toutes les occasions pour l'entendre parler. Vous auriez dû apporter votre diplôme de bachelier. Si vous l'aviez ici, vous pourriez vous inscrire [1] maintenant pour le mois de juillet.

—Ne pourrais-je pas vous accompagner à vos cours une fois ou deux?

—Cela est impossible. Chez nous, les professeurs font l'appel pour contrôler les absences; ici on doit montrer sa carte d'immatriculation [1] avant d'entrer dans les salles de classe. Du reste, on ne répète pas les leçons comme chez nous. Le professeur explique une ou deux fois par semaine un morceau du texte littéraire qu'on étudie pour montrer aux étudiants comment il faut étudier et l'étudiant doit préparer le texte entier. A la fin du cours, il passe un examen. S'il est reçu, il aura son diplôme; s'il échoue, il doit suivre le cours de nouveau. Si on suivait ce système chez nous, on collerait la moitié de nos étudiants.

—Agnès vient d'obtenir le certificat [2] d'études françaises, n'est-ce pas? Elle a dû travailler bien ferme.

—En effet, Agnès est très forte en français, mais tout de même, elle a dû consacrer beaucoup de temps à ses études.

---

[1] **se faire immatriculer:** to matriculate, i. e., to be accepted as a student in a university; **s'inscrire:** to register for a specific course or series of courses.

[2] Given to foreign students upon the successful completion of a year's course.

CONVERSATION

1. Qu'est-ce que la Sorbonne? 2. Quel diplôme faut-il avoir pour s'y inscrire? 3. Pour quels cours Jean est-il inscrit? 4. Que faut-il se procurer avant d'assister à une conférence? 5. Comment contrôle-t-on les absences dans une université américaine? 6. Quelle est la méthode d'enseignement à la Sorbonne? 7. Si un étudiant échoue à un examen, qu'est-ce qu'il est tenu de faire? 8. Quel certificat Agnès a-t-elle obtenu? 9. L'a-t-elle obtenu sans difficulté? 10. Parle-t-elle mieux le français que Paul?

COMPOSITION

"You haven't seen the certificate that I received at the Sorbonne?" asked Agnes. "I must show it to you."

"That must have cost you a lot of work."

"A year of work and a hundred francs. If I had had more time, I should have registered for the doctorate, but father would not let me spend more than a year in France. You ought to take the summer courses, Paul."

"I don't know whether I shall be able to stay in Paris all summer. Besides, I didn't bring my bachelor's diploma as I should have done (it). They are very strict at the Sorbonne, aren't they?"

"That depends. If you do not have a student's card, you cannot enter a lecture room. On the other hand, the professors do not call the roll. If you wish to absent yourself from your classes, that is your affair. A professor gives a lecture or he explains a passage from a literary text once a week in order to teach you how you must approach the subject. At the end of the course, you must take an examination and if you fail in it, you will have to repeat the course."

"What [an] admirable system! If we had it at home, I should not have spent so much time at the Dean's, explaining to him why I was not attending my classes."

"And you would not have passed your examinations. You would have had to remain another year at the university."

"And I should not have had the pleasure of lunching with you today either. Where shall we go?"

DRILL EXERCISE 17

1. John is to meet me at the Sorbonne. 2. If he should not come, should you wait for him? 3. I asked him for his address but he would not give it to me. 4. If I had had a diploma I should have brought it. 5. We had to take a French examination. 6. I should go to the lecture, if I had a student's card. 7. He must have failed in his English examination. 8. He did not know whether he would be able to come or not. 9. If I go to Europe, I shall spend more time in France than in England. 10. John was to spend his vacation in Spain last year, but he failed in his examinations in June. 11. He ought to have studied more (**davantage**).[1] 12. You ought to visit Fontainebleau, if you have the time. 13. When we were in Paris, we would often spend an afternoon in the Luxembourg garden. 14. Do you think that I should have telephoned to him? 15. What should you do in my place? 16. She would not have left, if she had known that I was waiting for her. 17. She must have forgotten our appointment. 18. We asked her to accompany us, but she would not do it. 19. Do you know whether they will give that play at the Odéon or at the Théâtre Français? 20. If they give it at the Théâtre Français, you must go [and] see it.

[1] **davantage** (not **plus**) is used to translate *more* when no expressed comparison follows. It usually stands at the end of a clause.

LESSON X

THE PAST TENSES

The Imperfect Tense

75. The imperfect tense is used:

1. To emphasize the continuance or repetition in the past of an activity or a condition. When the imperfect is used, there is no indication, in the clause in which it stands, as to when the activity or condition came to an end. Hence, the imperfect tense denotes what was happening or used to happen and is regularly equivalent to the English *was (were)* + *-ing* or *used to* + an infinitive.

Il était très malade, quand je l'ai vu.	He was very sick (and continued to be sick), when I saw him.
Il entrait dans un magasin, quand je l'ai vu.	He was entering a store, when I saw him.
J'allais le voir tous les jours.	I went to see him every day. (Nothing indicates when I ceased seeing him.)

   a) If there is any indication in the same clause that the activity or condition came to an end, the imperfect cannot be used.

Pendant deux ans, je l'ai vu tous les jours.	For two years I saw (used to but no longer do see) him every day.

2. As a descriptive tense, to state characteristics of persons or things.

La terre était couverte de neige.	The ground was covered with snow.
Il était grand et mince.	He was tall and thin.

3. To indicate an activity or a condition in the past that had been going on and was still going on. English usage here requires the progressive form of the pluperfect (past perfect), *had been + -ing*. The time element, if mentioned, is introduced by **depuis, depuis quand** or **il y avait . . . que**. (Cf. § 36.)

J'avais l'intention de lui écrire.	I had been intending to write to him.
Il y avait un an qu'il le disait. Il le disait depuis un an.	He had been saying it for a year.
Depuis quand m'attendiez-vous ?	How long had you been waiting for me?

4. In the *if* clause of a conditional sentence, when the main clause has the conditional.

Si vous l'invitiez à passer les vacances chez vous, il viendrait.	If you invited (should invite, were to invite) him to spend the vacation at your house, he would come.

The Past Indefinite

76. The past indefinite is regularly used to translate 1) the English present perfect tense (*have* + a past participle); 2) an English past tense, used narratively to denote a completed action or state; and 3) the English emphatic past tense (*did* + the infinitive).

J'ai vu votre frère hier.	I saw your brother yesterday.
Avez-vous fini votre travail?	Have you finished Did you finish } your work?

The Past Definite

77. The past definite denotes an action or state, completed in the past. It is essentially a literary tense and is usually replaced in conversational French by the past indefinite.

Louis XIV régna de 1643 à 1715.   Louis XIV reigned from 1643 to 1715.

The Pluperfect and Past Anterior

78. The pluperfect tense is used in general as in English except in the cases noted in § 75, 3.

Il avait déjà fini son travail.   He had already finished his work.

79. The past anterior is a purely literary tense rarely used except after **quand, aussitôt que** and **après que**. It is avoided in informal writing and conversation.

(Literary)
Quand il eut fini son travail, il partit.   When he had finished his work, he left.

(Informal)
Après avoir fini son travail, il est parti.   After having finished his work, he left.

VOLTAIRE ET FRÉRON

Depuis bien des années, Voltaire et Fréron se détestaient. Voltaire méprisait le journaliste sans talent qui se moquait méchamment de lui dans ses articles et le jour vint où il refusa de lui adresser la parole.

On organisait à Paris un grand banquet qui devait réunir tous les grands écrivains de la capitale. Un ami de Voltaire vint l'inviter à y assister. Voltaire hésita. Est-ce que Fréron y serait? Dans ce cas, il refuserait d'y aller. Consternation générale! Il était évident qu'on ne pouvait pas se passer de l'auteur le plus fameux de la

France et on ne pouvait pas non plus désinviter Fréron. Que faire ? C'est Fréron lui-même qui trouva une solution à la difficulté. Si Voltaire consentait à assister au banquet, lui, Fréron, promettait de ne pas dire plus de quatre mots pendant toute la soirée. Voltaire, qui tenait beaucoup à y aller, accepta.

La fête était superbe. Au dîner, on discuta pendant deux heures des questions de littérature et de politique. Voltaire, spirituel et ironique comme toujours, amusait tout le monde, tandis que Fréron restait silencieux dans son coin. Le repas touchait à sa fin. On avait servi le café et on passait des noisettes. Un garçon en offrit à Voltaire qui refusa.

—J'ai déjà mangé autant de noisettes que Samson a tué de Philistins, protesta-t-il.

Alors Fréron, qui attendait patiemment une occasion favorable pour placer ses quatre mots, s'écria :

—Avec les mêmes armes !

Est-il nécessaire d'expliquer que c'est avec la mâchoire d'un âne que Samson a massacré mille Philistins ?

CONVERSATION

1. Depuis quand Voltaire connaissait-il Fréron ? 2. Pourquoi le détestait-il ? 3. Quelle fête est-ce qu'on organisait à Paris ? 4. Pourquoi Voltaire a-t-il refusé d'assister à cette fête ? 5. Pourquoi son refus a-t-il causé une consternation générale ? 6. Quelle solution a-t-on trouvée à la difficulté ? 7. Décrivez la fête. 8. Qu'est-ce qu'un garçon a offert à Voltaire vers la fin du repas ? 9. De quelle façon Voltaire a-t-il répondu au garçon ? 10. Comment Fréron a-t-il profité de cet incident ? 11. Que savez-vous de Samson ?

COMPOSITION

Fréron was seated in his office, when a well-known Parisian author entered. He was evidently ill at ease and did not know how to broach the affair which had brought him there. Fréron, whom the embarrassment of his visitor amused, remained silent for a few moments. Then, smiling maliciously, he said to him :

"So old Voltaire did not like my last article and you have come to recall your invitation to me. I would willingly dispense with your invitation but that talentless philosopher would despise me more than ever if I did not attend your banquet. Therefore I insist upon going to it."

Then Fréron proposed a solution to the difficulty. If Voltaire consented to sit at table with him, he would promise not to say more than six words during the whole evening. The visitor accepted this proposition immediately, for he was sure that if Fréron could not talk, there would be nothing to fear. But he did not know the journalist.

Fréron arrived early at the festival and seated himself at the end of the table. For more than two hours he ate in silence, while Voltaire amused by his wit the celebrities who surrounded him. Voltaire was enjoying his triumph, while Fréron was waiting for a favorable moment to crush the rival who had been making fun of him for years.

This moment finally came.

"No thank you," Voltaire was saying to a waiter, "I have already eaten as many nuts as Samson killed (of) Philistines."

"With the jaw-bone of an ass!" shouted Fréron.

DRILL EXERCISE I

1. How long had Fréron been writing articles against Voltaire? 2. One day he refused to speak to him. 3. If Fréron went to the banquet, Voltaire would not go (to it). 4. Fréron took advantage of the occasion that he had been awaiting for a long time. 5. He used to go to his office every day. 6. If I should invite you to dine with me, should you come? 7. For two years he wrote every week articles in which [1] he made fun of Voltaire. 8. While the others were talking, Fréron remained silent. 9. While Paul was living in Paris, he made the acquaintance of Miss Martin. 10. The journalist was old and mean. 11. When they brought the coffee, he left the hall. 12. He returned, when the nuts were being passed. 13. Voltaire had been speaking for ten minutes. 14. Louis XIII was King of France in 1630. 15. At his death in 1643, Louis XIV became King of France.

[1] où.

DRILL EXERCISE II

Replace the infinitives in parentheses by the appropriate past tenses:

1. J'(*entrer*) dans la salle de l'auberge et me (*jeter*) dans un vieux fauteuil. 2. J'(*être*) triste et fatigué et ne (*tarder*) pas à m'assoupir. 3. Je (*dormir*) depuis quelques minutes, quand tout à coup je (*rouvrir*) les yeux et je (*voir*) sur le mur une ombre immobile. 4. C'(*être*) l'ombre d'une jeune fille. 5. Le profil en (*être*) si charmant que je (*sentir*), en le voyant, toute ma fatigue s'évanouir. 6. Je (*tourner*) la tête pour voir celle qui (*faire*) une si belle ombre. 7. Il n'y (*avoir*) personne dans la salle. 8. De nouveau je (*regarder*) le mur; l'ombre n'y (*être*) plus. 9. Je (*courir*) à la porte. 10. La neige, qui (*tomber*) abondamment, (*couvrir*) le sol et aucun pas n'(*être*) marqué dans la neige.

d'après Anatole France

VERB REVIEW

dormir, to sleep. Cf. § 188.
  s'endormir, to go to sleep
mentir, to lie
partir, to go away, leave
servir, to serve
  se servir de, to use
sentir, to feel; se sentir, to feel (*of health*)
  consentir, to consent
sortir, to go out

Note: All the verbs above are conjugated like **dormir**.

1. Mary went to sleep at half past ten. 2. He went out (*p. def.*) without replying. 3. What books are you using? 4. If you consented to do it, he would be very happy. 5. I shall sleep tomorrow until eleven o'clock. 6. They left very early yesterday. 7. I am afraid that he is lying. 8. I would feel very well, if I slept better. 9. Let's not go away now. 10. Don't use that; use this. 11. Do you think that you would go to sleep more easily? 12. I shall never consent to it. 13. She felt much better yesterday. 14. We used to go out every evening. 15. They were leaving the house, when we went out.

LESSON XI

SPECIAL USES OF FALLOIR, POUVOIR, SAVOIR, FAIRE

80. Falloir (cf. § 223) has two meanings:

1. *must, to be necessary, have to;*
   Falloir differs from **devoir**, in that it expresses coercion from external circumstances and not moral obligation.[1]

Il faut que je finisse mon travail avant six heures.	I must (am obliged *by some person or some circumstance—not by my sense of duty*) finish my work before six o'clock.

a) **Falloir** is followed by an infinitive, when the meaning is clear, without expressing the indirect object of **falloir**. In other cases (that is, for emphasis or to avoid ambiguity) use **falloir** + the subjunctive.

Il faut le lui donner.	I (you, he, we, etc.) must give it to him.
Il ne faut jamais être en retard.	One must never be late.
Il faut que je m'en aille maintenant.	I must go now.
Il faut que vous le lui donniez.	You must give it to him.

b) Used negatively, **falloir** means *must not. It is not necessary* is translated by **il n'est pas nécessaire**.

Il ne faut pas dépenser tant d'argent.	You (he, we, etc.) must not spend so much money.
Il n'est pas nécessaire de m'attendre.	It is not necessary to wait for me.

[1] This distinction is not always observed.

2. *to need, require, must have, it takes* + an expression of time, measure, price, etc.

Il me faut un nouveau chapeau.	I need (must have) a new hat.
Il lui faut dix minutes pour aller à la gare.	He needs (it takes him) ten minutes to go to the station.

81. Pouvoir (cf. § 225) *to be able, can, may, might, could.*

The required tense of **pouvoir** can usually be determined by substituting for *can, may,* etc., the equivalent tense of the verbal phrase *to be able*.

Pres. indic. **je puis (peux):**   I am able, can, may

     Puis-je partir?   Can (may) I go?

Imperf. indic. **je pouvais:**   was able, could

     Etant malade, il ne pouvait pas travailler.   As he was sick, he could not (was not able) to work.

Condl. **je pourrais:**   would be able, could

     Pourriez-vous m'accompagner?   Would you be able to (could you) accompany me?

Condl. perfect **j'aurais pu:**   should have been able, could have, might have.

     J'aurais pu vous aider.   I should have been able to help you (could have, might have, helped you).

82. Savoir (cf. § 226) has two meanings:

1. *to know how to, can, be able* + infinitive.
Savoir translates *can, to be able* in the sense of *to know how to;* **pouvoir** means *to be able* physically.

     Il sait jouer du piano.   He can (knows how to) play the piano.

Il ne peut (pourra) pas jouer ce soir, parce qu'il est malade.	He cannot (is unable to) play tonight, because he is sick.

2. *to know* (with the mind), *know* (as a fact), *know by heart*.

When *to know* is equivalent to *to be acquainted with, be familiar with,* it is translated by **connaître**.

Je sais ce qu'il a fait.	I know what he has done.
Je sais qu'il est ici.	I know that he is here.
Nous savons nos leçons.	We know our lessons.
Connaissez-vous M. Hébert?	Do you know Mr. Hébert?
Elle connaît très bien Paris.	She knows Paris very well.

83. Faire (cf. § 207).

1. **Faire** + infinitive in French has the meaning of *to cause, have, make, order* and an infinitive or past participle in English.

Je l'ai fait écrire.	I had him write (*or* I had it written).

2. If **faire** and the infinitive have only one object between them, a pronoun object precedes **faire** and a noun object follows the infinitive. If both **faire** and the infinitive have objects, the pronoun objects precede **faire** and the noun objects follow the infinitive. The object of **faire** in this case, whether it is a noun or pronoun, must be indirect in form.[1] The past participle of **faire** in these constructions is invariable.

Je les ai fait venir.	I sent for them (had them come).
J'ai fait venir mon ami.	I sent for my friend.
Je les lui ai fait lire.	I had him read them.

[1] Laisser, entendre and voir may also take this construction. They may also take a direct object, as in English. **Je lui (l') ai entendu lire ce poème.** I heard him read that poem.

Il a fait étudier les leçons aux[1] **élèves.** — He had the students study the lessons.
Faites-les-lui voir. — Have him see them.

UNE VISITE

—Savez-vous qu'il est déjà huit heures et que nous devons être chez M. Reval à neuf heures moins le quart?

—J'avais complètement oublié ce rendez-vous. Vous avez bien fait de me le rappeler. Il faut que je me dépêche, car il nous faudra une bonne demi-heure pour y aller. Heureusement, je connais bien le quartier.

Ils trouvèrent facilement l'adresse que M. Reval leur avait donnée et sonnèrent à la porte de son appartement.

—Bonsoir, Messieurs. Donnez-vous la peine d'entrer.

—Bonsoir, M. Reval. Permettez-moi de vous présenter mon ami M. Paul Somers.

—Je suis enchanté de faire votre connaissance.

—Et moi, Monsieur, il y a longtemps que je désire vous connaître. Jean ne parle que de vous depuis plus d'un an et il vient de me faire lire votre dernier roman que je trouve épatant. Vous devriez le faire traduire en anglais.

—Vous me flattez, Monsieur, mais je suis très content, si j'ai su vous plaire. Mais asseyez-vous donc, je vous prie. Puis-je vous offrir une cigarette? Et à vous, Jean?

—Non, merci. Est-ce que je pourrais fumer ma pipe?

—Mais certainement. Il ne faut pas faire de façons chez moi.

—Puis-je vous demander des nouvelles de Mme Reval?

—Elle sera désolée d'avoir manqué votre visite. Elle n'a jamais pu supporter l'été à Paris et j'ai dû l'envoyer à la campagne.

—Quand vous lui écrirez, vous serez bien aimable de me rappeler à son bon souvenir.

—Je ne manquerai pas de le faire. Ah! voici le café. J'ai aussi une liqueur délicieuse que je veux vous faire goûter à tous les deux.

CONVERSATION

1. Quel rendez-vous Paul avait-il oublié? 2. Combien de temps faut-il pour aller chez M. Reval? 3. Jean a-t-il trouvé facilement

---

[1] To avoid ambiguity, **par** may replace **à**. **Elle a fait lire ce livre par les élèves.** She had the students read this book.

son appartement? Pourquoi? 4. De quelle façon M. Reval a-t-il reçu ses invités? 5. Est-ce que Paul le connaissait? 6. Quelle est la profession de M. Reval? 7. M. Reval a-t-il offert des cigares à ses amis? 8. Pourquoi n'a-t-on pas vu Mme Reval? 9. En apprenant son absence, qu'est-ce que Jean a dit? 10. Qu'est-ce que M. Reval a servi à ses invités?

COMPOSITION

"You can't go out now," exclaimed John. "Don't you remember that Mr. Reval is to call on us this evening?"

"I know it. But I must mail this letter. It will take me only two minutes."

"It is not necessary to go to the post-office yourself. Have the boy take the letter. He must be in the office, for I saw him come in a few minutes ago. Ah! there's Mr. Reval. Good evening, Mr. Reval."

"Good evening, John. Have I kept you waiting long?"

"On the contrary. You could not arrive at a better time. We have finished dining and you can have coffee with us. You don't know my friend, Paul, I believe."

"Yes, I do. Miss Martin introduced him to me recently. But I am very glad to see you again, Mr. Somers."

"Let's sit down. We were hoping that Mrs. Reval would be able to come with you."

"She would have liked to come but she went out without her coat last night and caught cold."

"We are very sorry that she is indisposed. You won't fail to remember us to her?"

"And you, what have you been doing, since I saw you last week?"

"We went by auto to Fontainebleau yesterday with Dr. Martin. The Doctor knows the park and he was able to show us many things that we should never have been able to find ourselves. We were to go to Versailles to-day but we had to postpone our trip until (à) another time because of the rain. One must not visit Versailles in the rain, you know."

"Here is the coffee. Let me serve you. And here are some American cigarettes that I sent for expressly for you."

DRILL EXERCISE

1. Can you play tennis? 2. He could go with you, if he had time. 3. I am to be at the station at six o'clock. 4. We must give them to her. 5. How much money do you need? 6. I used to know Paris very well. 7. I could not see him last night, because I was sick. 8. You must not smoke here. 9. We are having him buy them. 10. It was not necessary to spend so much money. 11. May I see you a moment? 12. I shall have him taste this coffee. 13. John and Mary could have helped us. 14. He did not know that you knew her. 15. He must have stayed at home today. 16. It takes us a half hour to go to the university. 17. I am going to have a suit made. 18. They ought to have sent us the news. 19. He would know that, if he were here. 20. I shall have John read this novel. 21. He should have brought Mrs. Reval with him. 22. He was to bring her, but she could not come. 23. Have the coffee served now. 24. We must leave at once. 25. We had to remain here. 26. Could you lend me that novel?

LESSON XII

DEMONSTRATIVE ADJECTIVES AND PRONOUNS. ADVERBS

Demonstrative Adjectives

84. Table of the demonstrative adjectives.

Singular		Plural	
M. ce, cet	this, that	ces	these, those
F. cette	this, that	ces	these, those

85. The demonstrative adjectives agree in number and gender with the nouns they modify and are repeated before each noun. The masculine singular form **cet** is used before a vowel or **h** mute.

Cet homme et cette femme.   This man and that woman.

86. To distinguish *this* from *that* and *these* from *those,* **-ci** and **-là** may be added to the noun.

Ce livre-ci est plus intéressant que ce livre-là.   This book is more interesting than that book.

Demonstrative Pronouns

87. Forms of the demonstrative pronouns.

1. Variable forms.

Singular	Plural	
M. **celui**, this one, that one, the one, he	**ceux**	these, those, the ones, they
F. **celle**, this one, that one, the one, she	**celles**	

2. Invariable forms.

> ce, this, these, that, those, he, she, it, they.
> ceci, this.
> cela, ça, that.

88. The variable forms are never used alone. They are followed by:

1. a relative clause, or
2. a prepositional phrase generally introduced by **de** or
3. **-ci** or **-là**.

1. Ce livre est celui que vous avez déjà lu.	This book is the one that you have already read.
2. Mes amies et celles de ma sœur sont déjà arrivées.	My friends and my sister's (those of my sister) have already arrived.
3. Ceux-ci sont à moi; ceux-là sont à vous.	These are mine; those are yours.

89. **Ceci**, *this* and **cela**, *that* have as an antecedent a general idea or a thing indicated but not named. They cannot have a particular word as an antecedent.

Cela est très important.	That is very important.
Je n'aime pas ceci.	I do not like this.

90. **Ce** (*this, that, these, those, he, she, it, they*) is frequently used instead of **il** or **elle** as the subject of **être**. Cf. §§ 68–70.

91. **Ce** followed by a relative pronoun translates the English *what, that which*.

Dites-moi ce qu'il a fait.	Tell me what he did.
Je ne sais pas ce qui est arrivé.	I do not know what has happened.

Adverbs

92. There are in French three classes of adverbs: 1) simple adverbs; 2) adverbs formed from adjectives; 3) adjectives used as adverbs. All adverbs are invariable.

93. Simple adverbs include such common adverbs as: **ainsi,** *thus;* **alors,** *then;* **souvent,** *often;* **maintenant,** *now,* etc.

94. Adverbs from adjectives. Most adjectives may be converted into adverbs by adding **-ment** to the feminine singular. Adjectives ending in a vowel in the masculine singular add **-ment** to the masculine singular.

sûr	sûre	sûrement	surely
facile	facile	facilement	easily
absolu	absolue	absolument	absolutely
doux	douce	doucement	gently

1. Note the following common exceptions:

constant	constante	constamment	constantly
précis	précise	précisément	precisely
fou	folle	follement	madly
nouveau	nouvelle	nouvellement	newly

95. A few common adjectives are used as adverbs in fixed phrases.

Ces plumes m'ont coûté cher.	These pens cost me dear.
Cette pipe sent bon (mauvais).	This pipe smells good (bad).

Comparison of Adverbs

96. The comparative of an adverb is formed, like that of an adjective, by the use of **plus, moins, si** or **aussi** before the adverb. *Than* is translated by **que.** Cf. § 27.

Marie parle français plus (moins) facilement que Jean.	Mary speaks French more (less) easily than John.

1. *More than, less than,* as adverbs of quantity = **plus de, moins de.**

Il m'a donné plus de dix francs.	He gave me more than ten francs.

97. The superlative of an adverb is formed by placing invariable **le** before the comparative.

C'est lui qui travaille le mieux.   He is the one who works best.

98. The following adverbs are compared irregularly.

bien, well	mieux, better	le mieux, (the) best
mal, badly, ill	{ plus mal / pis } worse	{ le plus mal / le pis } (the) worst
beaucoup, much	plus, more	le plus, (the) most
peu, little	moins, less	le moins, the least

Note. **Beaucoup** may never be modified by another adverb except **pas**.

A LA RECHERCHE D'UNE PENSION

—Cette vie d'hôtel m'ennuie, dit Paul un jour. Tous ces étrangers parlent anglais et je n'aime pas cela. Ce qu'il me faut, c'est une bonne pension de famille. Ne pourriez-vous pas m'en trouver une?

—Il est très difficile de trouver ce qu'on désire, surtout en cette saison-ci. Mais on peut toujours essayer. J'ai plus d'une douzaine d'adresses qu'on m'a données au bureau de renseignements à la Sorbonne.

Jean était très bien installé dans une pension du Quartier Latin et Paul espérait trouver une chambre dans une maison assez près de celle qu'habitait son ami. Après avoir cherché un peu partout, ils finirent par découvrir une chambre disponible dans un appartement de la rue d'Assas. Elle était bien meilleure que toutes celles qu'ils avaient vues jusque là. De la fenêtre qui donnait sur la rue, on avait une belle vue sur le jardin du Luxembourg et la chambre elle-même était propre et gentiment meublée.

—Je prendrai celle-ci, dit Paul tout de suite en la voyant. J'y serai très bien.

—En effet. Et puis vous serez dans une famille française où il faudra parler français ou vous taire.

—Tant mieux. Ce n'est pas la peine de venir en France pour passer son temps avec un tas de touristes qui parlent français encore plus mal que moi. Ce voyage m'a coûté assez cher et il faut absolument que je profite autant que possible de mon séjour en France.

CONVERSATION

1. Où habite Paul depuis qu'il est à Paris? 2. Pourquoi veut-il chercher une pension? 3. Pourquoi est-il difficile de trouver une bonne pension à Paris en été? 4. Pourquoi Paul ne veut-il pas quitter le Quartier Latin? 5. Dans quelle rue a-t-il trouvé une pension? 6. Etait-elle plus ou moins satisfaisante que celles qu'il avait vues ailleurs? 7. Que voyait-on de la fenêtre de sa chambre? 8. Comment la chambre était-elle meublée? 9. Pourquoi Paul voulait-il être dans une famille française? 10. Pourquoi ne voulait-il pas passer son temps avec des touristes américains?

COMPOSITION

"Hello, John. I was just going to your house. Didn't you tell me that you had some addresses of pensions?"

"I have those that were given to me at the information bureau."

"Well, I think I should like a furnished room better than the hotel and I visited some yesterday. Unfortunately those that I saw cost more than thirty francs a day or they were badly situated. There must be others nearer the Luxembourg."

"Without doubt. But I don't know whether we shall be able to find what you want."

"A room with (the) running water and a bathroom, if that is possible."

"We won't find that easily, especially at less than thirty francs. However, I know a widow who usually has some rooms to rent. I'll take you to her house, if you wish."

Fortunately, Mrs. Leroux was at home.

"I have a nice room which opens on the Luxembourg Garden," she told them. "Behind this one, there are two smaller rooms but those are taken. This one is available, however. It has (the) running water and there is a bathroom in the apartment. You will be very comfortable here. It is not expensive either, at 600 francs a month."

"I'll take this one," said Paul. "Could I also take my meals with you? I should like to speak French as much as possible."

"That can be arranged easily. When will you come?"

"This afternoon, if that does not inconvenience you."

"Not at all. We shall expect you at dinner this evening."
"Thank you, Madame. Until (à) this evening, then."

DRILL EXERCISE

1. What we are looking for is a good boarding-house. 2. I am not absolutely sure that you will find what you want. 3. He to whom I was speaking is my French teacher. 4. We should speak French constantly, in order to perfect ourselves in the language. 5. That suits us perfectly. 6. I do not know what is amusing them. 7. That knife cuts better than this one. 8. These rooms are more nicely furnished than those. 9. But they are more expensive than the ones we saw yesterday. 10. Those of the Latin Quarter are more simple. 11. My apartment and Paul's are quite similar. 12. She who was here yesterday is extremely pretty. 13. What I need is three rooms with a bathroom. 14. This is true, but what he said is not true. 15. My suitcases and my brother's have already arrived. 16. In America, he used to speak French very badly, but he speaks it much better now. 17. What beautiful flowers! How good they smell! 18. They are prettier than those from our garden. 19. The ones he sent me last week are still more beautiful.

VERB REVIEW

voir, to see. Cf. § 228.
s'asseoir,[1] to seat oneself, sit down. Cf. § 222.

1. I shall see him, when he comes. 2. Sit down here and I shall see what I can do. 3. It is necessary that I see them. 4. If I were in

---

[1] Students will avoid mistakes in the use of s'asseoir, se coucher, se lever, se promener, etc., if they note that French has no intransitive verbs corresponding to the English verbs *to sit, to rise, to go to bed,* etc. The ideas contained in the English intransitive verbs are rendered in French by the transitive verbs **asseoir**, *to seat;* **coucher**, *to put to bed;* **lever**, *to raise;* **promener**, *to take to (for a) walk,* etc., used reflexively. Thus:

Elle était assise dans le salon.	She was sitting (= was seated) in the salon.
Elle s'asseyait quand je suis entré dans le salon.	She was sitting down (= was seating herself) when I entered the salon.
Elle s'est levée à 8 heures.	She arose (= raised herself) at 8 o'clock.

your place, I should see them before their departure. 5. He was sitting here, when I saw him. 6. I see nothing that interests me. 7. Let him sit down here, if he wants to do so. 8. He entered (*p. def.*) the room, saw (*p. def.*) me and sat (*p. def.*) down. 9. We used to see them every day seated in the park. 10. We shall sit down here, where we shall see everything. 11. They are sitting down now. 12. He had been sitting there for two hours.

LESSON XIII

NUMERALS. DATES

Cardinal Numbers

99. Table of the cardinals.

1. **Un**, une	21. vingt et un
2. deux	22. vingt-deux
3. trois	30. trente
4. quatre	40. quarante
5. cinq	50. cinquante
6. six	60. soixante
7. sept	70. soixante-dix
8. huit	71. soixante et onze
9. neuf	80. quatre-vingts
10. dix	81. quatre-vingt-un
11. onze	90. quatre-vingt-dix
12. douze	91. quatre-vingt-onze
13. treize	100. cent
14. quatorze	101. cent un
15. quinze	200. deux cents
16. seize	201. deux cent un
17. dix-sept	1000. mille
18. dix-huit	1001. mille un
19. dix-neuf	2000. deux mille
20. vingt	

100. Pronunciation of cardinals.

1. Final consonants of 5, 6, 7, 8, 9, 10, 17, 18, 19, are pronounced except before a word multiplied by them beginning with a consonant or **h** aspirate. The consonant is pronounced in **cinq hommes, le dix mai,** but it is silent in **cinq livres.**

2. No elision or linking occurs before **huit** or **onze**. Cf. **le onze juin; les huit livres**.
3. The t of **vingt** is pronounced only in the numbers from 21 to 29; t is silent in the numbers from 81 to 99 and in 101, 102, etc.
4. **Et** is regularly used in 21, 31, 41, 51, 61, 71.
5. The hyphen is used in all compound numbers under 100, except where **et** is used.

101. Quatre-vingt and multiples of **cent** take **s** when immediately followed by a noun, an adjective plus a noun, or when used as nouns of number.

 Quatre-vingts dollars.
 Deux cents (bons) prix.
But: Trois cent cinq francs.

102. Mille is invariable. **Mil** replaces **mille** in dates, but the form in hundreds is more frequently used, as in English.

Cinq mille francs.	Five thousand francs.
En { mil neuf cent vingt-six. / dix-neuf cent vingt-six.	In nineteen hundred twenty-six.

103. *A* or *one* are not translated before **cent** or **mille**.

Cent (mille) francs.	One hundred (one thousand) francs.

Ordinal Numbers

104. The ordinals, with the exception of **premier**, *first* and **second**, *second,* are formed in French by adding **-ième** to the last consonant of the cardinals. Final **q** in **cinq** becomes **qu** and final **f** of **neuf** becomes **v**. The form **deuxième** usually replaces **second** in a series of more than two.

 cinquième, neuvième, vingt et unième, trente-deuxième

105. Ordinals usually precede the word they modify and agree with it in gender and number. When a cardinal number is used with an ordinal, the cardinal number comes first.

La deuxième classe.	The second class.
Les quatre premières pages.	The first four pages.

106. The ordinals are used in general as in English, except that in dates and titles they are replaced by the cardinals for all numbers but **premier,** *first*.

Louis XIV; le vingt avril.	Louis Fourteenth; the twentieth of April.
Le premier février; Charles Ier.	The first of February; Charles First.

Collectives

107. The following collectives take **s** in the plural and are construed as ordinary nouns. They require **de** before the word they measure.

une **dizaine,** about ten	une **cinquantaine,** about fifty
une **douzaine,** a dozen	une **soixantaine,** about sixty
une **quinzaine,** about fifteen	une **centaine,** about a hundred
une **vingtaine,** about twenty	un **millier,** about a thousand
une **trentaine,** about thirty	un **million,** a million
une **quarantaine,** about forty	un **milliard,** a billion

Une douzaine de roses.	A dozen roses.
Un million de dollars.	A million dollars.

Fractions

108. Fractions are expressed by cardinals in the numerator and ordinals in the denominator, as in English. But the following forms are irregular: **un demi,** *a half;* **un tiers,** *a third;* **un quart,** *a quarter*.

Les cinq huitièmes de la terre.	Five-eighths of the earth.
Les trois quarts des habitants.	Three-fourths of the inhabitants.

1. **Demi,** *half,* as an adjective, is invariable before a noun and is joined to it by a hyphen. After a noun, it is variable.

Une demi-heure.	A half-hour.
Deux heures et demie.	Two hours and a half.

2. **La moitié,** *half,* is a noun and is the equivalent of the English *(the) half (of)*.

La moitié de mes amis.   Half of my friends.

109. *Once, twice, three times,* etc., are translated by **une fois, deux fois, trois fois,** etc.

Trois fois neuf font vingt-sept.   Three times nine make twenty-seven.

UN EMPRUNT

Vers la fin de 1819, l'avoué Grès se trouva obligé de vendre son étude. Son premier clerc, Derville, un homme actif et intelligent, voulait l'acheter mais il ne gagnait que cent trente francs par mois et ne connaissait d'autre capitaliste qu'un vieil usurier appelé le papa Gobseck. Sans beaucoup d'espoir il alla le trouver.

—Voici le fait, expliqua-t-il à l'usurier. L'étude de mon patron rapporte annuellement une vingtaine de mille francs; mais je crois qu'entre mes mains elle en vaudra quarante. Il veut la vendre cent cinquante mille francs. Si vous pouviez me prêter la moitié de cette somme. . . .

—Possible, dit Gobseck. Quel âge avez-vous?

—Vingt-cinq ans dans huit jours. Le dix-sept mai, pour être exact. Voici mon acte de naissance.

Gobseck prit le papier officiel et le lut.

—Nous allons tâcher d'arranger cette affaire. Je tire cinquante pour-cent de mes fonds, quelquefois cent, deux cents, quatre cents pour-cent.

Derville pâlit.

—Mais à cause de notre connaissance, je me contenterai de douze et demi pour-cent d'intérêt par . . .

Il hésita.

—Eh bien, pour vous je me contenterai de treize pour-cent par an. Cela vous va-t-il?

—Oui, répondit Derville. Ce sera dur les deux ou trois premières années, mais je serai libéré dans dix ans.

—Eh puis, continua Gobseck, mes confrères vous enverront leurs procès et ils en ont des centaines. Si vous en gagnez le tiers, vous serez plus riche que moi. Vous devriez presque me donner quinze pour-cent de mes soixante-quinze mille francs.

—Soit, mais pas davantage, dit Derville avec fermeté.

Gobseck parut content du marché, avança la somme voulue, et moins de trois mois après Derville avait son étude.

d'après Balzac

CONVERSATION

1. Qui était Derville? 2. Combien d'argent gagnait-il par mois? 3. Combien d'argent valait l'étude de son patron? 4. Combien voulait-il bien la vendre? 5. Pourquoi Derville s'est-il adressé à Gobseck? 6. Qui était Gobseck? 7. Quel pour-cent Gobseck tirait-il de ses fonds? 8. Quel pour-cent d'intérêt a-t-il demandé à Derville? 9. Combien de temps faudra-t-il à Derville pour payer sa dette à Gobseck? 10. Comment Gobseck aidera-t-il Derville à s'enrichir? 11. Combien d'argent a-t-il prêté enfin à Derville et à quel pour-cent? 12. Pourquoi a-t-il demandé quinze pour-cent au lieu de treize? 13. Quand est-ce que Derville a pu acheter son étude?

COMPOSITION

About (**vers**) 1820 Papa Gobseck was the richest of Parisian money-lenders and the stingiest. Hundreds of persons needing money applied to him and each one of them added a few thousand francs to the millions that he had already accumulated. He demanded (**se faire payer**) enormous interests, getting from his capital up to three hundred per cent. In spite of his eighty years he was as shrewd as a Norman. Derville knew it and his [1] heart beat fast when Gobseck opened the door for him.

[1] Cf. § 113.

"Well," said the miser, "your employer is selling his practice the second of February and you want Papa Gobseck to lend you the money necessary to buy it."

"Why not?" Derville answered firmly. "I am earning a hundred and fifty francs a month and I am not yet thirty years old. My employer's practice brings in now fifteen hundred francs monthly but in my hands it will be worth four times as much after the first year. I shall need eighty thousand francs. If you would be satisfied with ten and a half per cent (of) interest . . .

Gobseck did not answer.

"I will even give fourteen per cent a year, if you will send me the law suits of which you and your colleagues must have hundreds."

Gobseck offered him his hand. "Since I have been in business, no one has ever explained to me more clearly the motives of his visit. I will give you the money and for the sake of our acquaintanceship, I shall be satisfied with . . . fifteen per cent a year."

DRILL EXERCISE

1. Victor Hugo was born at Besançon in 1802 and died in Paris in 1885. 2. Francis I reigned from 1515 to 1547. 3. Marseilles has 700,000 inhabitants. 4. The Spanish republic was founded in 1931. 5. Alphonse XIII was the last King of Spain. 6. Thousands of tourists go to Europe every year. 7. ¼, 4/7, ⅔, 3/5. 8. The last six pages of this book are missing. 9. A second class ticket from New York to Paris costs about one hundred and eighty dollars. 10. That novel is in the twenty-first volume of the works of Balzac. 11. Six times nine make fifty-four. 12. You will read four and one half pages for to-morrow. 13. France has thirty-eight million inhabitants. 14. The fourteenth of July is the French national holiday. 15. The fête of Joan of Arc is celebrated the second Sunday in May. 16. I paid for this picture one hundred and five francs and for that one, two hundred francs. 17. Washington was born on February 22nd 1732. 18. There are about thirty students in our class. 19. Half of the automobiles in the United States cost less than eight hundred dollars each. 20. The third French republic was proclaimed the fourth of September 1870. 21. What famous battle took place in 1066?

VERB REVIEW

écrire, to write. Cf. § 206.
  décrire, to describe
lire, to read. Cf. § 208.

1. I was reading, while he was writing. 2. They wrote to him yesterday. 3. She has read that book. 4. John will read us his composition. 5. He would have written us. 6. It is necessary that you read more. 7. I should write him, if I had his address. 8. If he were here, he would read it to us. 9. She read (*p. def.*) too rapidly. 10. What are you writing? 11. John will write to us from Paris. 12. Describe what you saw. 13. Read me your description. 14. He wants me to write to her. 15. I read every evening. 16. We wrote (*p. def.*) them at once.

LESSON XIV

POSSESSIVE ADJECTIVES AND PRONOUNS. EXPRESSIONS OF TIME. DATES. AGE

Possessive Adjectives

110. Table of the possessive adjectives.

| Singular | | Plural | |
Masc.	Fem.	Masc. and Fem.	
mon	ma	mes	my
ton	ta	tes	your, thy
son	sa	ses	his, her
notre	notre	nos	our
votre	votre	vos	your
leur	leur	leurs	their

111. Possessive adjectives, contrary to English usage, agree in gender and number with the thing possessed, not with the possessor. They are repeated before each noun modified.

Son livre et son stylo. His (her) book and his (her) fountain pen.

1. To avoid ambiguity, the possessive adjective may be supplemented by **à** + a disjunctive pronoun.

Son livre à lui (à elle). His (her) book.

2. Emphatic *own* is translated by **propre** or by **à** + disjunctive pronoun.

Mon propre livre.
Mon livre à moi. } My own book.

112. **Mon, ton** and **son** are used instead of **ma, ta** and **sa** before a vowel or **h** mute.

| Mon amie. | My friend. |

113. The definite article generally replaces the possessive adjective referring to parts of the body, when there is no ambiguity as to the possessor.

Je me suis coupé le doigt.	I cut my finger.
Ils ont levé la [1] main droite.	They raised their right hands.
Le cœur lui battait fort.	His heart was beating fast.

Possessive Pronouns

114. Table of the possessive pronouns.

Singular	Plural	
le mien, *m.*	les miens	
la mienne, *f.*	les miennes	mine
le tien, *m.*	les tiens	
la tienne, *f.*	les tiennes	thine
le sien, *m.*	les siens	
la sienne, *f.*	les siennes	his, hers
le (la) nôtre, *m. and f.*	les nôtres	ours
le (la) vôtre, *m. and f.*	les vôtres	yours
le (la) leur, *m. and f.*	les leurs	theirs

115. Possessive pronouns agree in gender and number, as do the adjectives, with the thing possessed, not with the possessor.

| Mon auto et la sienne. | My auto and his (hers). |

116. *Mine,* etc. after the verb **être** is translated by **à** + a disjunctive pronoun, except when distinction of ownership is stressed. In this case, a possessive pronoun is generally used.

---

[1] The singular is generally used when each individual possesses but one of the objects named.

Ce livre est à moi.	This book is mine.
Ce livre-ci est le mien; celui-là est le vôtre.	This book is mine; that one is yours.

117. *A friend of mine,* (*his,* etc.) is paraphrased by *one of my* (*his,* etc.) *friends.*

Un de mes amis.	A friend of mine.
Un professeur de ses amis.	A professor who is a friend of his.

Expressions of Time

118. *It is* in telling the time of day is **il est.**

Il est quatre heures.	It is four o'clock.

119. *After* or *past* is expressed by: 1) **et** before **demi;** 2) **et** or **un** before **quart;** 3) nothing before **minutes. Minutes** may also be omitted.

Il est cinq heures et demie.	It is half past five.
Il est dix heures et (un) quart.	It is quarter after ten.
Il est midi vingt (minutes).	It is twenty minutes past twelve.

120. *Of* or *before* is expressed by **moins,** *less,* followed by the number of minutes. **Quart** may be used alone or preceded by **un** or **le.**

Il est neuf heures moins cinq (minutes).	It is five minutes of nine.
Il est minuit moins { le / un } quart.	It is quarter to twelve (midnight).

121. Note the following current expressions:

Quelle heure est-il?	What time is it?
A quelle heure est-il arrivé?	(At) what time did he arrive?
Il est midi et demi.	It is half past twelve (noon).
A onze heures précises.	At eleven o'clock sharp.
A huit heures du matin.	At eight A. M.

A dix heures du soir.	At ten P.M.
Il est tard.	It is late.
Je suis en retard.	I am late (behind time).
Le train est arrivé à l'heure.	The train arrived on time.
Nous sommes arrivés à temps pour prendre le train.	We arrived in time to catch the train.
Ma montre avance de deux minutes.	My watch is two minutes fast.
Ma montre retarde de deux minutes.	My watch is two minutes slow.
Quelle heure avez-vous à votre montre?	What time is it by your watch?

122. Date expressions.

Quel jour du mois est-ce (sommes-nous) aujourd'hui?	What day of the month is it to-day?
C'est (Nous sommes) aujourd'hui le quinze mai.	To-day is the fifteenth of May.
Il y a huit (quinze) jours.	A week (two weeks) ago.
Samedi passé.	Last Saturday.
D'aujourd'hui en huit.	A week from to-day.
La semaine prochaine.	Next week (*in the future*).
La semaine suivante.	The following week.

123. Age expressions.

Quel âge a-t-il?	How old is he?
Il a dix-huit ans. Il est âgé de dix-huit ans.	He is eighteen years old.
Il est plus (moins) âgé que moi de trois ans. Il a trois ans de plus (moins) que moi.	He is three years older (younger) than I.

UNE PROMENADE

En lisant le journal du soir, Paul remarqua la petite annonce suivante: Demain, dimanche, à quatre heures et demie précises les Grandes Eaux joueront à Versailles.

—Diable! s'écria-t-il. Jean m'a dit que ce spectacle devait avoir lieu de demain en huit. Il faut que je lui donne un coup de téléphone tout de suite.

En ce moment, Mme Leroux frappa à la porte.

—On vous demande au téléphone, M. Somers.

Paul alla à l'appareil et prit le récepteur:

—J'écoute.

—C'est vous, Paul? C'est moi, le Docteur Martin. Nous allons à Versailles demain après-midi voir les Grandes Eaux. Voulez-vous être des nôtres?

—Mais avec plaisir.

—Agnès emmène une étudiante de ses amies et Jean est naturellement de la partie. Nous irons vous prendre chez vous à deux heures et quart.

—Nous serons prêts. Allô, allô! Voilà qu'on a coupé la communication. Ces demoiselles du téléphone sont insupportables!

. . . .

—Le Docteur Martin se fait attendre, dit Paul le lendemain après-midi. Nous n'arriverons jamais à temps. Quelle heure avez-vous à votre montre, Jean? La mienne avance, peut-être, de quelques minutes.

—Nos amis sont certainement un peu en retard. Les voilà enfin.

L'auto stoppa et les deux jeunes gens y montèrent. Le docteur conduisit à toute vitesse et on entra dans le parc au moment où les fontaines commençaient à jouer.

—Comme c'est beau, dit Agnès, en montrant du doigt le grand bassin de Neptune. Autrefois ce beau jardin appartenait à Louis XIV pour son bon plaisir et celui des siens. Maintenant on voit bien qu'il est au peuple. Avez-vous jamais vu une foule pareille?

CONVERSATION

1. Quelle annonce Paul a-t-il vue dans le journal? 2. Pourquoi cette annonce l'a-t-elle surpris? 3. Qui l'a demandé au téléphone à ce moment-là? 4. Qu'est-ce que le Docteur Martin l'a invité à faire? 5. Comment irait-on à Versailles? 6. A quelle heure devait-on partir? 7. Comment la conversation téléphonique s'est-elle terminée? 8. Est-ce que le Docteur Martin est arrivé en avance chez Paul le lendemain? 9. Pourquoi n'est-on pas arrivé en retard à Versailles? 10. A quel moment est-on entré dans le parc? 11. Qui

a construit le parc de Versailles? 12. A qui appartient-il aujourd'hui? 13. Est-ce que les Grandes Eaux jouent souvent? 14. Quel jour de la semaine jouent-elles?

COMPOSITION

"What time is it by your watch, John? Mine is slow."

"It is twenty-minutes after four by mine. I wonder where the Martins can (well) be. I invited them a week ago to join us to-day and they promised to meet us here in front of the palace at quarter to four. I tried to telephone to Agnes last night but she was not at home."

"Well, we can't wait any longer. If they commence on time, we shall be late. If Agnes and that French friend of hers wish to waste their afternoon, I am not anxious to waste ours. Let's go."

The fountains were already playing, when they arrived in front of the first basin. The streams of water rose so high that it was necessary to raise one's eyes to see the tops of them. In the groves on both sides, one could glimpse other streams of water half hidden by the trees.

"What a magnificent spectacle!" exclaimed Paul. "This park once belonged to Louis XIV, didn't it?"

"Yes, but now it belongs to the French people, as you can very well see," said John, pointing to the crowd which was circulating on the terraces. "The French love Versailles, for here the living past of France surrounds them and the glory of the great king becomes, for a few hours, theirs."

That evening Dr. Martin called up John. "We had a breakdown near Meudon," he explained.

"That's too bad," said John. "Fortunately for you, the fountains play again three weeks from to-day."

DRILL EXERCISE

1. What day of the month is it to-day? 2. It is the 17th of August. 3. Paul telephoned to me last Wednesday. 4. He will arrive a week from to-day. 5. Paul is twenty-one years old. 6. He is one year younger than John and two years older than Agnes. 7. We saw the fountains at Versailles two weeks ago. 8. We did not arrive in time

to visit the palace. 9. A friend of ours was to accompany us. 10. Shall we take our auto or yours? 11. Why not mine? It is at the door. 12. He will call for you at seven o'clock sharp. 13. That is her own idea; what do you think of it? 14. She hurt her hand, when she fell. 15. I hope to spend my vacation in France next year. 16. Whose newspaper is this? It is not mine; it must be hers. 17. Who is the girl with Helen? It is a student friend of hers. 18. I am late, because my train did not arrive on time. 19. John's room is more comfortable than his friend's. 20. I like it better than theirs. 21. French newspapers have fewer pages than ours. 22. He wears a gold ring on (à) the little finger of his left hand.

VERB REVIEW

tenir, to hold. Cf. § 193.
    tenir à, to be anxious to, insist on
    appartenir, to belong
    maintenir, to maintain
    obtenir, to obtain
venir, to come. Cf. § 194.
    devenir, to become
    revenir, to come back, return
    se[1] **souvenir de**, to remember

1. They will come soon. 2. He was anxious to see the palace. 3. I did not remember her. 4. I am sorry that he is not coming. 5. To whom does this book belong? 6. It used to belong to them. 7. What has become of her? 8. He is coming back at six o'clock. 9. He will maintain that you are wrong. 10. He would insist on leaving, if he were sick. 11. They were coming to get us after (the) dinner. 12. They would come, if they were not busy. 13. He came back (*p. def.*) immediately. 14. He does not remember us. 15. He was insisting on it. 16. I shall tell him that, when he comes. 17. I am glad that he remembered it. 18. Did you get the connection (*of a telephone*)?

---

[1] Direct object. **Se** (indirect object) **rappeler**, *to recall, to remember*, is more frequently used referring to things than to persons and cannot be used with **me, te, nous**, or **vous** as direct object. **Je me le rappelle.** I remember it (him). But: **Je me souviens de vous.**

LESSON XV

THE RELATIVE PRONOUN

124. The forms of the relative pronoun are:

	Antecedent a person	Antecedent a thing	
Subject	qui	qui	*who, which, that*
Direct object.	que	que	*whom, which, that*
Object of de	dont	dont	*whose, of whom, of which*
		M. F.	
Object of prepositions other than de	qui	sing. lequel,[1] laquelle plur. lesquels, lesquelles	*whom, which*

Les élèves qui sont ici. — The pupils who are here.
Le livre que vous m'avez donné. — The book which you gave me.
La craie avec laquelle j'écris. — The chalk with which I am writing.

L'homme } **dont je parle.** — The man of whom } I am
Les livres } — The books of which } speaking.
Le monsieur à qui je parle. — The gentleman to whom I am speaking.

1. **Lequel,** etc. may be used in place of any of the other forms of the relative pronoun, when required for clearness.

La sœur de Jean laquelle vient d'arriver. — John's sister who has just arrived.

---

[1] Lequel, lesquels and lesquelles combine with de and à, giving **duquel, desquels, desquelles** and **auquel, auxquels, auxquelles.**

125. Relative pronouns are required in French, even though omitted in English.

> Les fleurs que je lui ai envoyées. The flowers I sent her.

126. Dont is equivalent to **de** plus a relative pronoun and translates the English *whose, of whom, of which,* etc. **Dont** must be immediately followed by the subject of the verb in the clause introduced by it and the noun which it modifies must be preceded by the definite article.

> La soirée dont je parlais. The party of which I was speaking.
>
> Mon cousin dont vous connaissez la sœur. My cousin whose sister you know.
>
> Un livre dont le prix est très élevé. A book whose price is very high.

1. When, in English, *whose, of whom, of which,* modifies a noun which is the object of a preposition, **dont** cannot be used. Instead, **de qui** (of persons) or **de** plus a form of **lequel** (of persons or things) must be used.

> Le monsieur avec le fils de qui (duquel) je me promenais. The gentleman with whose son I used to go walking.

127. The compound relative with indefinite antecedent referring to things, *that which, what,* has the following forms:

Subject	ce qui	*that which, what*
Direct object	ce que	*that which, what*
Object of de	ce dont	*that of which, of what*
Object of other prepositions	ce *prep.* quoi	*that to (with,* etc.*) which*

> Je ne sais pas ce qui vous amuse. I don't know what is amusing you.
>
> Ce qu'il m'a donné, c'est un bon conseil. What he gave me was some good advice.

Ce dont je parle.   What I am speaking of.
Ce avec quoi je travaille.   What I am working with.

128. The compound relative with definite antecedent, referring to persons or to things, *he who, she who, the one who, those who, whoever,* etc., is made up of the demonstrative pronoun (cf. §§ 87–88) and **qui, que, dont**. It has the following forms:

Subject	celui etc. qui
Direct object	celui etc. que
Object of **de**	celui etc. dont
Object of other prepositions	celui etc. *prep.* qui (lequel)

Celui qui parle.   He who (The one who, whoever) is speaking.
Ceux que nous avons trouvés.   Those which we found.
Celui dont vous parlez.   The one you are speaking of.
Celle avec qui vous vous promenez.   She with whom you are walking.

129. Où. The adverb **où** is often used instead of a relative pronoun preceded by a preposition meaning *to, at, in, on*.

La maison où (dans laquelle) je demeure.   The house in which I live.

MOYENS DE TRANSPORT

Cher Albert:

Merci de votre bonne lettre à laquelle j'aurais dû répondre il y a longtemps. Depuis que je vous ai écrit, j'ai quitté l'hôtel où j'étais descendu et je suis dans une famille française dont Jean m'a donné l'adresse. Je connais Paris assez bien et je parle assez couramment le français pour me tirer d'affaire partout.

Les moyens de transport ici sont à mon avis meilleurs et, ce qui est plus important, meilleur marché que ceux de chez nous. Je prends souvent les autobus dont les lignes traversent Paris dans tous les sens. Leur itinéraire est divisé en sections et le tarif varie selon la distance parcourue. Ils ont deux classes: les places à l'avant sont réservées aux voyageurs de première classe, les autres aux voyageurs de seconde, dont une huitaine doivent rester debout sur la plate-forme. Quand il n'y a plus de place, le receveur accroche une pancarte portant le mot "Complet" et on n'admet plus personne. Je trouve ce système excellent mais il a ses inconvénients. Par exemple, l'autre soir j'étais à Montmartre avec Agnès Martin, dont je vous ai parlé et avec qui je sors souvent. Le dernier autobus était bondé et nous avons dû prendre un taxi dans lequel on paye tarif double passé minuit. Quand l'auto s'est arrêtée devant le jardin au fond duquel se trouve l'appartement d'Agnès, j'ai découvert que je n'avais pas assez d'argent pour payer le chauffeur et j'ai dû en emprunter à Agnès.

Ecrivez-moi ce qui se passe chez vous et ce que vous allez faire cette automne.

Cordiale poignée de main de votre ami,
Paul

CONVERSATION

1. De qui Paul a-t-il reçu une lettre? 2. Où habite Paul? 3. A-t-il changé d'adresse récemment? 4. Comment parle-t-il français? 5. Y a-t-il beaucoup d'autobus à Paris? 6. Combien de classes ont-ils? 7. Quelles places sont réservées aux voyageurs de première classe? 8. Les voyageurs de seconde classe ont-ils des places assises? 9. Que fait-on, quand toutes les places sont prises? 10. Où Paul est-il allé avec Agnès un soir? 11. Pourquoi n'a-t-il pas pris un autobus pour le retour? 12. Est-ce que les taxis coûtent cher à Paris? 13. Où habite Agnès? 14. Qu'est-ce qui s'est passé, quand le taxi s'est arrêté devant la maison d'Agnès?

COMPOSITION

62 rue d'Assas
August 6th.

Dear Albert:

Your last letter finally reached me at Mme Leroux's whose address I beg you to note. I was glad to learn what is happening at your home and what you hope to do this fall.

I am beginning to know Paris fairly well, thanks to Agnes Martin to whose father you gave me a letter of introduction. John has also given me a lot of practical information without which I could not get along.

Yesterday Agnes and I went to see the Davis Cup matches at Auteuil. The stadium is near the Bois de Boulogne in a quarter quite far from the one we live in. After the matches, that I do not need to describe to you, we looked for a tramway of the line by which we had come. But the tramways were crowded and the autobuses all bore the sign [1] "Full." We waited for a quarter of an hour, and then we walked to the nearest subway station. There we found ourselves immediately in the middle of a crowd, from which it was impossible to get out. A subway train is composed of five cars of which the middle one (**celle du milieu**) is reserved for first class passengers. In that car one can generally find seats (**places assises**) but yesterday we were like sardines in a box. It was an experience that we shall long remember. I made my excuses to Agnes of course but I still wonder why I did not take a taxi.

Don't fail to write me soon.

Sincerely,
Paul

DRILL EXERCISE

1. Do you know what you are going to do? 2. Here is the hotel of which I spoke to you. 3. Miss Martin, whose brother you know, lives here. 4. She is the girl with whom I often go to the theatre. 5. The boarding-house in which I live is near here. 6. The woman in whose house I live is French. 7. The autobus that passes in front of the house is the one that goes to the St. Lazare station. 8. Those that stop here are usually full. 9. There are a dozen bridges by which one can cross the Seine. 10. The subway, whose lines cross Paris in all directions, is better than that of New York. 11. The conductor is the one who takes the tickets. 12. Tell me what you are thinking of. 13. I do not know what will interest you most in Paris. 14. The daughter of Mr. Martin, who has been here for a year, speaks French very well. 15. This is exactly what I need. 16. Here is the rue de Tournon, at the end of which is the Luxembourg Palace.

[1] la pancarte or l'écriteau *m.*

GRAMMATICAL EXERCISE

Replace the dash by a proper form of the relative pronoun:

1. Connaissez-vous cette église — on voit la façade? 2. C'est Notre Dame, — je vous ai parlé. 3. Quelle est cette tour au sommet — on voit une statue? 4. Dites-moi — vous voulez voir ensuite. 5. Savez-vous — me plaît ici? 6. Le guide — j'ai acheté n'est pas — vous m'avez recommandé. 7. L'édifice devant — nous nous trouvons est l'Hôtel de Ville. 8. Le monsieur à — je pense est un médecin. 9. L'autobus — nous sommes montés est — va à l'Opéra. 10. L'hôtel — je suis descendu est très comfortable.

VERB REVIEW

recevoir, to receive. Cf. § 220.
   apercevoir, to perceive (*with the senses*), notice, see, etc.
   s'apercevoir de, to perceive (*with the mind*), become aware of
   s'apercevoir que, to perceive, notice
   décevoir, to deceive
suivre, to follow. Cf. § 216.

1. He perceived that I was reading. 2. What courses were you taking? 3. I became aware of his sickness yesterday. 4. She used to receive Thursdays. 5. I am taking two courses in (de) English. 6. Her teacher wants Mary to receive the prize. 7. She will take a course in history next year. 8. When will you receive them? 9. He did not notice my presence. 10. I should take another course, if I had (the) time. 11. My father wants me to take a course in mathematics. 12. Madame Martin receives now on Tuesdays. 13. Follow me and I shall introduce you to him. 14. I am afraid he may not receive them. 15. His dog would follow him everywhere. 16. I shall follow your advice.

LESSON XVI

INTERROGATIVE PRONOUNS AND ADJECTIVES

The Interrogative Pronouns

130. The forms of the interrogative pronoun are:

	Referring to persons	Referring to things
Subject	qui? who? qui est-ce qui? who?	qu'est-ce qui? what?
Direct object	qui? whom? qui est-ce que? whom?	que? what? qu'est-ce que? what?
Object of prepositions	qui? whom? qui est-ce que? whom?	quoi? what?

Referring to both persons and things

	Sing.	Plural	
Masc.	lequel?[1]	lesquels?	which? which one?
Fem.	laquelle?	lesquelles?	

Qui (or qui est-ce qui) est arrivé?	Who has arrived?
Qu'est-ce qui vous intéresse?	What interests you?
Qui avez-vous vu?	Whom have you seen?
Qu'avez-vous trouvé? Qu'est-ce que vous avez trouvé?	What have you found?
De quoi parlaient-ils?	What were they talking about?

131. Lequel, laquelle, etc., agree in gender and number with the antecedent and are never followed directly by a noun.

---

[1] **Lequel, lesquels** and **lesquelles** combine with **de** and **à**, giving **duquel, desquels, desquelles** and **auquel, auxquels, auxquelles.**

Lequel est votre ami?   Which (one) is your friend?
Auquel de ces messieurs parlez-vous?   To which one of these gentlemen are you speaking?

132. *What?* (asking for a definition) is rendered in French by **qu'est-ce que c'est que?** (or **qu'est-ce que?**).[1] This locution should be distinguished from the interrogative adjective **quel? quelle?** etc., meaning *which?* or *what?*, in the sense of *which one?*

Qu'est-ce que c'est que le Musée de Cluny?   What is the Cluny Museum?
But: Quelle est la leçon?   What (which) is the lesson?

133. *Whose?* in interrogations is translated by **à qui?** to denote mere ownership; in other cases by **de qui? Dont** is never used interrogatively.

De qui êtes-vous le fils?   Whose son are you?
A qui est cette maison?   Whose house is this? (i. e., who owns it.)

Interrogative Adjectives

134. The forms of the interrogative adjective are:

	Sing.	Plural	
Masc.	quel?	quels?	} what? what a! which?
Fem.	quelle?	quelles?	

135. The interrogative adjective is followed directly by the noun modified or is used as a predicate adjective with the verb **être**.

Quelle vue superbe!   What a superb view!
Quel est votre sport préféré?   What is your favorite sport?
Quels cours suivez-vous?   What courses are you taking?

---

[1] In indirect questions: ce que c'est que. Je ne sais pas ce que c'est que ce musée-là.

LE MUSÉE CARNAVALET

—Que voulez-vous voir aujourd'hui? dit Jean, comme lui et Paul sortaient de la pension de ce dernier. Jean connaissait Paris à fond et naturellement voulait faire voir à son ami les principales curiosités de la capitale.

—Je voudrais visiter un des monuments historiques. Lequel suggérez-vous?

—Nous pourrions aller à Carnavalet. Qu'en dites-vous?

—Qu'est-ce que c'est que Carnavalet? Qu'est-ce qu'on y voit?

—C'est le musée historique de la ville de Paris. Il doit son nom à Mme de Kernovenoy qui y demeurait au seizième siècle. On l'a bien oubliée et son nom par corruption est devenu Carnavalet. On y voit de très curieux souvenirs de la Révolution Française, notamment divers articles provenant de la Bastille et de la Tour du Temple.

—De quel temple parlez-vous?

—De l'ancien monastère fortifié des Templiers dans la grosse tour duquel Louis XVI a été emprisonné en 1792. On conserve à Carnavalet des meubles et des articles de toilette dont la malheureuse famille royale s'est servie pendant sa captivité.

—Allons voir les souvenirs de Louis Capet. Vous voyez que je me rappelle tout de même mon histoire de France.

—Vous rappelez-vous aussi que l'Hôtel Carnavalet est l'ancienne demeure de Mme de Sévigné?

—Quoi! La vieille dame dont les lettres décrivent si bien la cour de Louis XIV? Non, vraiment, je ne savais pas chez qui j'allais. Qu'est-ce qui reste de l'ancien édifice?

—Une assez belle façade, les chambres habitées par Mme de Sévigné et par sa fille. Que sais-je encore? D'ailleurs vous verrez pour vous-même, puisque nous voilà.

—Quelle foule devant la porte! Qu'est-ce qui se passe?

—Tout simplement que beaucoup de touristes visitent Carnavalet et que nous avons mal choisi notre jour.

CONVERSATION

1. Est-ce que Paul connaît Paris mieux que Jean? 2. Comment se fait-il que Jean connaisse si bien la capitale? 3. A quel musée

a-t-il mené Paul un jour? 4. Qu'est-ce que c'est que Carnavalet? 5. Quels souvenirs historiques peut-on y voir? 6. Quand la Bastille a-t-elle été détruite? 7. Quel jour célèbre-t-on la destruction de la Bastille? 8. Qui a construit le Temple? 9. Quel roi de France a été détenu dans la Tour du Temple? 10. Qui a habité autrefois l'Hôtel Carnavalet? 11. Quels souvenirs de Mme de Sévigné se trouvent encore à Carnavalet? 12. Que savez-vous de Mme de Sévigné? 13. A quelle époque a-t-elle vécu? 14. Est-ce que beaucoup de touristes visitent Carnavalet?

COMPOSITION

"What fine weather!" said Paul to his friend. "Where shall we go to-day and what are we going to see?"

"Suppose we visit one of the museums that you haven't seen."

"All right. Which one?"

"One of those that I like best is Carnavalet."

"What is Carnavalet and what is to be found there?"

"You don't know what Carnavalet is? That surprises me, for the Hôtel Carnavalet was once the residence of a writer whose letters you must have read."

"Who lived in it?"

"Have you never heard (speak) of Mme de Sévigné? She lived nineteen years in this mansion."

"I remember now that Mme de Sévigné lived in the Quartier du Marais not far from the Temple but I had forgotten the name of her residence. By the way, what remains of the Temple?"

"Nothing. Napoleon I had the big tower torn down in 1811 and the rest was demolished under Napoleon III. However, you will see at Carnavalet a few objects that came from (**provenant de**) the rooms occupied by Louis XVI and his family during their imprisonment in the old monastery."

"When I recall the drama of the Temple, I don't think of Louis XVI nor of the queen."

"Of whom do you think?"

"Of the little dauphin. Did he die in the Temple? By whom was he killed? If he didn't die there, who was the child who died there in his place?"

"No one will ever know (it). But here we are at the door of the museum. What a crowd of tourists! The entrance is evidently free on Thursdays."

DRILL EXERCISE

1. Who was with you? 2. To whom were you talking? 3. What did they want? 4. What is that building? 5. Which one of those girls is your cousin? 6. Of whom are you thinking? 7. What did he talk about? 8. What day is it to-day? 9. Whom did you see last night? 10. What is amusing them? 11. Whose cousins are they? 12. Whose books are these? 13. Of which ones are you speaking? 14. What brings you here? 15. What were they trying to do? 16. What was he thinking of? 17. What is this street? 18. What are the reasons that he gave? 19. Of all these flowers which ones do you like the best? 20. What a magnificent view! 21. He does not know which one he will choose. 22. What novels of Hugo have you read? 23. Which ones do you prefer? 24. I do not know what he will do. 25. To what museum are you going to take me to-day? 26. To which one do you want to go? 27. Do you know what Carnavalet is? 28. I do not know what Carnavalet is.

VERB REVIEW

mourir, to die. Cf. § 191.
naître, to be born. Cf. § 210.

1. George Washington was born (*p. def.*) in 1732 and died (*p. def.*) in 1799. 2. They would die of hunger there. 3. She was born in 1903. 4. My uncle died yesterday. 5. I am sorry that he has died. 6. Born in 1899, he died two years ago. 7. Many will be born who will not understand these times. 8. We are born, grow old and die; that is life. 9. He was dying, when the doctor arrived. 10. She would have died, if they had not come.

LESSON XVII

INDEFINITE ADJECTIVES AND PRONOUNS

136. Indefinite Adjectives.

certain, certain
chaque, each, every
divers, divers, various

quelque, some; *pl.,* some, a few
quelconque } any (whatever, at all)
n'importe quel

137. Indefinite Pronouns.

    chacun, chacune, each, each one
    on, one, we, they, people
    n'importe qui, any one (at all)
    n'importe quoi, anything (whatever)
    personne . . . ne,[1] nobody, no one
    quelqu'un, quelques-uns } somebody, some one, some
    quelqu'une, quelques-unes
    quiconque, whoever
    rien . . . ne, nothing

138. Forms used either as adjectives or pronouns.

aucun . . . ne, no, no one
autre, other
même, same
nul . . . ne, no, nobody, none
pas un . . . ne, not one

plusieurs, several
tel, telle, such
tout, tous } all, every
toute, toutes

Uses of the Indefinites

139. Certain, in the sense of *certain, some,* precedes the noun. After a noun, it means *sure, positive.*

[1] For the use of **personne, rien, aucun** in negative sentences, cf. § 64.

| Certaines choses. | Certain things. |
| Une nouvelle certaine. | Trustworthy news. |

140. Quelques—not the partitive construction—translates *some,* in the sense of *a few. Few* in the sense of *not many* is translated by **peu de**.

J'ai des amis à Paris.	I have friends (*no indication as to how many*) in Paris.
J'ai quelques amis à Paris.	I have some (a few) friends in Paris.
J'ai peu d'amis à Paris.	I have few (not many) friends in Paris.

141. On (= *one, we, they, you, people,* etc.) requires the verb in the 3rd person singular. Its corresponding possessive adjective is **son** (= *one's, their, people's,* etc.) and its reflexive forms are **se** and **soi**. A construction with **on** frequently translates an English passive.[1]

Dîner à sept heures. On dansera.	Dinner at seven o'clock. There will be dancing.
Au printemps on porte toujours son imperméable.	In the spring we always wear our raincoats.
On ne doit pas toujours penser à soi.	People should not always think of themselves.

142. Même[2] means *same* before a noun and as a pronoun. After a noun or pronoun, it means *self, very, even.*

Les mêmes enfants.	The same children.
Moi-même.	Myself.
Ce jour même.	That very day.

143. Autre in the singular is used as in English. In the plural, **les autres** translates *the others;* **d'autres** translates *others.*

---

[1] Cf. § 49.
[2] Même is also used invariably as an adverb, meaning *even.* Il a même gagné le prix. He even won the prize.

Les uns / Quelques-uns } danseront; { les autres / d'autres } joueront au bridge.

Some will dance; { the others / others } will play bridge.

1. Distinguish between **un autre,** *another (a different one)* and **encore un,** *another (an additional one)*.

| Donnez-moi une autre tasse; celle-ci est fêlée. | Give me another (a different) cup; this one is cracked. |
| Donnez-moi encore une tasse de thé. | Give me another (an additional) cup of tea. |

2. Note the following idiomatic construction:

| Nous autres Américains. | We Americans. |

144. Quelque chose and **rien** require **de** before an adjective. The adjective is always masculine singular. Although **chose** is feminine, **quelque chose** is construed as masculine.

| Quelque chose d'intéressant est arrivé. | Something interesting has happened. |
| Rien de nouveau n'est arrivé. | Nothing new has happened. |

145. Quelconque, *any whatever, any at all,* follows its noun. Its plural is formed by adding **s. Quiconque,** *whoever,* is invariable and is usually replaced in informal writing or speaking by **celui qui,** etc.

| Donnez-moi deux livres quelconques. | Give me any two books whatever. |
| Quiconque (celui qui) le fera, le regrettera. | Whoever does it will be sorry. |

146. Tel is preceded (and not followed, as in English) by the indefinite article.

| Un tel homme. | Such a man. |

147. Tout is usually followed by the definite article.

Tous les jours.	Every day.
Toute la journée.	All day, the whole day.

148. L'un ... l'autre, etc., are used in various correlative constructions.

Elles se trompent l'une et l'autre.	They are both mistaken.
L'une et l'autre se trompent.	
Je choisirai l'un ou l'autre.	I shall choose one or the other.
Ils se souviennent les uns des autres.	They remember one another.

149. N'importe, *it does not matter,* + the interrogatives **quel, qui** or **quoi** has the force of *any one (anything) whatever.*

Dites-lui n'importe quoi.	Tell him anything (at all).
N'importe qui peut faire cela.	Any one can do that.
Donnez-moi n'importe quel livre.	Give me any book whatever.

UN GOÛTER

On s'était arrêté devant l'appartement des Martin au retour d'une visite au tombeau de Napoléon.

—A demain, Agnès, dit Paul.

—Au revoir, Mlle Hélène, dit Jean.

—Mais pas du tout, dit Agnès. Vous allez monter avec nous. Il n'y a personne à la maison mais nous trouverons bien quelque chose de bon dans la cuisine.

—Un véritable pique-nique, alors. Je ne sais rien de plus agréable.

—Il faudra que tout le monde m'aide, par exemple, ajouta Agnès. Si on est plusieurs, ce ne sera pas long.

Quelques minutes après, ils étaient tous occupés à préparer le repas. Agnès sortait la vaisselle et les autres mettaient le couvert.

—Dites donc, Agnès. Où faut-il mettre ces belles tranches de jambon que j'ai trouvées dans la glacière?

—Sur n'importe quel plat. Pas celui-là, cependant; il est fêlé. Il y en a certainement d'autres.

—Qui veut du pain?

—Tout le monde, naturellement. Aucun repas n'est complet sans pain. Pendant que je prépare le café, cherchez la crème. Il doit y en avoir un peu dans la glacière.

—Voici notre dessert: une crème au chocolat qui vous fait venir l'eau à la bouche. Si on avait seulement des gâteaux ou même des biscuits avec cette crème, ce serait parfait.

—Vous êtes bien difficile, si ces gâteaux que j'ai faits moi-même ne vous suffisent pas!

—Comment vais-je me faire pardonner une telle gaffe? se dit Jean, qui n'avait pas remarqué les gâteaux.

—Il nous faut encore une tasse, Paul, et il n'y a pas un morceau de sucre dans le sucrier.

—Tout est prêt maintenant et chacun peut prendre sa place à table.

—Dites donc, Agnès, si on faisait marcher la T.S.F.? Personne ne s'y oppose?

Ce fut un petit goûter bien gai; puis, la table desservie et la vaisselle lavée, on se dit au revoir les uns aux autres et les jeunes gens regagnèrent leur domicile.

CONVERSATION

1. Comment avait-on passé l'après-midi? 2. Pourquoi est-on monté chez Agnès? 3. Qui a aidé Agnès à préparer le repas? 4. Qu'est-ce que Jean a trouvé dans la glacière? 5. Qu'est-ce que c'est qu'une glacière? 6. Aimez-vous le dessert qu'on a servi? 7. Quelle gaffe Jean a-t-il faite? 8. Que sert-on avec le café? 9. Qu'est-ce que c'est qu'un sucrier? 10. A-t-on eu de la musique pendant le goûter? 11. Que faut-il faire après un repas?

COMPOSITION

"Nothing is more tiring than visiting a museum," exclaimed Jean on leaving the Army Museum with a few of his friends. "Besides, I am so thirsty that I could drink anything, even French coffee."

"There are few cafés in this quarter," said Paul, "and I don't know any of them."

"Listen," said Agnes, "we'll all go to our apartment. There is no one at home during the afternoon and there is always something to drink in the ice box. I might even find something to eat."

"Now," said Agnes, as they were going into the dining-room, "you must all help me. John and I shall look after the wine and the coffee; the rest of you will get out the dishes and set the table. If certain persons think that they are going to listen to the radio, while others are working, they are mistaken."

At the end of a few minutes, a delicious lunch was ready and each one had taken his place at the table.

"Your coffee is excellent," said Helen. "Will you give me another cup? And you, John, will you give me another glass. This one is cracked."

"I say, Paul, don't eat all the ham. Leave me one slice at least."

"Let him eat the ham. What tempts me is that vanilla cream."

"Which of these cakes do you wish, Paul? There are several kinds."

"Any kind at all. I don't care much for cakes."

"You are certainly hard to please. I made those cakes myself."

"After such a break, Paul, you will have to wash the dishes to earn your pardon."

DRILL EXERCISE

1. There are few furnished apartments in this quarter. 2. Did you ever see such a man? 3. Dinner is served at seven o'clock. 4. No one likes to make breaks. 5. Certain persons are very hard to please. 6. No one of them had seen Napoleon's tomb. 7. Agnes made those cakes this very day. 8. You remember him, do you not? 9. Some of our friends are coming to dine with us to-night. 10. You know several of them. 11. Any one can point out that address to you. 12. I must buy another fountain pen; mine is broken. 13. Do you wish another slice of ham? 14. There is nothing interesting in the paper tonight. 15. There are no more crackers on the table; have you any others? 16. We have need of each other. 17. You cannot visit the whole museum in a single afternoon. 18. You foreigners do not always understand us.

VERB REVIEW

conduire, to conduct, take, drive (*an auto*), etc. Cf. § 199.
introduire, to show in
construire, to construct, build
vivre, to live. Cf. § 218.

Note. *Live* in the sense of *to dwell* is translated by **demeurer** or by **habiter. J'habite (demeure à) New York.** I live in New York.

1. As long as I live, I shall remember it. 2. Will you drive me to the Post Office? 3. He used to live in France. 4. She is still living. 5. Don't drive so fast. 6. When was that building constructed? 7. Long live the Republic! 8. Louis XV and Louis XVI lived in the eighteenth century. 9. A guide is taking us to Versailles tomorrow. 10. He would not drive so fast, if you were with him. 11. Does she drive well? 12. He was still living when I arrived. 13. He used to drive very well. 14. Where are they living now? 15. I am sorry that he drives so fast.

LESSON XVIII

THE SUBJUNCTIVE MOOD (1)

THE SIGNIFICANCE OF THE SUBJUNCTIVE MOOD

150. Sentences may be divided roughly into two classes: a) those that merely make a statement, and b) those that stress an attitude or an opinion with regard to a statement, i. e., feeling inspired by the assertion, its necessity or importance, uncertainty as to its truth or to its future accomplishment. For example, *My father is in Chicago* is a simple statement; but *I am glad (it is possible) that my father is in Chicago* and *It is essential that my father should be in Chicago* stress the attitude of the speaker towards the statement.

While the English construction may vary in these sentences, the usage in French is as follows:

1. All true principal clauses in French take the indicative mood.
2. Dependent clauses after expressions stressing certainty, including **croire**, *to believe;* **penser**, *to think,* and **espérer**, *to hope,* take the indicative mood.
3. Dependent clauses after expressions stressing a) feeling or will; b) necessity or importance; c) uncertainty; and dependent clauses containing within themselves an element of uncertainty, take the subjunctive mood.

Je suis content que mon père soit à Chicago.	I am glad that my father is in Chicago. (*Feeling of speaker stressed.*)
Il faut que mon père soit à Chicago demain.	It is necessary for my father to be in Chicago tomorrow. (*Necessity is stressed.*)

| Croyez-vous que mon père soit à Chicago? | Do you think that my father is in Chicago? (*Attitude of uncertainty.*) |
| Quoique mon père soit à Chicago, vous ne pourrez pas le voir. | Although my father is (so far as I know) in Chicago, you will not be able to see him. |
| Je resterai jusqu'à ce qu'il vienne. | I shall wait until he comes. (*Uncertainty as to when or whether he will come.*) |//
But: Mon père est à Chicago.	My father is in Chicago. (*Simple statement.*)
Je sais que mon père est à Chicago.	I know that my father is in Chicago. (*Certainty is stressed.*)
Je crois (pense) que mon père est à Chicago.	I think that my father is in Chicago. (*The element of uncertainty in these verbs is not strong enough to require a subjunctive in the dependent clause.*)

Classified rules for the use of the subjunctive should be regarded as illustrations of this general principle.

THE SUBJUNCTIVE IN NOUN CLAUSES

151. The subjunctive is used in noun clauses after personal and impersonal verbs and expressions denoting:

1. necessity or importance (**il faut, il est nécessaire, il importe, il est important**);

| Il faut qu'il vienne tout de suite. | He must come at once. |

2. uncertainty, doubt (**il est possible, il se peut, douter; croire** and **penser**[1] when negative or interrogative);

| Il se peut que vous ayez raison. | It may be that you are right. |

[1] In conversational French **croire** and **penser** frequently take the indicative even when negative or interrogative.

a) But expressions denoting certainty unless negative or interrogative (être sûr, certain, évident, etc.; il paraît,[1] croire and penser when affirmative) take the indicative.

| Je suis sûr qu'il viendra. | I am sure he will come. |
| But: Il n'est pas sûr qu'il soit nommé. | It is not sure that he is nominated. |

3. emotion [2] (avoir peur,[3] craindre;[3] c'est dommage; être content, heureux, fâché, etc.; regretter);

| Je crains qu'il ne pleuve demain. | I fear it may rain to-morrow. |

4. will (aimer mieux, commander, défendre, demander, désirer, empêcher,[3] permettre, vouloir, valoir mieux).

| Il veut que nous l'accompagnions. | He wants us to go with him. |

Sequence of Tenses

152. The following sequence of tenses is observed in dependent subjunctive clauses:

Principal Clause	Dependent Clause	Corresponds to English
Present Future Condl.[4] Imperative	Present subj.	Present, future, or condl.
	Perfect subj.	Perfect, past or fut. perf.

---

[1] Il me (lui, nous, etc.) semble takes the indicative; il semble is usually followed by the subjunctive.

[2] espérer always takes the indicative.

[3] avoir peur, craindre, empêcher may take a redundant ne in the clause following, when the verb in the main clause is affirmative.

[4] The conditional may also be followed by an imperfect or pluperfect subjunctive in literary style.

Je suis content qu'il vienne.	I am glad that he is coming (will come).
Je regrette qu'il ne soit pas venu.	I am sorry that he did (has) not come.
Je voudrais que vous me donniez votre adresse.	I wish you would give me your address.
Vous serez content un jour que je vous aie aidé.	You will be glad some day that I helped you.
Empêchez qu'il (ne) sorte.	Prevent him from going out.

153. If the principal clause is in a past tense, the dependent clause is in the imperfect or pluperfect subjunctive.

These two tenses of the subjunctive are rarely used in conversation or in informal writing. For ways of avoiding their use, cf. § 157.

RETOUR EN AMÉRIQUE

Mon cher Jean:

Il se peut que la lettre que je vous ai écrite du Havre se soit égarée. En tout cas, je veux que vous sachiez encore une fois à quel point je vous suis reconnaissant de vos bontés pour moi pendant mon séjour à Paris. Il est regrettable que j'aie dû vous quitter si brusquement, mais mon père avait besoin de moi et il a bien fallu que je m'en aille.[1]

Nous avons fait une traversée magnifique. Il faisait si beau qu'on s'apercevait à peine de la marche du paquebot. Personne n'a eu le mal de mer. Je suis bien fâché que vous ne soyez pas revenu avec moi, car vous n'aurez certainement pas un voyage aussi agréable.

Les repas à bord étaient excellents. Il y avait des quantités de plats de toute espèce et on pouvait commander n'importe quoi. Il est possible que j'aie abusé de ce droit mais vous savez comme on a faim en mer.

Le paquebot était bondé. Il y avait parmi les touristes beaucoup d'étudiants et de professeurs. J'ai fait la connaissance de plusieurs jeunes filles charmantes. Le matin nous jouions au tennis; l'après-midi, nous allions au cinéma en attendant l'heure du thé; le soir nous dansions.

---

[1] For this tense, cf. § 158.

Je suis bien content que vous m'ayez donné un mot d'introduction pour votre ami Foulard. C'est un jeune homme tout à fait sympathique que j'espère revoir, puisqu'il est possible qu'il vienne à Toronto. C'est dommage que je ne puisse pas aller à la rencontre des Martin à New York, mais un grand voyage que je dois faire dans l'Ouest empêchera que je sois de retour avant la fin de décembre.

Toutes mes amitiés aux Martin et encore merci de vos bontés pour moi.

Bien sincèrement,
Paul

CONVERSATION

1. Pourquoi Paul est-il retourné en Amérique? 2. Où a-t-il pris le bateau? 3. Combien de fois a-t-il écrit à Jean? 4. Pourquoi lui a-t-il écrit? 5. Quelle sorte de traversée a-t-il faite? 6. Quel temps a-t-il fait pendant le voyage? 7. Est-ce que Paul a eu le mal de mer? 8. Comment a-t-il trouvé les repas à bord? 9. Y avait-il beaucoup de monde sur le paquebot? 10. Comment Paul s'est-il amusé? 11. Pour qui avait-il une lettre d'introduction? 12. Pourquoi espère-t-il revoir ce jeune homme? 13. Pourquoi ne pourra-t-il pas aller à la rencontre des Martin quand ils arriveront de France?

COMPOSITION

The steamer had already left Havre when Paul, coming out of his stateroom, met by chance an old friend.

"Well! Well! Frank Horton! What are you doing here?"

"Hello, Paul. What luck! I wrote you before my departure, as I knew you were to be in Europe this summer, but I never received an answer to my letter."

"I am sorry that I did not receive your letter. I fear it went astray. Anyhow, I am glad that you took this boat. It appears that there are lots of college students on board. We ought to have a good time."

"Yes, if I can avoid seasickness."

"I don't think that you will be sick. The first [few] days it would be better that you eat very little. However, if the weather remains fine, no one will be seasick."

"I hope that you are right. I mustn't waste the last days of my vacation."

"Why didn't you look me up in Paris?"

"I spent only three days there on my way back from Germany. But I should like to have you visit me in New York."

"I am sorry that I cannot accept your invitation but I must return to Toronto immediately."

"It is a pity that you are in such a hurry. I want you to meet some friends of mine."

"I should like very much to meet them. It is possible that I can do so later, as I am going to New York to meet the Martins in October."

"I am afraid that my friends will no longer be in the city. But you must come to my home anyway. . . . It is nearly seven o'clock. Do you wish to dine now?"

"As you wish."

DRILL EXERCISE

1. Is it possible that you do not know my friend? 2. I must present him to you at once. 3. It appears that he has just arrived. 4. I am afraid that she will be seasick. 5. It is important that you should visit Germany. 6. It may be that you are right. 7. Do you think that we shall have a good crossing? 8. They are sorry that Paul has left. 9. They cannot prevent him from leaving. 10. It would be better for you to get your tickets today. 11. We doubt that he is on the boat. 12. It is not certain that the weather will be fine. 13. She wished me to visit her in Paris, but I did not wish to do so. 14. I shall have to write to him at once. 15. He orders his dinner to be served at six o'clock. 16. One must not eat too much. 17. I believe that we shall have a good time. 18. Permit me to give you a letter of introduction for him. 19. I should like to have you bring me some white bread and a bottle of wine. 20. I hope that Fred will take the same boat.

VERB REVIEW

craindre, to fear, be afraid of. Cf. § 203.
   peindre, to paint
   plaindre, to pity

se plaindre de, to complain of (about)
plaire,[1] to please. Cf. § 211.
se taire, to be silent, to cease speaking

1. I am afraid that may not please him. 2. What were you afraid of? 3. I hope that this will please your mother. 4. What did he complain about? 5. After that, she was silent. 6. The trip pleases her very much. 7. If she should stay, that would please him. 8. He feared (*p. def.*) everybody. 9. I used to be afraid of nearly everything. 10. That will please your friends. 11. Don't pity me, if you please. 12. Fear nothing. 13. The performance pleased us very much. 14. I should do it, if it pleased him. 15. What will you fear, if you are not alone?

---

[1] Requires indirect object. **Cela plaît à sa mère.** This pleases his mother

LESSON XIX

THE SUBJUNCTIVE (II)

The Subjunctive in Adjectival Clauses

154. The subjunctive is used in adjectival clauses (i. e., those introduced by a relative pronoun):

1. When the clause indicates characteristics desired but not yet attained. The antecedent in the main clause is generally indefinite (i. e., it is accompanied by the indefinite article or the partitive forms **du, de la, de l', or des**).

Je cherche une maison qui vous convienne.	I am looking for a house which will (may) suit you.
Il veut choisir des cours qui soient faciles.	He wants to choose courses which are (may be) easy.
But: Il a choisi tous les cours qui sont faciles.	He has chosen all the easy courses.
J'ai trouvé une maison qui me convient.	I have found a house which suits me.

2. Frequently, but not necessarily, when the antecedent in the main clause is qualified by an adjective in the superlative degree or by **seul, premier** or **dernier**.

C'est la meilleure pièce que j'aie vue.	That is the best play that I have seen.
C'est le seul ami qui me soit fidèle.	He is the only friend who is true to me.

3. After a general negation in the main clause.

Je ne connais personne qui sache cela.	I do not know any one who knows that.
Il n'y a rien que vous puissiez faire.	There is nothing that you can do.

4. In compound relative and indefinite clauses, introduced by *whoever, whatever,* etc. The word order in the following examples should be noted.[1]

Qui que ce soit que vous ayez vu.	Whoever it is that you have seen.
Qui que vous soyez.	Whoever you may be.
Quoi que vous fassiez.	Whatever you do.
Quelles que soient ses raisons.	Whatever his reasons may be.
Quelque difficile que soit ce travail.	However difficult this work may be.
Quelque rapidement qu'il écrive.	However rapidly he writes.
Quelques raisons qu'il ait.	Whatever reasons he may have.

The Subjunctive in Adverbial Clauses

155. The subjunctive is used in adverbial clauses after the following conjunctions of:

1. time before which or up to which: **avant que,** *before;* **jusqu'à ce que,** *until;*

J'étudierai jusqu'à ce que vous arriviez.	I shall study until you arrive.

2. purpose: **pour que,** *in order that;* **afin que,** *in order that;* **de sorte (façon) que,** *so that;*[2]

Pour que vous ne manquiez pas le train, j'ai commandé un taxi.	In order that you may not miss the train, I have ordered a taxi.
Conduisez votre auto de sorte que vous n'ayez pas d'accidents.	Drive your auto so that you won't have any accidents.

---

[1] It should be noted that *whatever* as an adjective is translated by **quel, quelle, quels** or **quelles** when the verb is être; otherwise by **quelque(s)**.

[2] De sorte (façon) que takes the indicative in result clauses.

Il a parlé de façon que tout le monde l'a compris.	He spoke so that every one understood him.

3. emotion: **de crainte que,**[1] **de peur que,**[1] *for fear that, lest;*

| Je vous enverrai un chèque, de peur que vous n'ayez pas assez d'argent. | I shall send you a check, for fear that you haven't enough money. |

4. condition: **à moins que,**[1] *unless;* **pourvu que,** *providing that;*

| Il viendra, à moins qu'il ne soit malade. | He will come, unless he is sick. |

5. concession: **quoique, bien que,** *although;*

| Quoique la réunion soit importante, je ne peux pas y aller. | Although the meeting is important, I cannot go to it. |

6. negation: **sans que,** *without.*

| Il est parti, sans que je l'aie vu. | He left without my seeing him |

UN PIQUE-NIQUE

Agnès, Jean et le docteur faisaient un pique-nique près d'un des jolis étangs de Ville d'Avray que tout le monde connaît par les toiles de Corot.

—C'est dommage que Paul ait dû rentrer si tôt en Amérique, dit Agnès. C'est un des garçons les plus sympathiques que j'aie jamais connus.

—Je regrette qu'il ne soit pas ici aujourd'hui, répondit Jean. Il n'y a rien qui lui plaise autant qu'un pique-nique.

—Vous n'avez rien pu faire pour qu'il se décide à rester?

—Rien. Quoique j'aie fait mon possible, avant qu'il ait quitté Paris, pour le décider à prendre ce parti. Son père est malade, paraît-il, et bien qu'il n'y ait rien à craindre pour le moment, sa

---

[1] **De crainte que, de peur que** and **à moins que** are usually followed by a redundant **ne**. Cf. also § 151, 3 note.

mère veut qu'il revienne tout de suite. Il va me manquer énormément.

—Et à nous aussi.

—Tiens! Notre goûter est prêt, dit le docteur voyant qu'Agnès avait mis la nappe sous un arbre, asseyons-nous, à moins que vous n'ayez pas faim.

—Moi, j'ai toujours faim, dit Jean; surtout quand il s'agit d'un repas préparé par Agnès. Il n'y a personne qui sache faire la cuisine comme elle.

—Je lui dis toujours, dit son père, que je devrais lui trouver une bonne afin qu'elle ait plus de temps pour s'amuser. Mais j'ai beau insister, elle veut tout faire elle-même. Pourvu qu'elle soit contente, c'est l'important.

—Ne dis pas de bêtises, Papa. Il est convenu, tu sais bien, que je reste auprès de toi jusqu'à ce que tu prennes ta retraite. Alors nous ferons de grands voyages et peut-être que nous inviterons Jean à nous accompagner. Vous voulez bien, Jean?

—Voilà une bonne idée. J'accepte d'avance.

CONVERSATION

1. Où Jean et les Martin font-ils un pique-nique? 2. Qui a peint souvent cet endroit? 3. Pourquoi Paul n'a-t-il pas accompagné ses amis? 4. Pourquoi a-t-il quitté Paris? 5. Est-ce que son père est sérieusement malade? 6. Où Agnès a-t-elle mis la nappe? 7 Est-ce qu'Agnès sait faire la cuisine? 8. A-t-elle une bonne pour l'aider? 9. Pourrait-elle avoir une bonne, si elle le voulait? 10. Son père veut-il qu'elle fasse tout le travail de la maison? 11. Jusqu'à quand Agnès compte-t-elle rester auprès de son père? 12. Que veut-elle faire alors?

COMPOSITION

For half an hour, Dr. Martin and his daughter have been waiting for John and Paul who are to go on a picnic with them to Ville d'Avray.

"Unless those two boys come soon," said Agnes, "it will be dark before we reach the pond. It is seldom that they arrive late at an appointment. Do you think that something has happened to them?"

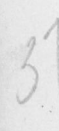

"I am sure that they will be here at any moment. There's the bell now. It must be they. What! John, all alone! Where is Paul?"

"That's quite a story. Paul received a cablegram from his mother this morning saying that his father is sick and that he must return home at once. So that he has just taken the train for Havre. He asked me to make his excuses to you and to say good-bye to you for him."

"We are very sorry," said Dr. Martin, "that this bad news has cut short his stay in Paris. Paul is one of the most likeable young men that I know and I shall miss him very much. Do you think his father is seriously sick?"

"No, although the cablegram was not very clear. Naturally Paul was quite upset. I helped him pack his trunk so that he wouldn't miss his train and I remained at the station with him until his train left."

"There is nothing we can do," said Agnes, "until he writes to us. Let's have our picnic anyway. I have prepared a lunch for four persons so that John will have to eat Paul's share."

DRILL EXERCISE

1. It is not easy to find a maid who knows how to cook. 2. We cannot find any one who knows him. 3. However hard this work may be, he will do it. 4. You must be here early in order that he can talk to you. 5. I shall stay until he returns. 6. This is the best opera I have seen. 7. Unless they are sick, they will be here. 8. He bought them without my seeing them. 9. Whoever you are and whatever reasons you may have, you cannot see him. 10. I shall write him so that he may know the day of my arrival. 11. Before they go away, send them some flowers. 12. They have found a teacher who suits them perfectly. 13. Provided it doesn't rain, we shall have a good time. 14. He left the city so that I didn't see him. 15. Although he may have said that, I don't believe it.

VERB REVIEW

fuir, to flee. Cf. § 189.
rire, to laugh. Cf. § 214.
  sourire, to smile

1. Why were they laughing? 2. He fled before I saw him. 3. Don't laugh; this is serious. 4. They were fleeing when you saw them. 5. I shall laugh anyway. 6. The army is fleeing before the enemy. 7. If you knew the story, you would laugh at it. 8. They had already fled. 9. Unless you smile, he will think that you are angry. 10. Everybody is smiling.

LESSON XX

THE SUBJUNCTIVE (III). THE PRESENT PARTICIPLE

The Subjunctive in Principal Clauses

156. The subjunctive occurs but rarely in principal clauses. When so used, it expresses a wish or an order.[1]

Vive le roi!	Long live the king.
Que Dieu vous bénisse!	God bless you!
Qu'il vienne, s'il le veut.	Let him come, if he wishes.

Substitutes for the Subjunctive

157. The imperfect subjunctive and the pluperfect subjunctive are rarely used in conversation or in informal writing. Their use is therefore to be avoided. The following suggestions show how this may be done:

1. Replace the subjunctive by an infinitive construction.[2]

   a) When the subject in the dependent clause is the same as the subject in the main clause, the conjunction introducing the dependent clause is replaced by a preposition as follows:

---

[1] Such clauses are really dependent clauses, with a main clause containing the verb *I wish* or a similar expression understood.

[2] Even in a present sequence, the infinitive construction is always preferable.

de, *to*	+ infin. replaces	que
afin de, *in order to*	+ infin. replaces	afin que
pour, *in order to*	+ infin. replaces	pour que
à moins de, *unless*	+ infin. replaces	à moins que
avant de, *before*	+ infin. replaces	avant que
de peur de, *lest*	+ infin. replaces	de peur que
de façon à, *so as*	+ infin. replaces	de façon que
sans, *without*	+ infin. replaces	sans que

Avoid: Use instead:

Je regrettais que je ne pusse pas y aller.   Je regrettais de ne pouvoir y aller.

Il est parti de bonne heure pour qu'il ne manquât pas le train.   Il est parti de bonne heure pour ne pas manquer le train.

Ils s'en sont allés sans qu'ils me dissent adieu.   Ils s'en sont allés sans me dire adieu.

Nous leur avons dit cela avant que nous partissions.   Nous leur avons dit cela avant de partir.

b) Even when the subject in the dependent clause is different from the subject in the main clause, the above construction may be used after **commander**,[1] **demander**,[1] **défendre**,[1] **dire**,[1] **empêcher**, **permettre**.[1][2]

J'ai empêché qu'il ne le fît.   Je l'ai empêché de le faire.
Il défend qu'ils fassent cela.   Il leur défend de faire cela.

2. The dependent clause may be replaced by a noun or an adjective construction.

Quoiqu'il fût riche, il n'était pas avare.   Quoique riche, il n'était pas avare.

Je les ai vus avant qu'ils soient partis.   Je les ai vus avant leur départ.

---

[1] Takes indirect object of the person: il défend à Marie de rester.
[2] With all of these verbs, the infinitive construction is preferable to the subjunctive even in a present sequence.

3. The sentence may be rephrased:

   a) by inserting an infinitive such as **apprendre, trouver, savoir,** etc.;

Il était content[1] que vous gagnassiez le prix.	Il était content d'apprendre que vous avez gagné le prix.
Elle voulait que nous allassions à l'église.	Elle voulait nous faire aller à l'église.
Je regrettais qu'il ne fût pas venu.	Je regrettais de savoir qu'il n'était pas venu.

   b) by replacing the construction which requires the subjunctive by a construction which does not require the subjunctive.

Il a fallu que nous restassions ici.	Nous avons dû rester ici.
Il viendrait à moins que nous ne fussions absents.	Il viendrait si nous n'étions pas absents.

158. A present or a perfect subjunctive is now frequently used in violation of the rules in place of the imperfect or pluperfect subjunctive.

Je voulais qu'il vienne (vînt).	I wanted him to come.
Il avait peur que je ne le fasse (fisse).	He was afraid that I would do it.

The Present Participle

159. The present participle is invariable in French. It is used as an English participle, a) to introduce a phrase modifying a noun or pronoun or b) preceded by **en,** *in, upon, while, during,* to modify a verb. When accompanied by **en,** the present participle always refers to the subject of the sentence.

---

[1] Etre content, heureux, fâché, etc. may also be followed by **de ce que** and the indicative. This construction is less usual. Il était content de ce que vous avez gagné le prix.

Prenant sa plume, elle s'est mise à écrire.	Taking her pen, she began to write.
(Tout) en parlant, il examinait ses auditeurs.	While speaking, he examined his hearers.
Tout en travaillant bien, il ne réussit pas.	Although he works hard, he does not succeed.
Je l'ai vue sortant de la maison.	I saw her (as she was) going out of the house.
Je l'ai vu, en sortant de la maison.	I saw him (as I was) going out of the house.
En partant de bonne heure, vous arrivez à quatre heures.	By leaving early, you arrive at four o'clock.

160. The present participle may also be used as an ordinary adjective. In such a case, it agrees like all adjectives.

Des enfants obéissants.	Obedient children.

PASTEUR

—Je dois visiter l'Institut Pasteur demain, dit le docteur Martin, et on a bien voulu permettre que je vous emmène. Il n'y a rien à Paris qui soit plus intéressant que ce laboratoire et je désire que vous le voyiez.

—Merci, Docteur, répondit Jean. Je suis très content que vous m'ayez procuré l'autorisation de vous accompagner. C'est Pasteur qui a découvert la vaccination contre la rage, n'est-ce pas?

—Oui. Et le premier essai qu'il a fait de son vaccin fut dramatique. Le 6 juillet 1885, un enfant conduit par sa mère, Mme Meister, vint au laboratoire. Attaqué l'avant-veille par un chien enragé, l'enfant avait reçu quatorze blessures. Le médecin de l'endroit, craignant que ses blessures ne fussent mortelles, l'avait envoyé à Paris. Il ne croyait pas qu'il fût possible de le sauver, à moins que le nouveau vaccin dont il avait entendu parler ne fît ce miracle. Pasteur hésita. Quoiqu'il eût appliqué son traitement préventif à des chiens, il voulait consulter deux médecins de ses amis avant de tenter ces mêmes inoculations sur un enfant. Ces médecins, sachant que sans Pasteur l'enfant était perdu, demandèrent que Pasteur essayât de le sauver. Le soir même on lui fit la première inoculation. Les semaines passèrent sans que la rage se déclarât. L'enfant était sauvé.

—Ce récit m'a beaucoup intéressé, dit Jean.

—Dans ce cas, il faut que vous lisiez la *Vie de Pasteur* par Vallery-Radot, qui est une des plus intéressantes biographies que je connaisse.

CONVERSATION

1. A quelle époque Pasteur a-t-il vécu? 2. Quel traitement médical a-t-il découvert? 3. Quel institut a-t-il fondé? 4. Quand a-t-il fait le premier essai de son vaccin sur un être humain? 5. Sur quels animaux l'avait-il essayé auparavant? 6. Qu'est-ce qui était arrivé au petit Meister? 7. Qui l'avait envoyé à Pasteur? 8. Pasteur était-il médecin? 9. Qui a-t-il consulté avant de faire des inoculations à l'enfant? 10. A-t-on sauvé l'enfant? 11. Qui a écrit la vie de Pasteur?

COMPOSITION

"I am sorry that our visit did not last longer," said John as he left the Pasteur Institute with Dr. Martin. "While going through these laboratories, I thought of the difficulties that Pasteur must have overcome, before the doctors accepted his treatment."

"Yes. Although [a] scientist, Pasteur was not a doctor and his enemies did their best to discredit him. An incident that occurred in 1885 is typical. A child ten years old came to the laboratory. Bitten in (**à**) the head by a mad dog thirty-seven days before, she was in a desperate condition. Pasteur realized that there was nothing that he could do. 'It is too late,' he said, 'for the preventive treatment to have the slightest chance of succeeding.' Although he knew that if the child died, his enemies would say that he was a charlatan, Pasteur hesitated only a moment. The child had taken his hands. 'Stay beside my bed,' she said. 'I am so glad that you are beside me. I shall be afraid, unless you stay with me.' Pasteur left the room sobbing. 'If there is only one chance in (**sur**) ten thousand, I must give the child that chance,' he said to himself. And he remained beside the bed until the child died. For suffering humanity, Pasteur compromised his future as a (**de**) scientist."

"That is the noblest action that I know," exclaimed John. "I must certainly read the biography of Pasteur."

DRILL EXERCISE I

Where possible, replace by other constructions the imperfect subjunctives that occur in the French passage above, rephrasing the sentences if necessary.

DRILL EXERCISE II

Replace wherever possible any subjunctives that you may have used in the Composition by other constructions, rephrasing the sentences if necessary. For example, the sentence beginning: "It is too late for the preventive treatment to have . . ." may be reworded as follows: "It is so late that the preventive treatment will not have . . ."

DRILL EXERCISE III

Recast the following sentences to avoid the use of the subjunctive.

1. Il a défendu que je sorte. 2. Il fit son possible pour empêcher que je ne réusisse. 3. Ecrivez-moi avant que vous vous en alliez. 4. Je ne crois pas qu'il soit malade. 5. J'attendrai que vous arriviez. 6. A moins que Pasteur ne le guérisse, il mourra. 7. Quoiqu'elle fût très malade, elle reçut le médecin avec un sourire. 8. Arrivez de bonne heure, afin que vous ne manquiez pas le premier acte. 9. Elle regrette qu'elle ne puisse pas venir. 10. Il a permis que je l'accompagne.

DRILL EXERCISE IV

1. When he saw the child, he knew that she would die. 2. While going to the Institute, the doctor told him the story of Pasteur. 3. I saw her, as I was leaving the house. 4. Seeing that it was raining, I took my umbrella. 5. The man working in the garden is the gardener. 6. If you work hard, you will be able to finish your task. 7. Weeping, the child told her story. 8. Pasteur said a few consoling words to her. 9. While consoling her, he tried to hide his fears from her. 10. When he left, she was smiling.

VERB REVIEW

cueillir, to pick, gather. Cf. § 187.
  accueillir, to welcome, receive
pleuvoir, to rain. Cf. § 224.

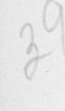

1. If it doesn't rain, we shall gather some flowers. 2. It was raining in torrents, when we arrived. 3. They welcomed us with open arms. 4. She is picking flowers in the garden. 5. It rained yesterday morning. 6. We should gather some carnations, if it were not raining. 7. Do you think that it will rain? 8. They were picking roses. 9. It is raining; I fear we shall not pick any flowers. 10. I think it will rain; let it rain. 11. It would rain, I am sure of it, if we took a walk. 12. He always receives us with pleasure.

LESSON XXI

THE INFINITIVE

The Infinitive after Other Verbs

161. Verbs in French may be followed by a) an infinitive without a preposition; b) **de** + an infinitive, or c) **à** + an infinitive.

1. The following common verbs govern an infinitive directly without a preposition:

aimer,[1] to like, love	laisser, to let
aimer mieux, to prefer	oser, to dare
aller, to go	paraître, to appear
croire, to believe	pouvoir, to be able
désirer, to desire	préférer, to prefer
devoir, must, ought	savoir, to know (how)
entendre, to hear	sembler, to seem
envoyer, to send	valoir mieux, to be preferable
espérer, to hope	venir, to come
faire, to do, make	voir, to see
falloir, to be necessary	vouloir, to wish

2. The following common verbs take **de** before a following infinitive:

cesser, to cease	se dépêcher, to hasten
conseiller, to advise	dire, to say, tell
craindre, to fear	empêcher, to prevent
décider, to decide	essayer, to try
défendre, to forbid	éviter, to avoid
demander, to ask	se hâter, to hasten

---

[1] **Aimer** may also be followed by **à**, except in the conditional.

être obligé (forcé), to be
  obliged to
oublier, to forget
offrir, to offer
permettre, to permit
prier, to pray, request

promettre, to promise
refuser, to refuse
regretter, to regret
remercier, to thank
tâcher, to try

3. The following common verbs take **à** before a following infinitive:

aider, to aid
apprendre, to learn
chercher, to seek
commencer,[1] to begin
consentir, to consent
continuer,[1] to continue

réussir, to succeed
engager, to urge
enseigner, to teach
forcer, to force
obliger, to oblige
inviter, to invite

Voulez-vous nous accompagner?	Do you wish to go with us?
Il a promis de venir me voir.	He has promised to come to see me.
Nous commençons à (de) parler français.	We are beginning to speak French.

À OR DE WITH THE INFINITIVE AFTER NOUNS AND ADJECTIVES

162. A noun or adjective is followed by **à** + infinitive, when the infinitive may be made passive in English.

Son écriture est difficile à lire.	His handwriting is hard to read (to be read).
Cela est facile à faire.	That is easy to do (to be done).
Voici un livre à vendre.	Here is a book for sale (to be sold).

163. A noun or adjective is followed by **de** + infinitive, when the passive construction is not possible in English.

Il est facile de faire cela.	It is easy to do that.
J'ai pris la liberté de vous écrire.	I have taken the liberty of writing to you.

[1] May also be followed by **de**.

Il est difficile de chanter bien.	It is difficult to sing well.
Vous avez besoin (tort, etc.) de vous méfier.	You need (are wrong, etc.) to be suspicious.

164. A few adjectives are regularly followed by **à** + an infinitive.

Je suis prêt à partir.	I am ready to go.

The Infinitive after Other Prepositions

165. All prepositions except **en** are followed by the infinitive in French. **En** is followed by the present participle.

Il est parti sans nous dire adieu.	He left without saying good-bye to us.
En entrant dans la classe.	On entering the classroom.

166. Pour is used with the infinitive:

1. to translate *in order to;*

Il faut travailler pour réussir.	You must work in order to succeed.

2. after verbs of motion when purpose is stressed;

Etes-vous venu pour travailler?	Have you come in order to work?
But: Il est venu me voir hier soir.	He came to see me last night.

3. after **assez** and **trop**.

Il a assez de temps pour vous voir.	He has time enough to see you.
Je suis trop occupé pour aller au théâtre.	I am too busy to go to the theatre.

167. Par after **commencer** and **finir** is equivalent to the English *by* with the present participle.

| Il a commencé par étudier le français. | He began by studying French. |
| But: Il a commencé à étudier le français. | He began to study French. |

168. Après requires the perfect infinitive; **sans,** either the present or the perfect infinitive.

| Après avoir dîné, nous sommes allés en ville. | After dining, we went to town. |
| Il est parti sans { dire / avoir dit } adieu à personne. | He left without saying good-bye to any one. |

The Infinitive as a Noun

169. The infinitive may be used as the subject or the object of a verb.

| Dire qu'il est riche, serait inexact. | To say that he is rich would be inexact. |

The Infinitive for a Subordinate Clause

170. For the use of the infinitive replacing a subordinate clause, cf. § 157.

LES MARTIN S'EN VONT

—Alors vous partez, vous aussi, Monsieur Martin?

—Il le faut bien, Jean. Voilà huit mois que je m'amuse ici sans songer à mes clients.

—Et puis, ajouta Marie, le mauvais temps ne tardera pas à venir. Les marronniers du Luxembourg commencent déjà à jaunir. Les pluies vont bientôt s'abattre sur ce triste Paris et on sera obligé de chausser ses caoutchoucs et de mettre son pardessus pour sortir. Il est vraiment temps de s'en aller.

—Que dites-vous là? Mais c'est justement en automne et en hiver qu'il faut voir Paris. Les touristes sont tous partis ou prêts à partir. Les vrais Parisiens, après avoir passé l'été au bord de la mer ou à la montagne se dépêchent de regagner leur domicile. Les théâtres commencent à afficher des pièces nouvelles. Vous êtes trop intelligente, Marie, pour ne pas savoir qu'un étranger ne peut pas connaître le véritable Paris sans y avoir passé un hiver.

—Vous avez raison. Mais cela n'empêche pas que j'aie bien souffert du froid l'année dernière dans mon appartement mal chauffé. Vous étiez sans doute trop occupé pour vous apercevoir du temps qu'il faisait. Et vous aurez encore plus à faire cette année-ci, n'est-ce pas?

—Oui. Je vais commencer par travailler à la Bibliothèque Nationale et à partir du premier novembre, je reprendrai mes cours à la Sorbonne. J'espère passer mes examens au mois de mai.

—Bonne chance, Jean, et au revoir. Vous n'oublierez pas de venir nous dire adieu à la gare demain?

—Je n'y manquerai pas. A demain, Docteur.

CONVERSATION

1. Depuis combien de temps les Martin sont-ils à Paris? 2. Pourquoi le docteur Martin est-il obligé de retourner à New York? 3. Quel temps fait-il à Paris en hiver? 4. Qu'est-ce qu'on est obligé de porter, quand on sort? 5. Y a-t-il beaucoup de touristes à Paris en hiver? 6. Où les Parisiens passent-ils l'été? 7. Pourquoi est-il désirable d'être à Paris pendant l'hiver? 8. Pourquoi Marie n'aime-t-elle pas l'hiver à Paris? 9. Où est-ce que Jean va travailler? 10. Quand passera-t-il ses examens?

COMPOSITION

"It was nice of you to invite us to take tea with you this afternoon," said Marie, "and I am glad that you chose this little tea room near the Luxembourg."

"I remember that you like to come here," answered John. "Even if the chestnut trees are beginning to turn yellow, the garden is still pleasant to look at. And you, Doctor Martin, don't you regret leaving Paris?"

"Naturally, but if I don't hurry (to go) back to New York, I shall have no patients to care for. My colleague has just written me, urging me to return as soon as possible."

"I must take up my studies again, too, without waiting for the opening of the university. I am going to try to finish my thesis before the first of April and in order to do that, I shall be obliged to spend most of my time in the libraries."

"I hope that you won't be too busy to go to the theatre occasionally," said Marie. "Don't forget that you have promised to keep me informed about the new plays."

"I shall not fail to do so. It is too bad that Pagnol's new comedy hasn't been given yet. After seeing *Topaze,* you will be sorry to miss this one."

"There is one thing," said Dr. Martin, "that I shall not regret."

"What?"

"The continual rains that force you to put on your rubbers and carry an umbrella, every time you leave your poorly heated apartment."

"I wonder, Doctor, what you say when you return to your overheated apartment in New York, after taking a walk in the snow!"

"A good retort, John," exclaimed Marie. "And now, good-bye. We have our trunks to pack, you know."

"Until tomorrow, then. I'll say good-bye to you at the station."

DRILL EXERCISE

1. I shall try to see you tonight. 2. Let me go with you. 3. Father made us put on our overcoats. 4. John is afraid that he will not pass his examinations. 5. The snow continued to fall all night. 6. You will end by taking a room in the Latin Quarter. 7. This novel is easy to read. 8. They have decided to leave Paris. 9. I shall send for a taxi. 10. Have you seen *Tartuffe* played at the Odéon? 11. I don't know how to find the National Library. 12. Smoking is forbidden in the reading-room. 13. Ask her to lend you her guide-book. 14. It is not easy to find a well heated apartment. 15. He began by telling us that he had no money. 16. In order to learn to speak French well, one should go to France. 17. Permit me to help you pack your trunk. 18. It did not rain enough to spoil our walk. 19. You must not leave Europe without seeing the Riviera. 20. Before going to see *Topaze,* I read the play. 21. To say that I like to work would not be quite true. 22. After taking tea with Marie, he went to the library.

23. We hope to see you at the station. 24. In a week I shall be ready to leave. 25. Unless you lose your way, you will be there at six-thirty.

VERB REVIEW

acquérir, to acquire. Cf. § 185.
courir, to run. Cf. § 186.

1. John ran to his class. 2. Let's not run so fast. 3. He was running, when I saw him. 4. He acquired (*p. def.*). 5. Has he acquired a good reputation? 6. He is acquiring a great deal of experience. 7. Let him run. 8. I would not run so fast, if I were you. 9. One acquires experience in a large city. 10. You are late, you must run fast.

APPENDIX

THE VERB

APPENDIX

THE VERB

The Regular Verbs

171. First Conjugation	172. Second Conjugation	173. Third Conjugation

Infinitive Mood

Present

donn **er,** *to give*	fin **ir,** *to finish*	vend **re,** *to sell*

Participles

Present Participle

donn **ant,** *giving*	fin **iss ant,** *finishing*	vend **ant,** *selling*

Past Participle

donn **é,** *given*	fin **i,** *finished*	vend **u,** *sold*

Indicative Mood

Present

I give, am giving, etc.	*I finish, am finishing, etc.*	*I sell, am selling, etc.*
je donn **e**	je fin **i s**	je vend **s**
tu donn **es**	tu fin **i s**	tu vend **s**
il donn **e**	il fin **i t**	il vend [1]

[1] The **t** of this ending is missing, but the same is true of so many of this class of verbs that **vendre** seems a better model for the third conjugation than does **rompre,** *to break,* which is often given. For **rompre** and its compounds, **interrompre** *to interrupt,* **corrompre** *to corrupt,* add a **t** to this ending: **rompt, interrompt, corrompt.**

First Conjugation	Second Conjugation	Third Conjugation
nous donn **ons**	nous fin **iss ons**	nous vend **ons**
vous donn **ez**	vous fin **iss ez**	vous vend **ez**
ils donn **ent**	ils fin **iss ent**	ils vend **ent**

Imperfect

I was giving, used to give, etc.	I was finishing, used to finish, etc.	I was selling, used to sell, etc.
je donn **ais**	je fin **iss ais**	je vend **ais**
tu donn **ais**	tu fin **iss ais**	tu vend **ais**
il donn **ait**	il fin **iss ait**	il vend **ait**
nous donn **ions**	nous fin **iss ions**	nous vend **ions**
vous donn **iez**	vous fin **iss iez**	vous vend **iez**
ils donn **aient**	ils fin **iss aient**	ils vend **aient**

Past Definite

I gave, etc.	I finished, etc.	I sold, etc.
je donn **ai**	je fin **is**	je vend **is**
tu donn **as**	tu fin **is**	tu vend **is**
il donn **a**	il fin **it**	il vend **it**
nous donn **âmes**	nous fin **îmes**	nous vend **îmes**
vous donn **âtes**	vous fin **îtes**	vous vend **îtes**
ils donn **èrent**	ils fin **irent**	ils vend **irent**

Future

I shall give, etc.	I shall finish, etc.	I shall sell, etc.
je donner **ai**	je finir **ai**	je vendr **ai**
tu donner **as**	tu finir **as**	tu vendr **as**
il donner **a**	il finir **a**	il vendr **a**
nous donner **ons**	nous finir **ons**	nous vendr **ons**
vous donner **ez**	vous finir **ez**	vous vendr **ez**
ils donner **ont**	ils finir **ont**	ils vendr **ont**

First Conjugation	Second Conjugation	Third Conjugation

Conditional

I should give, etc.	*I should finish*, etc.	*I should sell*, etc.
je donner **ais**	je finir **ais**	je vendr **ais**
tu donner **ais**	tu finir **ais**	tu vendr **ais**
il donner **ait**	il finir **ait**	il vendr **ait**
nous donner **ions**	nous finir **ions**	nous vendr **ions**
vous donner **iez**	vous finir **iez**	vous vendr **iez**
ils donner **aient**	ils finir **aient**	ils vendr **aient**

Subjunctive Mood

Present

(That) I (may) give, etc.	*(That) I (may) finish*, etc.	*(That) I (may) sell*, etc.
(que) je donn **e**	fin **isse**	vend **e**
(que) tu donn **es**	fin **isses**	vend **es**
(qu')il donn **e**	fin **isse**	vend **e**
(que) nous donn **ions**	fin **issions**	vend **ions**
(que) vous donn **iez**	fin **issiez**	vend **iez**
(qu')ils donn **ent**	fin **issent**	vend **ent**

Imperfect

(That) I (might) give, etc.	*(That) I (might) finish*, etc.	*(That) I (might) sell*, etc.
(que) je donn **asse**	fin **isse**	vend **isse**
(que) tu donn **asses**	fin **isses**	vend **isses**
(qu')il donn **ât**	fin **ît**	vend **ît**
(que) nous donn **assions**	fin **issions**	vend **issions**
(que) vous donn **assiez**	fin **issiez**	vend **issiez**
(qu')ils donn **assent**	fin **issent**	vend **issent**

First Conjugation	Second Conjugation	Third Conjugation

Imperative Mood

Present

Give, etc.	*Finish,* etc.	*Sell,* etc.
donn e [1]	fin i s	vend s
donn ons	fin iss ons	vend ons
donn ez	fin iss ez	vend ez

Auxiliary Verbs

174. Avoir (*aux.* avoir). **175.** Etre (*aux.* avoir).

Infinitive

Present

avoir, *to have*   être, *to be*

Participles

Present Participle

ayant, *having*   étant, *being*

Past Participle

eu, *had*   été, *been*

Indicative

Present

I have, am having, etc.		*I am, am being,* etc.	
j'ai	nous avons	je suis	nous sommes
tu as	vous avez	tu es	vous êtes
il a	il ont	il est	ils sont

[1] This form becomes "donn **es**" when followed by **-y** or **-en.**

Imperfect

I had, was having, etc.   *I was, was being*, etc.

j' avais	nous avions	j' étais	nous étions
tu avais	vous aviez	tu étais	vous étiez
il avait	ils avaient	il était	ils étaient

Past Definite

I had, etc.   *I was*, etc.

j' eus	nous eûmes	je fus	nous fûmes
tu eus	vous eûtes	tu fus	vous fûtes
il eut	ils eurent	il fut	ils furent

Future

I shall have, etc.   *I shall be*, etc.

j' aurai	nous aurons	je serai	nous serons
tu auras	vous aurez	tu seras	vous serez
il aura	ils auront	il sera	ils seront

Conditional

I should have, etc.   *I should be*, etc.

j' aurais	nous aurions	je serais	nous serions
tu aurais	vous auriez	tu serais	vous seriez
il aurait	ils auraient	il serait	ils seraient

Subjunctive

Present

(That) I (may) have, etc.   *(That) I (may) be*, etc.

(que) j'aie   (que) je sois
(que) tu aies   (que) tu sois
(qu') il ait   (qu') il soit
(que) nous ayons   (que) nous soyons
(que) vous ayez   (que) vous soyez
(qu')ils aient   (qu')ils soient

Imperfect

(That) I (might) have, etc.   (That) I (might) be, etc.

  (que) j'eusse   (que) je fusse
  (que) tu eusses   (que) tu fusses
  (qu') il eût   (qu') il fût
  (que) nous eussions   (que) nous fussions
  (que) vous eussiez   (que) vous fussiez
  (qu')ils eussent   (qu')ils fussent

Imperative

Have, etc.   Be, etc.

       ayons   soyons
aie   ayez   sois   soyez

Compound Tenses

176. The compound tenses are formed from the past participle of a given verb and an auxiliary verb (usually **avoir**, sometimes **être**). Cf. §§ 44–46.

177. Avoir (donné).   **178.** Etre (arrivé).

Infinitive

Perfect

To have given   To have arrived
avoir donné   être arrivé(e)(s)

Participle

Perfect

Having given   Having arrived
ayant donné   étant arrivé(e)(s)

Indicative

Past Indefinite

I have given, etc.   I have arrived, etc.
j'ai donné   je suis arrivé(e)
tu as donné   tu es arrivé(e)
etc.   etc.

Pluperfect

I had given, etc.   I had arrived, etc.
j'avais donné   j'étais arrivé(e)
etc.   etc.

Past Anterior

I had given, etc.   I had arrived, etc.
j'eus donné   je fus arrivé(e)
etc.   etc.

Future Perfect

I shall have given, etc.   I shall have arrived, etc.
j'aurai donné   je serai arrivé(e)
etc.   etc.

Conditional Perfect

I should have given, etc.   I should have arrived, etc.
j'aurais donné   je serais arrivé(e)
etc.   etc.

Subjunctive

Perfect

(That) I (may) have given, etc.   (That) I (may) have arrived, etc.
(que) j'aie donné   (que) je sois arrivé(e)
etc.   etc.

Pluperfect

(That) I (might) have given, etc.   (That) I (might) have arrived, etc.
(que) j'eusse donné   (que) je fusse arrivé(e)
etc.   etc.

Orthographical Changes

179. Verbs in –cer.

Placer, to place

Pres. Part.	Pres. Ind.	Impf. Ind.	Past Def.	Impf. Subj.
plaçant	place	plaçais	plaçai	plaçasse
	places	plaçais	plaças	plaçasses
	place	plaçait	plaça	plaçât
	plaçons	placions	plaçâmes	plaçassions
	placez	placiez	plaçâtes	plaçassiez
	placent	plaçaient	placèrent	plaçassent

180. Verbs in –ger.

Manger, to eat

Pres. Part.	Pres. Ind.	Impf. Ind.	Past Def.	Impf. Subj.
mangeant	mange	mangeais	mangeai	mangeasse
	manges	mangeais	mangeas	mangeasses
	mange	mangeait	mangea	mangeât
	mangeons	mangions	mangeâmes	mangeassions
	mangez	mangiez	mangeâtes	mangeassiez
	mangent	mangeaient	mangèrent	mangeassent

181. Verbs in –yer.

Employer, to use; payer, to pay

Pres. Ind.	Fut.	Cond.	Pres. Subj.
emploie, etc.	emploierai, etc.	emploierais, etc.	emploie, etc.
paye, } etc. paie,	payerai, } etc. paierai,	payerais, } etc. paierais,	paye, } etc. paie,

182. Verbs with stem-vowel *e* or *é*.

1. **Mener,** *to lead;* **céder,** *to yield.*

Pres. Ind.	Fut.	Cond.	Pres. Subj.
mène	mènerai	mènerais	mène
mènes	mèneras	mènerais	mènes
mène	mènera	mènerait	mène
menons	mènerons	mènerions	menions
menez	mènerez	mèneriez	meniez
mènent	mèneront	mèneraient	mènent

Céder with the stem-vowel *é*:

cède, etc.   céderai, etc.   céderais, etc.   cède, etc.

2. Verbs in *-eler* and *-eter*.

Appeler, *to call*

Pres. Ind.	Fut.	Cond.	Pres. Subj.
appelle	appellerai	appellerais	appelle
appelles	appelleras	appellerais	appelles
appelle	appellera	appellerait	appelle
appelons	appellerons	appellerions	appelions
appelez	appellerez	appelleriez	appeliez
appellent	appelleront	appelleraient	appellent

Jeter, *to throw*

jette, etc.   jetterai, etc.   jetterais, etc.   jette, etc.

Note.—A few verbs in *-eler, -eter* take the grave accent like **mener,** e. g., **acheter,** *to buy:*

achète, etc.   achèterai, etc.   achèterais, etc.   achète, etc.

Exceptions like **acheter:**

geler, *to freeze.*

Irregular Verbs in -er

183. Aller, *to go.*

1. *Infinitive* **aller;** *fut.* irai, iras, ira, etc.; *condl.* irais, etc.
2. *Pres. Part.* **allant;** *impf. indic.* allais, etc.; *pres. subj.* aille, ailles, aille, allions, alliez, aillent.
3. *Past Part.* **allé;** *past indef.* je suis allé, etc.
4. *Pres. Indic.* **vais,** vas, va, allons, allez, vont; *impve.* va, allons, allez.
5. *Past Def.* **allai,** allas, alla, allâmes, allâtes, allèrent; *impf. subj.* allasse, allasses, allât, allassions, allassiez, allassent.

Like **aller:**

s'en aller, *go away.*

184. Envoyer, *to send.*

1. *Infinitive* **envoyer;** *fut.* enverrai, etc.; *condl.* enverrais, etc.
2. *Pres. Part.* **envoyant;** *impf. indic.* envoyais, envoyais, envoyait, envoyions, envoyiez, envoyaient; *pres. subj.* envoie, envoies, envoie, envoyions, envoyiez, envoient.
3. *Past Part.* **envoyé;** *past indef.* j'ai envoyé, etc.
4. *Pres. Indic.* **envoie,** envoies, envoie, envoyons, envoyez, envoient; *impve.* envoie, envoyons, envoyez.
5. *Past Def.* **envoyai,** envoyas, envoya, envoyâmes, envoyâtes, envoyèrent; *impf. subj.* envoyasse, envoyasses, envoyât, envoyassions, envoyassiez, envoyassent.

Like **envoyer:**

renvoyer, *send away, dismiss.*

Irregular Verbs in -ir

185. Acquérir, *to acquire.*

1. *Infinitive* **acquérir;** *fut.* acquerrai, acquerras, etc.; *condl.* acquerrais, etc.
2. *Pres. Part.* **acquérant;** *impf. indic.* acquérais, etc.; *pres.*

subj. acquière, acquières, acquière, acquérions, acquériez, acquièrent.

3. *Past Part.* **acquis;** *past indef.* j'ai acquis, etc.
4. *Pres. Indic.* **acquiers,** acquiers, acquiert, acquérons, acquérez, acquièrent; *impve.* acquiers, acquérons, acquérez.
5. *Past Def.* **acquis,** acquis, acquit, acquîmes, acquîtes, acquirent; *impf. subj.* acquisse, acquisses, acquît, acquissions, acquissiez, acquissent.

Like **acquérir:**

  conquérir, *conquer.*

186. Courir, *to run.*

1. *Infinitive* **courir;** *fut.* courrai, courras, etc.; *condl.* courrais, etc.
2. *Pres. Part.* **courant;** *impf. indic.* courais, etc.; *pres. subj.* coure, coures, coure, courions, couriez, courent.
3. *Past Part.* **couru;** *past indef.* j'ai couru, etc.
4. *Pres. Indic.* **cours,** cours, court, courons, courez, courent; *impve.* cours, courons, courez.
5. *Past Def.* **courus,** courus, courut, courûmes, courûtes, coururent; *impf. subj.* courusse, courusses, courût, courussions, courussiez, courussent.

Like **courir** are its compounds:

  accourir, *run up, hasten.*   parcourir, *run over.*

187. Cueillir, *to gather, pick.*

1. *Infinitive* **cueillir;** *fut.* cueillerai, etc.; *condl.* cueillerais, etc.
2. *Pres. Part.* **cueillant;** *impf. indic.* cueillais, etc.; *pres. subj.* cueille, cueilles, cueille, cueillions, cueilliez, cueillent.
3. *Past Part.* **cueilli,** *past indef.* j'ai cueilli, etc.
4. *Pres. Indic.* **cueille,** cueilles, cueille, cueillons, cueillez, cueillent; *impve.* cueille, cueillons, cueillez.
5. *Past Def.* **cueillis,** cueillis, cueillit, cueillîmes, cueillîtes, cueillirent; *impf. subj.* cueillisse, cueillisses, cueillît, cueillissions, cueillissiez, cueillissent.

Obs.: The present indicative, future, and conditional are like those of **donner**.

Like **cueillir**:

accueillir, *welcome*.
recueillir, *gather, collect*.

188. Dormir, *to sleep*.

1. *Infinitive* **dormir**; *fut.* dormirai, etc.; *condl.* dormirais, etc.
2. *Pres. Part.* **dormant**; *impf. indic.* dormais, etc.; *pres. subj.* dorme, dormes, dorme, dormions, dormiez, dorment.
3. *Past Part.* **dormi**; *past indef.* j'ai dormi, etc.
4. *Pres. Indic.* **dors,** dors, dort, dormons, dormez, dorment; *impve.* dors, dormons, dormez.
5. *Past Def.* **dormis,** dormis, dormit, dormîmes, dormîtes, dormirent; *impf. subj.* dormisse, dormisses, dormît, dormissions, dormissiez, dormissent.

Like **dormir**:

All the compounds of **dormir** and the following verbs with their compounds:

bouillir *boil*
mentir *lie*
partir *set out, leave*
se repentir *repent*
sentir *feel*
servir *serve*
sortir *go out*

Observe the Present Indicative of the following types, which are represented in the above list:

bouillir: bous, bous, bout, bouillons, bouillez, bouillent.
mentir: mens, mens, ment, mentons, mentez, mentent.
partir: pars, pars, part, partons, partez, partent.
se repentir: repens, repens, repent, repentons, repentez, repentent.
sentir: sens, sens, sent, sentons, sentez, sentent.
servir: sers, sers, sert, servons, servez, servent.
sortir: sors, sors, sort, sortons, sortez, sortent.

189. Fuir, *to flee, fly*.

1. *Infinitive* **fuir**; *fut.* fuirai, etc.; *condl.* fuirais, etc.
2. *Pres. Part.* **fuyant**; *impf. indic.* fuyais, etc.; *pres. subj.* fuie, fuies, fuie, fuyions, fuyiez, fuient.

3. *Past Part.* **fui;** *past indef.* j'ai fui, etc.

4. *Pres. Indic.* **fuis,** fuis, fuit, fuyons, fuyez, fuient; *impve.* fuis, fuyons, fuyez.

5. *Past Def.* **fuis,** fuis, fuit, fuîmes, fuîtes, fuirent; *impf. subj.* fuisse, fuisses, fuit, fuissions, fuissiez, fuissent.

Like **fuir:**

s'enfuir, *flee, escape.*

190. Haïr, *to hate.*

1. *Infinitive* **haïr;** *fut.* haïrai, etc.; *condl.* haïrais, etc.

2. *Pres. Part.* **haïssant;** *impf. indic.* haïssais, etc.; *pres. subj.* haïsse, haïsses, haïsse, haïssions, haïssiez, haïssent.

3. *Past Part.* **haï;** *past indef.* j'ai haï, etc.

4. *Pres. Indic.* **hais,** hais, hait, haïssons, haïssez, haïssent; *impve,* hais, haïssons, haïssez.

5. *Past. Def.* **haïs,** haïs, haït, haïmes, haïtes, haïrent; *impf. subj.* haïsse, haïsses, haït, haïssions, haïssiez, haïssent.

191. Mourir, *to die.*

1. *Infinitive* **mourir;** *fut.* mourrai, mourras, etc.; *condl.* mourrais, etc.

2. *Pres. Part.* **mourant;** *impf. indic.* mourais, etc.; *pres. subj.* meure, meures, meure, mourions, mouriez, meurent.

3. *Past Part.* **mort;** *past indef.* je suis mort, etc.

4. *Pres. Indic.* **meurs,** meurs, meurt, mourons, mourez, meurent; *impve.* meurs, mourons, mourez.

5. *Past Def.* **mourus,** mourus, mourut, mourûmes, mourûtes, moururent; *impf. subj.* mourusse, mourusses, mourût, mourussions, mourussiez, mourussent.

192. Ouvrir, *to open.*

1. *Infinitive* **ouvrir;** *fut.* ouvrirai, etc.; *condl.* ouvrirais, etc.

2. *Pres. Part.* **ouvrant;** *impf. indic.* ouvrais, etc.; *pres. subj.* ouvre, ouvres, ouvre, ouvrions, ouvriez, ouvrent.

3. *Past Part.* **ouvert;** *past indef.* j'ai ouvert, etc.

4. *Pres. Indic.* **ouvre,** ouvres, ouvre, ouvrons, ouvrez, ouvrent; *impve.* ouvre, ouvrons, ouvrez.

5. *Past Def.* **ouvris,** ouvris, ouvrit, ouvrîmes, ouvrites, ouvrirent; *impf. subj.* ouvrisse, ouvrisses, ouvrît, ouvrissions, ouvrissiez, ouvrissent.

Like **ouvrir:**

couvrir, *cover.*
découvrir, *discover.*
offrir, *offer.*
souffrir, *suffer.*

193. Tenir, *to hold.*

1. *Infinitive* **tenir;** *fut.* tiendrai, tiendras, etc.; *condl.* tiendrais, etc.

2. *Pres. Part.* **tenant;** *impf. indic.* tenais, etc.; *pres. subj.* tienne, tiennes, tienne, tenions, teniez, tiennent.

3. *Past Part.* **tenu;** *past indef.* j'ai tenu, etc.

4. *Pres. Indic.* **tiens,** tiens, tient, tenons, tenez, tiennent; *impve.* tiens, tenons, tenez.

5. *Past Def.* **tins,** tins, tint, tînmes, tîntes, tinrent; *impf. subj.* tinsse, tinsses, tînt, tinssions, tinssiez, tinssent.

Like **tenir** are its compounds:

s'abstenir, *abstain.*
appartenir, *belong.*
contenir, *contain.*
détenir, *detain.*
entretenir, *entertain.*
maintenir, *maintain.*
obtenir, *obtain.*
retenir, *retain.*
soutenir, *sustain.*

194. Venir, *to come.*

1. *Infinitive* **venir;** *fut.* viendrai, viendras, etc.; *condl.* viendrais, etc.

2. *Pres. Part.* **venant;** *impf. indic.* venais, etc.; *pres. subj.* vienne, viennes, vienne, venions, veniez, viennent.

3. *Past Part.* **venu;** *past indef.* je suis venu, etc.

4. *Pres. Indic.* **viens,** viens, vient, venons, venez, viennent; *impve.* viens, venons, venez.

5. *Past Def.* **vins,** vins, vint, vînmes, vîntes, vinrent; *impf. subj.* vinsse, vinsses, vînt, vinssions, vinssiez, vinssent.

Like **venir** are its compounds:

devenir, *become.*
parvenir, *attain.*
prévenir, *prevent.*

provenir, *proceed (from,* **de**).
revenir, *come back.*
se souvenir, *remember*

195. Vêtir, *to clothe.*

1. *Infinitive* **vêtir**; *fut.* vêtirai, etc.; *condl.* vêtirais, etc.
2. *Pres. Part.* **vêtant**; *impf. indic.* vêtais, etc.; *pres. subj.* vête, vêtes, vête, vêtions, vêtiez, vêtent.
3. *Past Part.* **vêtu**; *past indef.* j'ai vêtu, etc.
4. *Pres. Indic.* **vêts,** vêts, vêt, vêtons, vêtez, vêtent; *impve.* vêts, vêtons, vêtez.
5. *Past Def.* **vêtis,** vêtis, vêtit, vêtîmes, vêtîtes, vêtirent; *impf. subj.* vêtisse, vêtisses, vêtît, vêtissions, vêtissiez, vêtissent.

Irregular Verbs in –re

196. Battre, *to beat.*

Loses one **t** in the present indicative singular: **Bats, bats, bat;** otherwise like **vendre.**

Like **battre:**

abattre, *fell.*
combattre, *fight, oppose.*

197. Boire, *to drink.*

1. *Infinitive* **boire**; *fut.* boirai, etc.; *condl.* boirais, etc.
2. *Pres. Part.* **buvant**; *impf. indic.* buvais, etc., *pres. subj.* boive, boives, boive, buvions, buviez, boivent.
3. *Past Part.* **bu**; *past indef.* j'ai bu, etc.
4. *Pres. Indic.* **bois,** bois, boit, buvons, buvez, boivent; *impve.* bois, buvons, buvez.
5. *Past Def.* **bus,** bus, but, bûmes, bûtes, burent; *impf. subj.* busse, busses, bût, bussions, bussiez, bussent.

198. Conclure, *to conclude.*

1. *Infinitive* **conclure;** *fut.* conclurai, etc.; *condl.* conclurais, etc.

2. *Pres. Part.* **concluant;** *impf. indic.* concluais, etc.; *pres. subj.* conclue, conclues, conclue, concluions, concluiez, concluent.

3. *Past Part.* **conclu;** *past indef.* j'ai conclu, etc.

4. *Pres. Indic.* **conclus,** conclus, conclut, concluons, concluez, concluent; *impve.* conclus, concluons, concluez.

5. *Past Def.* **conclus,** conclus, conclut, conclûmes, conclûtes, conclurent; *impf. subj.* conclusse, conclusses, conclût, conclussions, conclussiez, conclussent.

199. Conduire, *to conduct,* etc.

1. *Infinitive* **conduire;** *fut.* conduirai, etc.; *condl.* conduirais, etc.

2. *Pres. Part.* **conduisant;** *impf. indic.* conduisais, etc.; *pres. subj.* conduise, conduises, conduise, conduisions, conduisiez, conduisent.

3. *Past Part.* **conduit;** *past indef.* j'ai conduit, etc.

4. *Pres. Indic.* **conduis,** conduis, conduit, conduisons, conduisez, conduisent; *impve.* conduis, conduisons, conduisez.

5. *Past Def.* **conduisis,** conduisis, conduisit, conduisîmes, conduisîtes, conduisirent; *impf. subj.* conduisisse, conduisisses, conduisît, conduisissions, conduisissiez, conduisissent.

Like **conduire:**

construire, *construct.*
détruire, *destroy.*
introduire, *introduce.*
produire, *produce.*
réduire, *reduce.*
traduire, *translate.*

200. Etre, *to be.*

See § **175** for the full conjugation.

201. Connaître, *to know,* etc.

1. *Infinitive* **connaître;** *fut.* connaîtrai, etc.; *condl.* connaîtrais, etc.

2. *Pres. Part.* **connaissant**; *impf. indic.* connaissais, etc.; *pres. subj.* connaisse, connaisses, connaisse, connaissions, connaissiez, connaissent.

3. *Past Part.* **connu**; *past indef.* j'ai connu, etc.

4. *Pres. Indic.* **connais**, connais, connaît, connaissons, connaissez, connaissent; *impve.* connais, connaissons, connaissez.

5. *Past Def.* **connus**, connus, connut, connûmes connûtes, connurent; *impf. subj.* connusse, connusses, connût, connussions, connussiez, connussent.

Like **connaître**:

reconnaitre, *recognize*	paraître, *appear.*	disparaître, *disappear.*
	apparaître, *appear.*	reparaitre, *reappear.*

202. Coudre, *to sew.*

1. *Infinitive* **coudre**; *fut.* coudrai, etc.; *condl.* coudrais, etc.

2. *Pres. Part.* **cousant**; *impf. indic.* cousais, etc.; *pres. subj.* couse, couses, couse, cousions, cousiez, cousent.

3. *Past Part.* **cousu**; *past indef.* j'ai cousu, etc.

4. *Pres. Indic.* **couds**, couds, coud, cousons, cousez, cousent; *impve.* couds, cousons, cousez.

5. *Past Def.* **cousis**, cousis, cousit, cousîmes, cousîtes, cousirent; *impf. subj.* cousisse, cousisses, cousît, cousissions, cousissiez, cousissent.

203. Craindre, *to fear.*

1. *Infinitive* **craindre**; *fut.*, craindrai, etc.; *condl.* craindrais, etc.

2. *Pres. Part.* **craignant**; *impf. indic.* craignais, etc.; *pres. subj.* craigne, craignes, craigne, craignions, craigniez, craignent.

3. *Past Part.* **craint**; *past indef.* j'ai craint, etc.

4. *Pres. Indic.* **crains**, crains, craint, craignons, craignez, craignent; *impve.* crains, craignons, craignez.

5. *Past Def.* **craignis**, craignis, craignit, craignîmes, craignîtes, craignirent; *impf. subj.* craignisse, craignisses, craignît, craignissions, craignissiez, craignissent.

Like **craindre**:

in –aindre:
  contraindre, *constrain.*
  plaindre, *pity.*
in –eindre:
  atteindre, *attain.*
éteindre, *extinguish.*
peindre, *paint.*
in –oindre:
  joindre, *join.*

204. Croire, *to believe.*

1. *Infinitive* **croire**; *fut.* croirai, etc.; *condl.* croirais, etc.
2. *Pres. Part.* **croyant**; *impf. indic.* croyais, etc.; *pres. subj.* croie, croies, croie, croyions, croyiez, croient.
3. *Pres. Part.* **cru**; *past indef.* j'ai cru, etc.
4. *Pres. Indic.* **crois,** crois, croit, croyons, croyez, croient; *impve.* crois, croyons, croyez.
5. *Past Def.* **crus,** crus, crut, crûmes, crûtes, crurent; *impf. subj.* crusse, crusses, crût, crussions, crussiez, crussent.

205. Dire, *to say, tell.*

1. *Infinitive* **dire**; *fut.* dirai, etc.; *condl.* dirais, etc.
2. *Pres. Part.* **disant**; *impf. indic.* disais, etc.; *pres. subj.* dise, dises, dise, disions, disiez, disent.
3. *Past Part.* **dit**; *past indef.* j'ai dit, etc.
4. *Pres. Indic.* **dis,** dis, dit, disons, dites, disent; *impve.* dis, disons, dites.
5. *Past Def.* **dis,** dis, dit, dîmes, dîtes, dirent; *impf. subj.* disse, disses, dît, dissions, dissiez, dissent.

Like **dire**:

contredire,[1] *contradict.*
dédire,[1] *retract, deny.*
interdire,[1] *interdict.*
médire[1] (de), *slander.*
prédire,[1] *predict.*
redire, *say again.*

206. Ecrire, *to write.*

1. *Infinitive* **écrire**; *fut.* écrirai, etc.; *condl.* écrirais, etc.
2. *Pres. Part.* **écrivant**; *impf. indic.* écrivais, etc.; *pres. subj.* écrive, écrives, écrive, écrivions, écriviez, écrivent.

[1] The 2d plur. pres. indic. and impve. is: Contre**disez**, dé**disez**, inter**disez**, etc.

3. *Past Part.* **écrit;** *past indef.* j'ai écrit, etc.

4. *Pres. Indic.* **écris,** écris, écrit, écrivons, écrivez, écrivent; *impve.* écris, écrivons, écrivez.

5. *Past Def.* **écrivis,** écrivis, écrivit, écrivîmes, écrivîtes, écrivirent; *impf. subj.* écrivisse, écrivisses, écrivît, écrivissions, écrivissiez, écrivissent.

Like **écrire** are all verbs, in **-(s)crire:**

décrire, *describe.*   prescrire, *prescribe.*
inscrire, *inscribe.*

207. Faire, *to do, make.*

1. *Infinitive* **faire;** *fut.* ferai, etc.; *condl.* ferais, etc.

2. *Pres. Part.* **faisant;** *impf. indic.* faisais, etc.; *pres. subj.* fasse, fasses, fasse, fassions, fassiez, fassent.

3. *Past Part.* **fait;** *past indef.* j'ai fait, etc.

4. *Pres. Indic.* **fais,** fais, fait, faisons, faites, font; *impve.* fais, faisons, faites.

5. *Past Def.* **fis,** fis, fit, fîmes, fîtes, firent; *impf. subj.* fisse, fisses, fît, fissions, fissiez, fissent.

Like **faire:**

satisfaire, *satisfy.*

208. Lire, *to read.*

1. *Infinitive* **lire;** *fut.* lirai, etc.; *condl.* lirais, etc.

2. *Pres. Part.* **lisant;** *impf. indic.* lisais, etc.; *pres. subj.* lise, lises, lise, lisions, lisiez, lisent.

3. *Past Part.* **lu;** *past indef.* j'ai lu, etc.

4. *Pres. Indic.* **lis,** lis, lit, lisons, lisez, lisent; *impve.* lis, lisons, lisez.

5. *Past Def.* **lus,** lus, lut, lûmes, lûtes, lurent; *impf. subj.* lusse, lusses, lût, lussions, lussiez, lussent.

209. Mettre, *to place, put.*

1. *Infinitive* **mettre;** *fut.* mettrai, etc.; *condl.* mettrais, etc.

2. *Pres. Part.* **mettant;** *impf. indic.* mettais, etc.; *pres. subj.* mette, mettes, mette, mettions, mettiez, mettent.

3. *Past Part.* **mis;** *past indef.* j'ai mis, etc.

4. *Pres. Indic.* **mets,** mets, met, mettons, mettez, mettent; *impve.* mets, mettons, mettez.

5. *Past Def.* **mis,** mis, mit, mîmes, mîtes, mirent; *impf. subj.* misse, misses, mît, missions, missiez, missent.

Like **mettre:**

admettre, *admit.*
commettre, *commit.*
omettre, *omit.*
permettre, *permit.*

promettre, *promise.*
remettre, *put back, hand to.*
soumettre, *submit.*

210. Naître, *to be born.*

1. *Infinitive* **naître;** *fut,* naîtrai, etc.; *condl.* naîtrais, etc.

2. *Pres. Part.* **naissant;** *impf. indic.* naissais, etc.; *pres. subj.* naisse, naisses, naisse, naissions, naissiez, naissent.

3. *Past Part.* **né;** *past indef.* je suis né, etc.

4. *Pres. Indic.* **nais,** nais, naît, naissons, naissez, naissent; *impve.* nais, naissons, naissez.

5. *Past. Def.* **naquis,** naquis, naquit naquîmes, naquîtes, naquirent; *impf. subj.* naquisse, naquisses, naquît, naquissions, naquissiez, naquissent.

211. Plaire, *to please.*

1. *Infinitive* **plaire;** *fut.* plairai, etc.; *condl.* plairais, etc.

2. *Pres. Part.* **plaisant;** *impf. indic.* plaisais, etc.; *pres. subj.* plaise, plaises, plaise, plaisions, plaisiez, plaisent.

3. *Past Part.* **plu;** *past indef.* j'ai plu, etc.

4. *Pres. Indic.* **plais,** plais, plaît, plaisons, plaisez, plaisent; *impve.* plais, plaisons, plaisez.

5. *Past Def.* **plus,** plus, plut, plûmes, plûtes, plurent; *impf. subj.* plusse, plusses, plût, plussions, plussiez, plussent.

Like **plaire:**

se taire,[1] *to be silent*

[1] **Il tait** has no circumflex accent.

212. Prendre, *to take*.

1. *Infinitive* **prendre;** *fut.* prendrai, etc.; *condl.* prendrais, etc.
2. *Pres. Part.* **prenant;** *impf. indic.* prenais, etc.; *pres. subj.* prenne, prennes, prenne, prenions, preniez, prennent.
3. *Past Part.* **pris;** *past indef.* j'ai pris, etc.
4. *Pres. Indic.* **prends,** prends, prend, prenons, prenez, prennent; *impve.* prends, prenons, prenez.
5. *Past Def.* **pris,** pris, prit, primes, prîtes, prirent; *impf. subj.* prisse, prisses, prît, prissions, prissiez, prissent.

Like **prendre** are its compounds:

apprendre, *learn*.	reprendre, *take back*.
comprendre, *understand*.	surprendre, *surprise*.
entreprendre, *undertake*.	

213. Résoudre, *to resolve*.

1. *Infinitive* **résoudre;** *fut.* résoudrai, etc.; *condl.* résoudrais, etc.
2. *Pres. Part.* **résolvant;** *impf. indic.* résolvais, etc.; *pres. subj.* résolve, résolves, résolve, résolvions, résolviez, résolvent.
3. *Past Part.* **résolu** and **résous;** *past indef.* j'ai résolu, etc.
4. *Pres. Indic.* **résous,** résous, résout, résolvons, résolvez, résolvent; *impve.* résous, résolvons, résolvez.
5. *Past Def.* **résolus,** résolus, résolut, résolûmes, résolûtes, résolurent; *impf. sub.* résolusse, résolusses, résolût, résolussions, résolussiez, résolussent.

214. Rire, *to laugh*.

1. *Infinitive* **rire;** *fut.* rirai, etc.; *condl.* rirais, etc.
2. *Pres. Part.* **riant;** *impf. indic.* riais, etc.; *pres. subj.* rie, ries, rie, riions, riiez, rient.
3. *Past Part.* **ri;** *past indef.* j'ai ri, etc.
4. *Pres. Indic.* **ris,** ris, rit, rions, riez, rient; *impve.* ris, rions, riez.

5. *Past Def.* **ris,** ris, rit, rîmes, rîtes, rirent; *impf. subj.* risse, risses, rît, rissions, rissiez, rissent.

Like **rire:**

sourire, *smile.*

215. Suffire, *to suffice.*

1. *Infinitive* **suffire;** *fut.* suffirai, etc.; *condl.* suffirais, etc.
2. *Pres. Part.* **suffisant;** *impf. indic.* suffisais, etc.; *pres. subj.* suffise, suffises, suffise, suffisions, suffisiez, suffisent.
3. *Past Part.* **suffi;** *past indef.* j'ai suffi, etc.
4. *Pres. Indic.* **suffis,** suffis, suffit, suffisons, suffisez, suffisent; *impve.* suffis, suffisons, suffisez.
5. *Past Def.* **suffis,** suffis, suffit, suffîmes, suffîtes, suffirent; *impf. subj.* suffisse, suffisses, suffît, suffissions, suffissiez, suffissent.

216. Suivre, *to follow.*

1. *Infinitive* **suivre;** *fut.* suivrai, etc.; *condl.* suivrais, etc.
2. *Pres. Part.* **suivant;** *impf. indic.* suivais, etc.; *pres. subj.* suive, suives, suive, suivions, suiviez, suivent.
3. *Past Part.* **suivi;** *past indef.* j'ai suivi, etc.
4. *Pres. Indic.* **suis,** suis, suit, suivons, suivez, suivent; *impve.* suis, suivons, suivez.
5. *Past Def.* **suivis,** suivis, suivit, suivîmes, suivîtes, suivirent; *impf. subj.* suivisse, suivisses, suivît, suivissions, suivissiez, suivissent.

217. Vaincre, *to conquer.*

1. *Infinitive* **vaincre;** *fut.* vaincrai, etc.; *condl.* vaincrais, etc.
2. *Pres. Part.* **vainquant;** *impf. indic.* vainquais, etc.; *pres. subj.* vainque, vainques, vainque, vainquions, vainquiez, vainquent.
3. *Past Part.* **vaincu;** *past indef.* j'ai vaincu, etc.
4. *Pres. Indic.* **vaincs,** vaincs, vainc, vainquons, vainquez, vainquent; *impve.* vaincs, vainquons, vainquez.

5. *Past Def.* **vainquis,** vainquis, vainquit, vainquîmes, vainquîtes, vainquirent; *impf. subj.* vainquisse, vainquisses, vainquît, vainquissions, vainquissiez, vainquissent.

Like **vaincre**:

convaincre, *convince.*

218. Vivre, *to live.*

1. *Infinitive* **vivre;** *fut.* vivrai, etc.; *condl.* vivrais, etc.
2. *Pres. Part.* **vivant;** *impf. indic.* vivais, etc.; *pres. subj.* vive, vives, vive, vivions, viviez, vivent.
3. *Past Part.* **vécu;** *past indef.* j'ai vécu, etc.
4. *Pres. Indic.* **vis,** vis, vit, vivons, vivez, vivent; *impve.*, vis, vivons, vivez.
5. *Past Def.* **vécus,** vécus, vécut, vécûmes, vécûtes, vécurent; *impf. subj.* vécusse, vécusses, vécût, vécussions, vécussiez, vécussent.

Irregular Verbs in –oir

219. Avoir, *to have.*

See § 174 for the full conjugation of this verb.

220. Recevoir, *to receive.*

1. *Infinitive* **recevoir;** *fut.* recevrai, etc.; *condl.* recevrais, etc.
2. *Pres. Part.* **recevant;** *impf. indic.* recevais, etc.; *pres. subj.* reçoive, reçoives, reçoive, recevions, receviez, reçoivent.
3. *Past Part.* **reçu;** *past indef.* j'ai reçu, etc.
4. *Pres. Indic.* **reçois,** reçois, reçoit, recevons, recevez, reçoivent; *impve.* reçois, recevons, recevez.
5. *Past Def.* **reçus,** recus, reçut, reçûmes, reçûtes, reçurent; *impf. subj.* reçusse, reçusses, reçût, reçussions, reçussiez, reçussent.

Like **recevoir**:

apercevoir, *perceive.* concevoir, *conceive.* décevoir, *deceive.*

221. Devoir, *to owe.*

1. *Infinitive* **devoir**; *fut.* devrai, etc.; *condl.* devrais, etc.
2. *Pres. Part.* **devant**; *impf. indic.* devais, etc.; *pres. subj.* doive, doives, doive, devions, deviez, doivent.
3. *Past Part.* **dû** (*f.* due, *pl.* du(e)s); *past indef.* j'ai dû, etc.
4. *Pres. Indic.* **dois,** dois, doit, devons, devez, doivent; *impve.* ——.
5. *Past Def.* **dus,** dus, dut, dûmes, dûtes, durent; *impf. subj.* dusse, dusses, dût, dussions, dussiez, dussent.

222. Asseoir, *to seat.*

1. *Infinitive* **asseoir**; *fut.* assiérai, etc.; *condl.* assiérais, etc.
2. *Pres. Part.* **asseyant**; *impf. indic.* asseyais, etc.; *pres. subj.* asseye, asseyes, asseye, asseyions, asseyiez, asseyent.
3. *Past Part.* **assis**; *past indef.*, j'ai assis, etc.
4. *Pres. Indic.* **assieds,** assieds, assied, asseyons, asseyez, asseyent; *impve.* assieds, asseyons, asseyez.
5. *Past Def.* **assis,** assis, assit, assîmes, assîtes, assirent; *impf. subj.* assisse, assisses, assît, assissions, assissiez, assissent.

Like **asseoir**:

s'asseoir, *sit down.*

223. Falloir, *must,* etc. (impers.).

1. *Infinitive* **falloir**; *fut.* il faudra; *condl.* il faudrait.
2. *Pres. Part.* ——; *impf. indic.* il fallait; *pres. subj.* il faille.
3. *Past Part.* **fallu**; *past indef.* il a fallu.
4. *Pres. Indic.* il **faut**; *impve.* ——.
5. *Past Def.* il **fallut**; *impf. subj.* il fallût.

224. Pleuvoir, *to rain* (impers.).

1. *Infinitive* **pleuvoir**; *fut.* il pleuvra; *condl.* il pleuvrait.
2. *Pres. Part.* **pleuvant**; *impf. indic.* il pleuvait; *pres. subj.* il pleuve.
3. *Past Part.* **plu**; *past indef.* il a plu.

4. *Pres. Indic.* il **pleut**; *impve.* ———.

5. *Past Def.* il **plut**; *impf. subj.* il plût.

225. Pouvoir, *to be able,* etc.

1. *Infinitive* **pouvoir**; *fut.* pourrai, etc.; *condl.* pourrais, etc.

2. *Pres. Part.* **pouvant**; *impf. indic.* pouvais, etc.; *pres. subj.* puisse, puisses, puisse, puissions, puissiez, puissent.

3. *Past Part.* **pu**; *past indef.* j'ai pu.

4. *Pres. Indic.* **puis** *or* **peux**, peux, peut, pouvons, pouvez, peuvent; *impve.* ———.

5. *Past Def.* **pus,** pus, put, pûmes, pûtes, purent; *impf. subj.* pusse, pusses, pût, pussions, pussiez, pussent.

Obs.: The first sing. pres. indic. in negation is usually **je ne peux pas,** or **je ne puis;** in questions, only **puis-je?;** otherwise **puis** or **peux.**

226. Savoir, *to know,* etc.

1. *Infinitive* **savoir**; *fut.* saurai, etc.; *condl.* saurais, etc.

2. *Pres. Part.* **sachant**; *impf. indic.* savais, etc.; *pres. subj.* sache, saches, sache, sachions, sachiez, sachent.

3. *Past Part.* **su**; *past indef.* j'ai su, etc.

4. *Pres. Indic.* **sais,** sais, sait, savons, savez, savent; *impve.* sache, sachons, sachez.

5. *Past Def.* **sus,** sus, sut, sûmes, sûtes, surent; *impf. subj.* susse, susses, sût, sussions, sussiez, sussent.

227. Valoir, *to be worth.*

1. *Infinitive* **valoir**; *fut.* vaudrai, etc.; *condl.* vaudrais, etc.

2. *Pres. Part.* **valant**; *impf. indic.* valais, etc.; *pres. subj.* vaille, vailles, vaille, valions, valiez, vaillent.

3. *Past. Part.* **valu**; *past indef.* j'ai valu, etc.

4. *Pres. Indic.* **vaux,** vaux, vaut, valons, valez, valent; *impve.* vaux, valons, valez.

5. *Past. Def.* **valus,** valus, valut, valûmes, valûtes, valurent;

impf. subj. valusse, valusses, valût, valussions, valussiez, valussent.

228. Voir, *to see.*

1. *Infinitive* **voir**; *fut.* verrai, etc.; *condl.* verrais, etc.
2. *Pres. Part.* **voyant**; *impf. indic.* voyais, etc.; *pres. subj.* voie, voies, voie, voyions, voyiez, voient.
3. *Past Part.* **vu**; *past indef.* j'ai vu, etc.
4. *Pres. Indic.* **vois**, vois, voit, voyons, voyez, voient; *impve.* vois, voyons, voyez.
5. *Past Def.* **vis**, vis, vit, vîmes, vîtes, virent; *impf. subj.* visse, visses, vît, vissions, vissiez, vissent.

229. Vouloir, *to wish,* etc.

1. *Infinitive* **vouloir**; *fut.* voudrai, etc.; *condl.* voudrais, etc.
2. *Pres. Part.* **voulant**; *impf. indic.* voulais, etc.; *pres. subj.* veuille, veuilles, veuille, voulions, vouliez, veuillent.
3. *Past. Part.* **voulu**; *past indef.* j'ai voulu, etc.
4. *Pres. Indic.* **veux**, veux, veut, voulons, voulez, veulent; *impve.* veux, voulons, voulez.
5. *Past Def.* **voulus**, voulus, voulut, voulûmes, voulûtes, voulurent; *impf. subj.* voulusse, voulusses, voulût, voulussions, voulussiez, voulussent.

Note.—The regular *impve.* **veux, voulons, voulez** is rare; **veuillez,** *have the kindness* to, generally serves as second plural imperative.

230. REFERENCE LIST OF IRREGULAR VERBS

Note.—For verbs in -cer, cf. § 179; for verbs in -ger, cf. § 180; for verbs in -yer, cf. § 181; for verbs with stem-vowel e or é, cf. § 182.

A

abattre 196
abstenir 193
accourir 186
accueillir 187
acquérir 185
admettre 209
aller 183
apercevoir 220
apparaître 201
appartenir 193
apprendre 212
asseoir 222
atteindre 203
avoir 174

B

battre 196
boire 197
bouillir 188

C

combattre 196
commettre 209
comprendre 212
compromettre ... 209
concevoir 220
conclure 198
conduire 199
connaître 201
conquérir 185
consentir 188
construire 199
contenir 193
contraindre 203
convaincre 217
convenir 194
coudre 202
courir 186
couvrir 192
craindre 203
croire 204
cueillir 187

D

décevoir 220
découvrir 192
décrire 206
desservir 188
détenir 193
détruire 199
devenir 194
devoir 221
dire 205
disparaître 201
dormir 188

E

écrire 206
endormir 188
enfuir 189
entreprendre 212
entretenir 193
envoyer 184
éteindre 203
être 175

F

faire 207
falloir 223
fuir 189

H

haïr 190

I

inscrire 206
introduire 199

J

joindre 203

L

lire 208

M

maintenir 193
mentir 188

mettre 209
mourir 191

N

naître 210

O

obtenir 193
offrir 192
omettre 209
ouvrir 192

P

paraître 201
parcourir 186
partir 188
parvenir 194
peindre 203
permettre 209
plaindre 203
plaire 211
pleuvoir 224
poursuivre 216
pouvoir 225
prédire 205
prendre 212

prescrire 206
prévenir 194
prévoir 228
produire 199
promettre 209
provenir 194

R

recevoir 220
reconnaître 201
reconstruire 199
recueillir 187
redevenir 194
réduire 199
remettre 209
renaître 210
rendormir 188
renvoyer 184
reparaître 201
repartir 188
repentir 188
reprendre 212
reproduire 199
résoudre 213
ressentir 188
retenir 193
revenir 194
revivre 218
revoir 228
rire 214

S

satisfaire 207
savoir 226
sentir 188
servir 188
sortir 188
souffrir 192
soumettre 209
sourire 214
soutenir 193
souvenir 194
suffire 215
suivre 216
surprendre 212
survivre 218

T

taire 211
tenir 193
traduire 199

V

vaincre 217
valoir 227
venir 194
vêtir 195
vivre 218
voir 228
vouloir 229

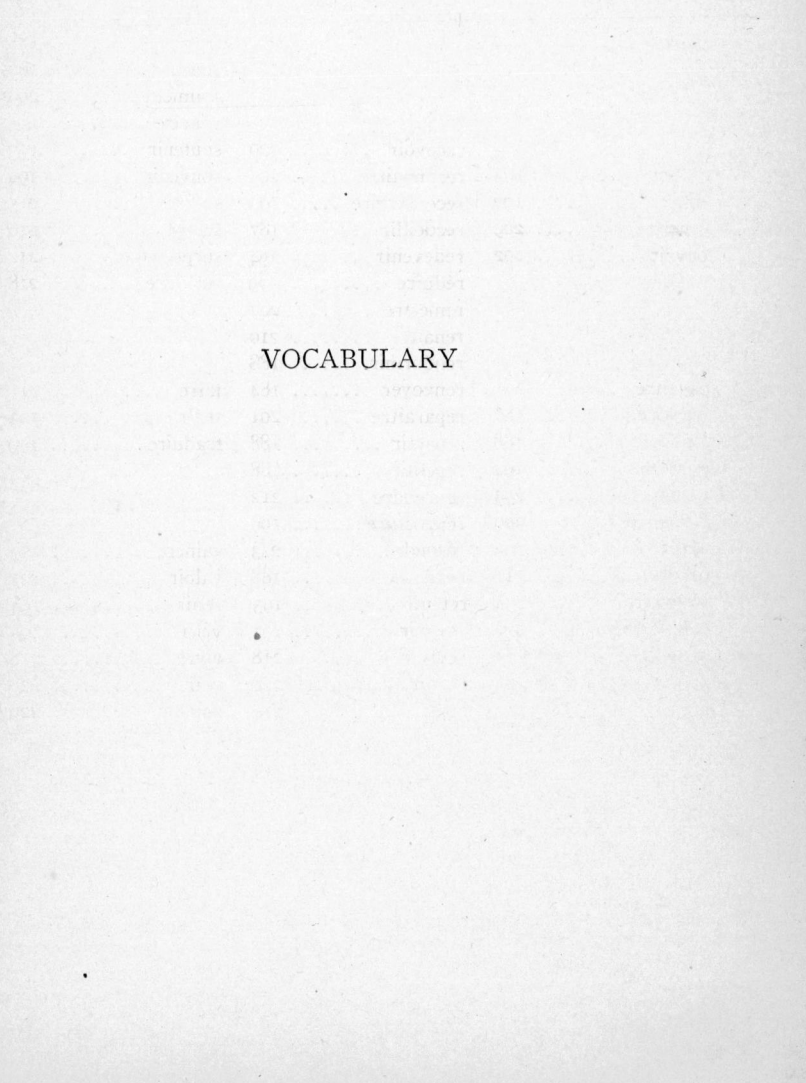

VOCABULARY

VOCABULARY

French–English

A

à at, to, in, with
s'abattre to swoop down, descend
abondamment abundantly
abord, see **d'abord**
absence *f.* absence
absolument absolutely
abuser de to abuse, make bad use of
accent *m.* accent
accepter to accept
accident *m.* accident
accompagner to accompany
accourir to come running up
accrocher to hang up
acheter to buy
acte *m.* act; certificate; **— de naissance,** birth certificate
acteur *m.* actor
actif active
adieu *m.* good-bye
admettre to admit
adresse *f.* address
adresser to address; **s'— à** to address oneself to, apply to; **— la parole à** to speak to
affaire *f.* affair, matter; **se tirer d'—** to get along
affiche *f.* placard, poster
afficher to advertise by poster or placard, announce
affreux frightful
afin de *prep.* in order to
afin que *conj.* in order that
âge *m.* age

agir to act; **il s'agit de** it is a question of
agréable agreeable, pleasant
aider to aid, help
ailleurs elsewhere; **d'—** moreover, besides
aimable amiable, kind; **vous serez bien — de** you will be kind enough to
aimer to love, like
ainsi thus
air *m.* air, appearance; **avoir l'—** to seem, look
ajouter to add
Allemagne *f.* Germany
aller to go, be going; to suit; **s'en —** to go away
allô hello
alors then
américain American
Amérique *f.* America
ami *m.* **amie** *f.* friend
amitié *f.* friendship; **mes —s à** my regards to
amuser to amuse; **s'—** to amuse oneself, enjoy oneself, have a good time
an *m.* year
ancien old, former, ancient
âne *m.* ass
anecdote *f.* anecdote
anglais English
Angleterre *f.* England
animal *m.* animal
année *f.* year
annonce *f.* announcement, advertisement

annoncer to announce
annuellement annually
apercevoir to perceive; **s'— de** to perceive, become aware of, notice
appareil *m.* apparatus; telephone
appartement *m.* apartment
appartenir to belong
appel *m.* call; **faire l'—** to call the roll
appeler to call; **s'—** to be named
appétit *m.* appetite
appliquer to apply
apporter to bring
apprendre to learn
après *adv.* afterwards; *prep.* after; **d'—** according to, after
après-midi *m. or f.* afternoon
arbre *m.* tree
argent *m.* money
arme *f.* arm, weapon
arranger to arrange
arrêter to stop; **s'—** to stop
arrivée *f.* arrival
arriver to arrive; to happen
arrondissement *m.* ward (*administrative division of a city*)
article *m.* article
articuler to articulate, pronounce
ascenseur *m.* elevator, lift
asseoir to seat; **s'—** to sit down, be seated. *For use, cf. p. 80 note.*
assez enough; quite, rather, fairly
assis seated
assister à to attend, be present at
s'assoupir to doze, become drowsy
attachant interesting, captivating
attaquer to attack
attendre to await, wait, wait for; **se faire —** to keep some one waiting, be late
auberge *f.* inn
aucun *with neg.* not any, no, any
auditoire *m.* audience
aujourd'hui to-day
auparavant before, previously
auprès de near to, with
au revoir good-bye

aussi also; as; so; such; **— bien que** as well as
aussitôt immediately; **— que** as soon as
autant as much, as many
auteur *m.* author
autobus *m.* autobus
automne *m. or f.* autumn
automobile, auto *f.* automobile
autorisation *f.* authorization, permission
autour de around, about
autre other, another; **d'—s** others
autrefois formerly, once
avance *f.* advance; **d'—** in advance; **en —** ahead of time
avancer to advance; (*of a watch*) be fast
avant *m.* front part; **à l'—** forward
avant *adv.*, **— de** *prep.*, **— que** *conj.* before
avant-veille *f.* two days before
avec with
avis *m.* opinion; **à mon —** in my opinion
avocat *m.* lawyer
avoir to have; to get; **— beau + infin.** to be useless to, be in vain; **— besoin** to have need; **— chaud** to be hot; **— faim** to be hungry; **— froid** to be cold; **— lieu** to take place; **— peur** to be afraid; **— raison** to be right; **— soif** to be thirsty; **— tort** to be wrong; **y —** to be; **il y a** there is, there are
avoué *m.* attorney

B

bachelier *m.* bachelor (*university*)
bain *m.* bath; **salle de —s** *f.* bathroom
baisser to lower; **se —** to stoop, bend
bal *m.* ball
banc *m.* bench; **— de paresse** dunce's seat

banquet *m.* banquet
baronne *f.* baroness
bassin *m.* basin
Bastille *f. prison in Paris, destroyed July 14, 1789*
bateau *m.* boat
beau, bel, belle beautiful, fine, handsome; avoir beau + *infin.* to be useless, to be in vain
beaucoup many, much
bergère *f.* easy chair
besoin *m.* need; avoir — de to need, have need of
bêtement foolishly, stupidly
bêtise *f.* silliness; dire des —s talk nonsense
beurre *m.* butter
bibliothèque *f.* library
bien *adv.* well, indeed; very; comfortable; much, many; — que although; aussi — que as well as; — à vous, sincerely yours
bien *m.* good, good thing; dire du — de to speak well of
bientôt soon
bière *f.* beer
billet *m.* ticket; prendre un — to buy or get a ticket
biographie *f.* biography
biscuit *m.* cracker
Bismarck, Otto von *German statesman 1815–1898*
blanc, blanche white
blessure *f.* wound
blond blond, light
bock *m.* glass (*holding a quarter of a liter of beer*)
boire to drink
boisson *f.* drink, beverage
bon, bonne good, kind
bonbon *m.* candy
bondé crowded, full
bonne *f.* maid
bonsoir *m.* good evening
bonté *f.* goodness, kindness
bord *m.* shore; board; à — on board
bouche *f.* mouth; faire venir l'eau à la — to make one's mouth water
bout *m.* end; bit
bouteille *f.* bottle
bras *m.* arm
Brie *m. cheese made in the district of Brie, lying slightly east of Paris*
brun brown; (*of beer*) dark
brusquement abruptly, suddenly
buffet *m.* buffet, refreshment room
bureau *m.* desk; office; ticket-office

C

ça that *see* cela
cadeau *m.* gift
café *m.* coffee; café; prendre le — to have coffee
cahier *m.* note-book
campagne *f.* country
Canada *m.* Canada
caoutchouc *m.* rubber, overshoe
Capet *name of the third French dynasty, by which Louis XVI was officially designated after the abolition of royalty during the Revolution*
capitale *f.* capital
capitaliste *m.* capitalist
captivité *f.* captivity
car for
caractéristique characteristic
Carnavalet *see Lesson XVI*
carnet *m.* note-book
carte *f.* card; bill of fare
cas *m.* case; en tout — in any case
casquette *f.* cap
cause *f.* cause; à — de because of, for the sake of
causer to cause; to chat
causeur, causeuse talkative
cavalier *m.* partner (*at dance*); gentleman
ce, cette this, that; ces these, those.
ce *pron.* it, that; — qui, — que that which, what

céder to yield, give up
cela that (*contracted to* **ça** *in familiar speech*)
célébrer to celebrate
celui, celle the one, he, that, this; **ceux, celles** those; **celui-ci** this one, the latter; **celui-là** that one, the former.
cent hundred
centaine *f.* (about a) hundred
cependant however
certainement certainly
certificat *m.* certificate
ces these, those
cesser to cease
ceux *see* celui
chacun each, each one, every one
chaire *f. desk and chair of professor on raised platform;* rostrum
chaleur *f.* heat
chambre *f.* room, bedroom
chance *f.* chance, luck; **bonne —** good luck
changer to change
Chantilly *a château once the property of the Condé family, now a museum belonging to the Institut de France. Situated 20 miles northeast of Paris near the town of Chantilly*
chapeau *m.* hat
chaque each, every
charmant charming
château *m.* château, castle
chaud *adj.* hot, warm
chaud *m.* warmth; **avoir —** to be warm; **faire —** to be warm, hot (*of weather*)
chauffer to heat
chauffeur *m.* chauffeur
chausser to put on (*of shoes*)
chemin *m.* way, road; **— de fer** railroad
cher, chère dear, expensive
chercher to look for, seek, search, get; **envoyer —** to send for
cheveux *m. pl.* hair

chez to, at, in, with, at the house of
chien *m.* dog
chocolat *m.* chocolate
choisir to choose
chose *f.* thing
cigare *m.* cigar
cigarette *f.* cigarette
cinéma *m.* "movies," motion picture theatre
cinq five
cinquante fifty
circuler to circulate, pass
cirer to wax, shine, polish
classe *f.* class; **salle de —** *f.* class room
clerc *m.* clerk (*of lawyer or notary*)
client *m.* patient
coin *m.* corner
colis *m.* parcel; **— postal** parcel post
coller to fail, "flunk"
combien how many, how much
comédie *f.* comedy
commander to order, command
comme how! as, like, as if
commencer to begin
comment how? in what manner?
communication *f.* communication; connection (*at telephone*); **couper la —** cut one off (*at telephone*)
complet complete, full (*of autobus or street car*)
complet *m.* suit (*of clothes*)
complètement completely
comprendre to understand
compter to count; to expect; to intend
concierge *m.* janitor
condamner to condemn
conduire to lead, drive, conduct, accompany
conférence *f.* lecture; **salle de —s** lecture room
confortable comfortable
confrère *m.* confrere, colleague
connaissance *f.* acquaintance, ac-

quaintanceship; **faire la — de** to make the acquaintance of
connaître to know, be acquainted with
connu well known
consacrer to devote
consentir to consent, agree
conserver to preserve, keep
consommation *f.* drink,
consternation *f.* consternation
construire to construct
consulter to consult
content glad, content, satisfied
contenter to content; **se — de** to be satisfied with
continuer to continue
contraire *m.* contrary; **au —** on the contrary
contre against
contrôler to control, check, verify
contrôleur *m.* controller, inspector, check- or ticket-taker
convenir to agree, admit
conversation *f.* conversation
copier to copy
cordial cordial
Corot, J. B. *French landscape painter 1796–1875*
côte *f.* coast
côté *m.* side; **à —** beside it, next door
côtelette *f.* chop
coucher to put to bed; **se —** to go to bed
coup *m.* blow; **— d'œil** glance; **— de téléphone** ring, call; **tout à —** suddenly
couper to cut; (*of telephone*) cut off
cour *f.* yard, court
couramment fluently
courber, se — to bend
courir to run
cours *m.* course; **— de vacances** Summer courses; **faire un —** to give a course; **suivre un —** to take (attend) a course
cousin *m.* **cousine** *f.* cousin

coûter to cost
couvert covered
couvert *m.* cover; table-cloth and covers; **mettre le —** to set the table
couvrir to cover
craindre to fear
cravate *f.* necktie
crayon *m.* pencil
crème *f.* cream
crier to cry, shout
croire to believe, think
cuisine *f.* kitchen; cooking; **faire la —** to cook
curieux curious
curiosité *f.* curiosity

D

d'abord first, at first
dame *f.* lady
dans in, into, within
danser to dance
davantage more
de of, from, by, with, than
se débarrasser de to get rid of
debout *adv.* standing, erect
décembre *m.* December
décider de to decide; **— à** to persuade, induce; **se — à** to make up one's mind, decide
déclamer to declaim, recite
déclarer to declare; **se —** to declare itself, break out
déconcerter to disconcert
décontenancer to put out of countenance, disconcert
découvrir to discover
décrire to describe
défendre to defend; to forbid
déjà already
déjeuner *m.* breakfast; lunch; **petit —** breakfast
déjeuner to breakfast; to lunch
délicieux delicious
demain tomorrow; **de — en huit** a week from tomorrow; **à —** good-bye until tomorrow

demander to ask, ask for; to want
démarrer (*of an auto*) to start, get away
demeure *f.* residence, dwelling
demeurer to live, dwell
demi half; — **-heure** *f.* half hour; — *m.* glass (*holding half a liter*)
démodé out of fashion, antiquated
demoiselle *f.* miss, young lady; — **du téléphone** telephone girl
se dépêcher to hurry
depuis since, for, from; — **quand** since when? how long?
déranger to inconvenience, put out
dernier last
descendre to descend, go or come down, get out; stop (*at a hotel*); *trans.* to bring down
désinviter to disinvite, withdraw an invitation
désirable desirable
désirer to desire
désolé very sorry, grieved
dès que as soon as
dessert *m.* dessert
desservir, to clear the table
destruction *f.* destruction
détail *m.* detail
détenir to detain, imprison, confine
détester to hate
détruire to destroy
dette *f.* debt
deux two
deuxième second
devant before, in front of
devenir to become
deviner to guess
devoir to owe; must, ought, am to
diable *m.* devil; —! *exclamation indicating surprise or impatience*
dicter to dictate
diction *f.* diction; public speaking
difficile difficult, hard to please
difficulté *f.* difficulty
dimanche *m.* Sunday
dîner *m.* dinner
dîner to dine
diplôme *m.* diploma

dire to say; — **du bien de** to speak well of; **dites donc!** say! I say! **vous m'en direz des nouvelles** I am sure you'll like it.
discuter to discuss
disponible available, free, unoccupied
distance *f.* distance
distinguer to distinguish
divers various
se divertir to enjoy oneself
diviser to divide
dix ten
docteur *m.* doctor
doigt *m.* finger
domicile *m.* domicile, residence
dommage *m.* damage, loss; **c'est —** it's a pity, it's too bad
donc therefore, then; *used after an imperative to emphasize a command or request*
donner to give; — **sur,** to open on, give on; **donnez-vous la peine d'entrer** please come in
dont whose, of which, of whom
dormir to sleep
double double
doute *m.* doubt
doux, douce sweet, soft, gentle, pleasant, mild
douzaine *f.* dozen
dramatique dramatic
droit *m.* right
dur hard

E

eau *f.* water; — **courante** running water; **Grandes Eaux** large fountains (at Versailles); **faire venir l'— à la bouche** *see* **bouche**
échouer to fail
éclat *m.* outburst; — **de rire** burst of laughter
éclater to burst, break out
écouter to listen
s'écrier to exclaim
écrire to write

écrivain *m.* writer
édifice *m.* building
effectivement indeed, really, in fact
effet *m.* effect; en — indeed, that is true
s'égarer to go astray
église *f.* church
eh bien! well!
élégant elegant, stylish, well dressed
élève *m. and f.* pupil, student
elle she, her; — -même herself
embarrasser to embarrass
emmener to take away, take along
empêcher to prevent
emprisonner to imprison
emprunt *m.* loan
emprunter to borrow
en *pron.* of it, of them, some, any
en *prep.* in, while, upon, as
enchanté delighted
encore, still, yet, besides; — un, another; — une fois once more
endroit *m.* place
enfant *m.* child
enfin at length, at last, finally
ennuyer to bore, tire
énorme enormous
énormément enormously
enragé mad
enrichir to make rich; s'— to become rich
enseignement *m.* instruction
ensuite next
entendre to hear
enthousiasme *m.* enthusiasm
entier entire, whole
entr'acte *m.* intermission; pendant les —s between the acts
entre between, among, in
entrecôte *m.* beefsteak
entrée *f.* entrance
entrer to enter, come in
envoyer to send, — chercher to send for
épatant splendid
épeler to spell
épinards *m. pl.* spinach

époque *f.* period, time
escale *f. nav.* putting into port; avec une — à touching at
Espagne *f.* Spain
espagnol Spanish
espèce *f.* sort, kind
espérer to hope
espoir *m.* hope
Esquimau *m.* Eskimo, "Eskimo Pie"
essai *m.* trial, test
essayer to try
essuyer to wipe
estrade *f.* platform
et and
étage *m.* story (*of building*); au deuxième — on the third floor
étang *m.* pond
Etats-Unis *m.* United States
été *m.* summer
étranger *m.* foreigner; *adj.* foreign, strange
être *m.* being
être to be; — à to belong to; — bien, to be comfortable; voulez-vous — des nôtres? will you join us? n'est-ce pas? is it not so? soit! agreed! so be it!
étude *f.* study; practice (*of lawyer*)
étudiant *m.* étudiante *f.* student
étudier to study
Europe *f.* Europe
eux them
s'évanouir to vanish
évidemment evidently, of course
évident evident
évoquer to evoke, recall
exact exact
examen *m.* examination; passer un — to take an examination
excellent excellent
exemple *m.* example; par — for instance, for example; *exclam.* indeed! however!
expédier to send
expérience *f.* experience, experiment

expliquer to explain
exposition *f.* exposition; — **Universelle** World's Exposition

F

fable *f.* fable
façade *f.* façade
fâché angry, sorry
facilement easily
façon *f.* way, manner; **il ne faut pas faire de** —**s** you must not stand on ceremony
facteur *m.* porter (*at station*)
faim *f.* hunger; **avoir** — to be hungry
faire to make; to do; to have, cause; — **l'appel,** to call the roll; — **beau (temps)** to be fine weather; — **un bout de toilette** to clean up a bit; — **du cent à l'heure** to make a hundred kilometers an hour; — **la connaissance de** to make the acquaintance of; — **la cuisine** to cook; — **son possible** to do one's best; — **(la) queue** to stand in line, — **signe** to motion; — **voir** to show; **se** — **attendre** to keep people waiting; **se** — **tard** to get late; **comment se fait-il que . . . ?** how does it happen that . . . ?
fait *m.* fact, case
falloir must, to be necessary, to need
fameux famous
famille *f.* family
fatigué tired
fatigue *f.* fatigue, weariness
fauteuil *m.* armchair; seat (*in theatre*)
faveur *f.* favor
favorable favorable
fêler to crack
femme *f.* woman
fenêtre *f.* window
ferme *adv.* hard

ferme *f.* farm
fermeté *f.* firmness
fête *f.* festival, fête; entertainment.
feuille *f.* leaf; sheet of paper
feuilleter to turn the pages of, run through (*conjugated like* **jeter**)
fier, fière proud
fille *f.* daughter; **jeune** — girl, young lady
fils *m.* son
fin *f.* end; **toucher à sa** — to draw to a close
finir to finish, end; — **par** to end by, to finally . . .
flatter to flatter
fleur *f.* flower
fois *f.* time; **une** — once
fond *m.* bottom; further end; **à** — thoroughly
fonder to found
fonds *m. pl.* funds, capital
fontaine *f.* fountain
fort strong, clever; **être** — **en** be good at, know very well
fortifier to fortify
foule *f.* crowd
foyer *m.* lobby (*of a theatre*)
frais, fraîche cool, fresh; youthful
franc *m.* franc
français French
France *f.* France
frapper to strike, knock
frère *m.* brother
Fréron, Elie *French critic and enemy of Voltaire. 1718-1776*
frit fried
froid *m.* cold
front *m.* forehead
fruit *m.* fruit
fumer to smoke
furieux furious

G

gaffe *f.* blunder, "break"
gagner to win; to earn
garçon *m.* boy; waiter
garder to keep

gare *f.* railroad station
gâteau *m.* cake
geler to freeze
général general
généreux generous
genou *m.* knee
gens *m. pl.* people; jeunes — young people, young men
gentil nice
gentiment nicely
Georges George
gigot *m.* leg of mutton
glace *f.* ice; une —, des —s ice cream
glacière *f.* ice-box, refrigerator
goûter *m.* lunch (*in afternoon*)
goûter to taste
gouvernement *m.* government
grand great, big, tall
grillade *f.* grill, broiled meat
gros (se) big, large, coarse, heavy
groseille *f.* currant
guère hardly
guérir to cure
guide *m.* guide; guide-book

H

(* indicates aspirate h)

habiter to inhabit, live in, dwell
* hall *m.* large hall; — de la gare main hall in station
* hasard *m.* chance; par — by chance
* hâte *f.* haste
* haut high; loud
* Havre (Le) *French port on the English Channel*
Hélène Helen
hésiter to hesitate
heure *f.* hour, o'clock, time; de bonne — early
heureusement happily, fortunately
heureux happy, pleased
hier yesterday; — soir last night, last evening
histoire *f.* history, story
historique historical
hiver *m.* winter
homme *m.* man
honneur *m.* honor
* hors-d'œuvre *m.* hors-d'œuvre
hôtel *m.* hotel; mansion; Hôtel de Ville City Hall
* huée *f.* hoot, shout
* huit eight
* huitaine *f.* about eight
humain human
* hurler to howl, yell

I

ici here
idée *f.* idea
il he, it
imaginer to imagine, conceive, devise
immatriculation *f.* matriculation, registration (*see note page 60*); carte d'—, matriculation card
immobile motionless
important important; c'est l'— that's the main thing
importer to matter; n'importe no matter
impossible impossible
incident *m.* incident
inconvénient *m.* drawback, disadvantage
indécis undecided
infliger to inflict
inintelligible unintelligible
inoculation *f.* inoculation
inquiet uneasy, anxious
inscrire, s'inscrire to register (*see note page 60*)
insister to insist
installer to install, settle, seat
institut *m.* institute
insupportable unbearable
intelligent intelligent
intéressant interesting
intéresser to interest
intérêt *m.* interest
interrompre to interrupt
introduction *f.* introduction

invité *m.* guest
inviter to invite
ironique ironical
itinéraire *m.* itinerary, route

J

jamais never; ever
jambon *m.* ham
jardin *m.* garden
jaunir to turn yellow
je I
Jean John
jeter to throw, cast; throw away
jeune young; — **fille** *f.* girl
joli pretty
jouer to play; — **à** to play (*a game*)
jour *m.* day; **huit** —s a week
journal *m.* newspaper
journaliste *m.* journalist
journée *f.* day
juillet *m.* July
juin *m.* June
jusque even to; — **là**, up to that time; **jusqu'à** *prep.* as far as, until, till; **jusqu'à ce que** *conj.* until
juste just; exactly
justement precisely, exactly

L

l' see **le, la**
la the; her, it
là there; — **-bas** down there, over there
laboratoire *m.* laboratory
LaFontaine, Jean de *French fabulist 1621–1695*
laisser to leave; to allow
lait *m.* milk
laitue *f.* lettuce
lancer to throw, cast
langue *f.* tongue; language
latin Latin
laver to wash; **se** — to wash oneself

le the; him, it
leçon *f.* lesson
légume *m.* vegetable
lendemain *m.* next day
lequel, laquelle *etc.* which, which one
lettre *f.* letter
leur their; to them
lever to lift, raise; **se** — to rise, get up
libéré free from debt
libre free
lieu *m.* place; **avoir** — to take place; **au** — **de** in place of, instead of
ligne *f.* line
liqueur *f.* liqueur
lire to read
littéraire literary
littérature *f.* literature
livre *m.* book
location *f.* advance sale of tickets; **prendre des places en** — buy tickets in advance, get reserved seats
longtemps long, a long time
Louis XIV *king of France 1643–1715*
Louis XVI *king of France in 1774, guillotined in 1793*
lui to him, to her, him; — **-même** himself
lundi *m.* Monday
Luxembourg (le) *palace built for Marie de Medici and now occupied by the French senate. It is surrounded by a public garden*
lycée *m.* lycée (*school covering high school and junior college work*)

M

machoire *f.* jaw bone
Madame, Mme *f.* madam, Mrs.
Mademoiselle, Mlle *f.* Miss
magnifique magnificent

mai *m.* May
main *f.* hand; à la — in his hand
maintenant now
mairie *f.* town-hall, mayor's offices
mais but
maison *f.* house; à la — at home
mal *m.* evil, ill; — de mer seasickness
mal *adv.* badly, bad
malade sick, ill
malheureux unfortunate
malle *f.* trunk
manger to eat
manquer to miss; to fail; il me manque I miss him
marche *f.* walk, motion, speed
marché *m.* market; bargain, deal; meilleur — cheaper
marcher to walk; run (*of trains, machines*); faire — la T.S.F. to start the radio
mari *m.* husband
marquer to mark
marronnier *m.* chestnut-tree
massacrer to massacre
matin *m.* morning; le — in the morning
mauvais bad, poor
méchamment maliciously, spitefully
médecin *m.* doctor, physician
médical medical
meilleur better; le — best
même *adj.* same, very; *adv.* even; tout de —, quand — anyhow, just the same
mener to lead, take
mépriser to despise
mer *f.* sea; en — at sea; mal de — *m.* seasickness
merci *m.* thanks, thank you, (no) thank you
mère *f.* mother
méthode *f.* method
mettre to put, place; put on; — le couvert to set the table; se — à to begin to; se — à table to sit down at table
métro, métropolitain *m.* subway

meuble *m.* piece of furniture; *pl.* furniture
meublé furnished
mien (le), mienne (la) mine
mieux better; tant — so much the better
milieu *m.* middle
mille thousand
minuit *m.* midnight
minute *f.* minute
miracle *m.* miracle
misérable miserable, wretched
moi me, to me
moindre less, least, slightest
moins less, fewer; au — at least; à — que unless
mois *m.* month
moitié *f.* half
moment *m.* moment; en (à) ce — at this moment
mon, ma, mes my
monastère *m.* monastery
monde *m.* world; people; tout le — everybody
monsieur, M. Mr., Sir, gentleman
montagne *f.* mountain
monter to go up, come up, climb, get into; *tr.* to carry up
Montmartre *m. a Bohemian quarter of Paris*
montre *f.* watch
montrer to show; — du doigt to point to
monument *m.* monument
se moquer de to make fun of, laugh at
morceau *m.* piece, lump; passage (*of text*)
mort dead
mortel mortal, fatal
mot *m.* word; note
mouchoir *m.* handkerchief
mourir to die
mouton *m.* mutton
moyen *m.* means, way
mur *m.* wall
musée *m.* museum
musique *f.* music

N

naissance *f.* birth; acte de — *m.* birth certificate

naître to be born

Napoléon III *emperor of France from 1852 to 1870*

nappe *f.* table-cloth; mettre la — to spread the table-cloth

national national

naturellement naturally, of course

ne not

nécessaire necessary

n'est-ce pas? is it not so? don't you? won't they? *etc.*

neige *f.* snow

nettoyer to clean

neuf nine

neuf, neuve new

ni . . . ni neither . . . nor

nièce *f.* niece

noisette *f.* hazel-nut

nom *m.* name

nombreux numerous

non no, not; — plus *after neg.* either

notamment particularly, in particular

notre our; le nôtre ours; être des nôtres *see* être

nous we, us, to us

nouveau, nouvelle new; de nouveau, again

nouveau *m.* new student

nouvelles *f. pl.* news; recevoir de ses — to hear from him; vous m'en direz des — I am sure you'll like it

novembre *m.* November

O

obliger to oblige

observer to observe

obtenir to obtain

occasion *f.* occasion, chance

occupé occupied, busy

Odéon *m. a theatre in the Latin Quarter of Paris, subsidized by the French government*

œil (*pl.* yeux) *m.* eye; coup d'— *m.* glance

œuf *m.* egg

officiel official

offrir to offer

ombre *f.* shadow

on one, you, they, people

opéra *m.* opera, opera-house

opposer, s'— à to oppose

orchestre *m.* orchestra

ordinaire ordinary, common; d'— usually

ordinairement ordinarily

ordre *m.* order

organiser to organize, plan, arrange

oser to dare

ou or; — bien or else

où where; *after expressions of time* when

oublier to forget

ouest *m.* west

oui yes

ouvert open

ouvreuse *f.* usher

ouvrir to open

P

pain *m.* bread

pâlir to turn pale

pancarte *f.* placard, sign

papa *m.* papa

papier *m.* paper

paquebot *m.* steamship, liner

par by

paraître to appear, seem

parc *m.* park

parce que because

parcourir to travel over, cover, go through

pardessus *m.* overcoat

pardonner to pardon

pareil like, similar

paresse *f.* idleness; banc de — *m.* dunce's seat

parfait perfect
parfum *m.* perfume; flavor
Paris *m.* Paris
parisien Parisian, of Paris
parler to speak
parmi among
parole *f.* word; **adresser la —** à to speak to
parti *m.* decision, resolution; **prendre ce —** to decide to do this, to make that decision
partie *f.* match, game, party
partir to leave, go away; **à — de** beginning with, from
partout everywhere; **un peu —** almost everywhere
pas *m.* step
pas not; no, not any; **— du tout** not at all
Pas de Calais (Le) *department in northeastern France*
passage *m.* passage
passé after
passé *m.* past
passer to pass; to spend (*time*); **— un examen** to take an examination; **se —** to happen; **se — de** to do without
Pasteur, Louis *French scientist 1822-1895*
patiemment patiently
patron *m.* employer
pauvre poor, needy
payer to pay, pay for
pays *m.* country
peindre to paint
peine *f.* pain, trouble; **à —** hardly, scarcely; **ce n'est pas la —** it is not worth while; **donnez-vous la — d'entrer** please come in
peinture *f.* painting
pendant during; **— que** while
penser to think
pension *f.* boarding house
perdre to lose; **perdu** lost; done for, doomed
père *m.* father
permettre to permit

personne *f.* person; *with* **ne** nobody
petit little, small
peu little, few; **un —** a little; **— à —** little by little, gradually
peuple *m.* people
peut-être perhaps
Philistin *m.* Philistine
pièce *f.* room; play
pied *m.* foot; **à —** on foot
pipe *f.* pipe
pique-nique *m.* picnic; **faire un —** to have a picnic
pire *adj.* worse; **le —** the worst
pis *adv.* worse; **tant —** so much the worse
place *f.* place; seat (*in theatre*); room (*space*)
placer to place
plaire to please
plaisir *m.* pleasure
plat *m.* plate, dish, platter
plate-forme *f.* platform
pluie *f.* rain
plume *f.* pen
plupart *f.* most, the greater part
plus more; **ne . . . —** no longer; **non —** *after neg.* either
plusieurs several; **si on est —** if there are several of us
plutôt rather
poignée *f.* shake (*of hand*)
point *m.* point; **sur le — de** on the point of, about to
politique *f.* politics
pomme *f.* apple; **— de terre** potato
porc *m.* pork
porte *f.* door
porter to carry; to bear; to wear
porteur *m.* porter
portion *f.* portion
poser to place, put
possible possible; **faire son —** to do one's best
postal postal, post
potage *m.* soup
pour for, in order to; **— que** in order that
pourboire *m.* tip

pour-cent *m.* percent
pourquoi why
pourvu que provided that, if only
pouvoir to be able, can; **il se peut** it may be
précis exact, precise; **à six heures —es** at six o'clock sharp
préférer to prefer
premier first
prendre to take, get; to call for; **— le café** to have coffee; **— un billet** to buy (get) a ticket
préparer to prepare
près near, nearby; **— de** near
présent present
présenter to present, introduce
presque almost
prêt ready
prêter to lend
préventif preventive
prier to pray, ask, beg; **je vous (en) prie** I beg of you
prince *m.* prince
principal principal
procès *m.* lawsuit
procurer, se — to obtain, procure
professeur *m.* professor, teacher
profession *f.* profession
profil *m.* profile
profiter to profit; **— de** to profit by, take advantage of
programme *m.* program
projet *m.* plan
promenade *f.* walk, ride; pleasure trip; **faire une —** to take a walk
se promener to walk, promenade
promettre to promise
proposer to propose
propre clean, neat
protester to protest
provenir to come originally from
proviseur *m.* principal, head-master
public *m.* public
puis then, besides
puisque since
punir to punish
punition *f.* punishment

Q

quai *m.* quai; platform
quand when; **— même** anyhow; **depuis —** since when? how long?
quant à as for
quantité *f.* quantity
quarante forty
quart *m.* quarter, fourth
quartier *m.* quarter (*of city*); **Quartier Latin** *the university quarter of Paris*
quatorze fourteen
quatre four
que whom, that, which
que? which? what?
que *conj.* that, than, as; **ne . . . —** only
quel, quelle what, what a
quelque some
quelquefois sometimes
quelqu'un some one; *pl.* some
qu'est-ce que? qu'est-ce que c'est que? what is?
qu'est-ce qui? what
question *f.* question
queue *f.* tail; line; **faire (la) —** to stand in line
qui who, whom, that, which
quinze fifteen
quinzaine *f.* about fifteen
quitter to leave
quoi which, what
quoique although

R

raconter to relate
radio *f.* radio
rage *f.* madness, hydrophobia
raison *f.* reason; **avoir —** to be right
rang *m.* row
rapide rapid, fast; *m.* express train
rappeler to recall; **se —** to remember, recall; **rappelez-moi au bon**

souvenir de remember me to . . .
rapporter to bring back; to bring in, pay
rarement seldom, rarely
se rasseoir to sit down again
récemment recently
récepteur *m.* receiver (*of telephone*)
receveur *m.* conductor
recevoir to receive; **être reçu à un examen** to pass an examination
recherche *f.* search; **à la — de** in search of
récit *m.* story, account
réclamer to demand
recommander to recommend
reconnaissant grateful
reconnaître to recognize
refaire to do *or* make again
refus *m.* refusal
refuser to refuse
regagner to regain; to return to
regard *m.* glance
regarder to look, look at
Régence (La) *a café on the avenue de l'Opéra. It dates from the 18th century*
région *f.* region
regrettable regrettable
regretter to regret, be sorry
remarquer to notice
remercier to thank
remonter to go up again
rencontre *f.* meeting; **aller à la — de** to go to meet
rencontrer to meet
rendez-vous *m.* appointment
rendre to render; to give back, return; **se — à** to go to
renseignement *m.* a piece of information; *pl.* information
rentrer to come *or* go home, return
renversé leaning back, reclining
repas *m.* meal
répéter to repeat; to recite
répondre to answer, reply
reprendre to take back, recover; take up again, resume, pick up
représentant *m.* representative
réserver to reserve
reste *m.* rest, remainder; **du —** moreover
rester to remain; **— tranquille** keep quiet
rétablir to reestablish, restore
retard *m.* delay; **en —** late, behind time
retenir to retain, reserve
retour *m.* return, return trip; **être de —** to be back
retourner to return, go back; **se —** to turn around
retraite *f.* retreat, retirement; **prendre sa —** to retire (*from business*)
retrouver to find again, join, meet
réunir to unite, bring together
réussir to succeed
réveiller to awaken; **se —** to wake up
revenir to come back, return
revoir to see again; **au —** good-bye
révolution *f.* revolution
riche rich
rideau *m.* curtain
ridicule ridiculous
ridiculus sum *Latin phrase, meaning* "I am ridiculous"
rien nothing, anything
rire *m.* laugh, laughter; **éclat de — *m.*** burst of laughter
rire to laugh
risquer to risk
roman *m.* novel
rôti *m.* roast
Rouen *city in Normandy between Le Havre and Paris*
rouvrir to open again
royal royal
rue *f.* street; **— des Saints-Pères,** *street on the edge of the Latin Quarter*

S

sa *see* son
saint holy
Saint-Lazare: Gare — *railroad station in Paris*
saison *f.* season
saisir to seize, catch
salade *f.* salad
salle *f.* hall, room; — à manger dining-room; — de bains bathroom; — de classe classroom; — de conférences, lecture hall
salon *m.* salon, parlor, living-room
Samson *Hebrew judge noted for his strength. See Judges XIII–XVI*
sans *prep.* without; — que *conj.* without
satisfaisant satisfactory
sauver to save
savoir to know (*facts*); know how; find out; que sais-je encore? I don't know what else.
scène *f.* scene
se himself, herself, itself, themselves
second second
seconde *f.* second class (ticket)
section *f.* section
séjour *m.* stay
selon according to
semaine *f.* week
sembler to seem, appear
sens *m.* sense; direction
sentir to feel
séparer to separate
sept seven
sérieusement seriously
sérieux serious
serrer to clasp; se — la main to shake hands
service *m.* service; course (*at dinner*)
servir to serve; se — de to use
ses *see* son
seul alone, single
seulement only

Sévigné, Mme de *famous for her letters picturing French society 1626–1696*
si if; so
si yes (*contradicting a negation*)
sien (le), sienne (la) his, hers; les —s one's relations and friends
signe *m.* sign; faire — to motion
silencieux silent
simplement, tout — simply, merely
sincèrement sincerely
sirop *m.* fruit syrup (*served with plain or charged water and ice*)
sœur *f.* sister
société *f.* society
soif *f.* thirst; avoir — to be thirsty
soir *m.* evening; hier — last night, last evening
soirée *f.* evening, evening party
soit *subj.* of être so be it, agreed
soixante sixty
sol *m.* ground
solution *f.* solution
somme *f.* sum
sommet *m.* summit, top
son, sa, ses his, her, its
songer to dream, think
sonner to ring
Sorbonne (La) *college of Arts and Sciences of the University of Paris; so called from its founder, Robert de Sorbon*
sorte *f.* sort, kind
sortie *f.* exit, gate
sortir to go out, come out, leave; *tr.* to take out
soudain suddenly
souffrir to suffer
soulier *m.* shoe
sourire to smile
sous under
souvenir *m.* remembrance, souvenir
se souvenir de to remember
souvent often
spectacle *m.* spectacle, performance
spectateur *m.* spectator
spirituel witty
station *f.* station

statue *f.* statue
stopper to stop (*of an automobile*)
succéder to succeed, follow
sucre *m.* sugar
sucrier *m.* sugar-bowl
suffire to suffice
suggérer to suggest
suite *f.* succession, series, continuation; **tout de —** right away, at once
suivant following
suivre to follow; to attend (*a course*)
superbe superb, splendid
supporter to endure
sur on, upon
surprendre to surprise, take *or* catch by surprise
surtout especially, above all
syllabe *f.* syllable
sympathique congenial, likeable
système *m.* system

T

table *f.* table
tâcher to try
se taire to be silent
talent *m.* talent
talon *m.* heel; stub (*of ticket*)
tandis que while, whereas
tant so much, so many; **— mieux** so much the better; **— pis** so much the worse
tante *f.* aunt
tapisser to upholster, cover
tard late; **se faire —** to be getting late
tarder to delay, be long in
tarif *m.* tariff, rate
tas *m.* pile, heap
tasse *f.* cup
taxi *m.* taxi
tel, telle such, like
téléphone *m.* telephone; **donner un coup de — à** call up
téléphoner to telephone

téléphonique telephonic, over the telephone
tellement so, so much
temple *m.* temple; **Le Temple** *see Lesson XVI*
Templiers (les) *Knights Templar, religious and military order for the protection of pilgrims to the Holy Land; suppressed in 1312*
temps *m.* time; weather; **à —** in time; **combien de —?** how long?
tenir to hold, keep; **— à** to want to, be eager to; **être tenu de** to be required to
tennis *m.* tennis
tenter to attempt, try
terminer, se — to end, finish
terrasse *f.* terrace; *sidewalk in front of a café where tables are placed*
terre *f.* earth, ground; **par —** on the ground
tête *f.* head
texte *m.* text
thé *m.* tea
théâtre *m.* theatre
tiers *m.* third
timidement timidly
tirer to draw, get, obtain; **se — d'affaire** to get along
toile *f.* canvas, painting
toilette *f.* toilet; **faire un bout de —** to clean up a bit
tombeau *m.* tomb
tomber to fall
tordant very funny
tôt soon
toucher to touch; **— à sa fin** to draw to a close
toujours always, still
tour *f.* tower
touriste *m.* tourist
tourner to turn; **se —** to turn
tout, tous, toute(s) all, whole, every
tout *adv.* wholly, quite, very; **— à coup** suddenly; **— à fait** quite, wholly; **— de même** just the

same, all the same; **— de suite** at once; **— en** while
traduire to translate
train *m.* train
traitement *m.* treatment
tranche *f.* slice
tranquille quiet; rester **—** to keep quiet
transport *m.* transportation
travail *m.* work
travailler to work; **— ferme** to work hard
traversée *f.* crossing
traverser to cross, go through
treize thirteen
trente thirty
très very
triste sad, dreary
troisième third
trop too, too much, too many
trouver to find; to think; se **—** to find oneself, to be; **comment le trouvez-vous?** what do you think of it?
T.S.F. (= **téléphonie sans fil**) *f.* radio
tuer to kill
tumulte *m.* tumult

U

un, une a, an, one
universel universal; **Exposition Universelle** World's Fair
université *f.* university
usurier *m.* usurer, money-lender

V

vacances *f. pl.* vacation; **cours de —** *m. pl.* Summer courses
vacarme *m.* uproar
vaccination *f.* vaccination
vaccin *m.* vaccine
vaisselle *f.* dishes
valise *f.* suitcase, valise
valoir to be worth
varier to vary
veau *m.* veal
velours *m.* velvet, velours
vendeur *m.* vendeuse *f.* seller, vender, clerk
vendre to sell
venir to come; **— de** to have just
verbe *m.* verb
véritable true, veritable
vers *m.* verse, line of poetry
vers towards, about
Versailles *f. town west of Paris, famous for its château built by Louis XIV and its parks*
vestiaire *m.* cloak room
viande *f.* meat
vie *f.* life
vieux, vieil, vieille old
ville *f.* city, town
Ville d'Avray *village between Paris and Versailles*
vin *m.* wine
vingt twenty
vingtaine *f.* about twenty, some twenty
visite *f.* visit
visiter to visit
vite quick, fast
vitesse *f.* speed; **à toute —** at full speed
vivre to live
voici here is, here are
voilà there is, there are, behold, there! **me —!** here I am!
voir to see, look at; **faire —** to show
voisin *m.* neighbor
voiture *f.* carriage, coach
voix *f.* voice
voler to steal
Voltaire *French poet and philosopher 1694–1778*
votre, vos your; **le vôtre** yours
vouloir to be willing; to wish, want; **— bien** to be willing, be kind enough to; **en — à** to be angry with, have a grudge against

vous you, to you; **bien à —** sincerely yours; **— -même** yourself
voyage *m.* voyage, trip, journey; **faire un —** to have *or* take a trip; **grand —** long trip
voyageur *m.* traveler, passenger
vrai true, real

vraiment truly, really
vue *f.* view

Y

y there; to (at, in, etc.) it, them
yeux *pl. of* œil

VOCABULARY

English-French

Preposition in parentheses ( ), refers to the preposition required before a dependent infinitive.

A

a, an un, une
abashed décontenancé
able; be — pouvoir 225
about (*around*) autour de; (*concerning*) de, sur, à propos de, au sujet de; (*nearly*) à peu près, environ; (*towards*) vers
absent; to — oneself s'absenter
absolutely absolument
accent accent *m.*
accept accepter
accident accident *m.*
accompany accompagner
accumulate accumuler
acquaintance, acquaintanceship connaissance *f.;* make the — of faire la connaissance de
acquainted; be — with connaître 201
acquire acquérir 185
act acte *m.*
action action *f.*
active actif (ve)
actor acteur *m.*
add ajouter
address adresse *f.*
admirable admirable
advantage; take — of profiter de
advice conseils *m. pl.;* a piece of — un conseil
advise conseiller (de)
affair affaire *f.*
afraid; be — craindre (de) 203, avoir peur

after après; *conj.* après que
afternoon après-midi *m. or f.*
again encore une fois, de nouveau
against contre
Agnes Agnès
ago il y a
ah! ah!
Alfonso Alphonse
all tout(e), tous, toutes; — at once tout d'un coup; not at — pas du tout
allow laisser, permettre 209
almost presque
alone seul
along *see* get
already déjà
also aussi
although quoique, bien que *with subjunc.;* tout en *with pres. part.*
always toujours
America Amérique *f.*
American américain
among parmi, entre
amuse amuser; — oneself s'amuser
amusing amusant
ancestors aïeux *m. pl.,* ancêtres *m. pl.*
and et
anew de nouveau
angry fâché; be — with en vouloir à, être fâché contre *or* avec
another (*different*) autre; (*one more*) encore un
answer réponse *f.*
answer répondre (à)

anxious; be — to tenir à 193
any *partitive* de, en; *adj.* quelque, (*with neg.*) aucun, pas un; **— at all** n'importe quel; **— way** en tout cas, quand même
anyhow en tout cas
any one quelqu'un, (*with neg.*) personne; **— at all** n'importe qui
anything tout, n'importe quoi; (*with neg.*) rien
any way en tout cas; (*in spite of all*) quand même
apartment appartement *m.*
aperitive apéritif *m.*
apology excuse *f.;* **present his —s** faire ses excuses
apparently apparemment
appear paraître 201, se montrer
appetite appétit *m.*
apply s'adresser à
appointment rendez-vous *m.*
approach s'approcher de; (*a subject or study*) aborder
April avril *m.*
arise se lever
arm bras *m.;* **with open —s** à bras ouverts
army armée *f.*
arrange arranger, organiser
arrival arrivée *f.*
arrive arriver
art art *m.*
article article *m.*
as *adv.* aussi, (*with neg.*) si; que; **— many —, — much —** autant que; **— ... —** aussi (si) ... que; **— for** quant à
as *conj.* comme, puisque; **— soon —** aussitôt que, dès que
ashamed; be — avoir honte
ask demander (de) *with personal indirect object,* prier (de) *with personal direct object;* **— for** demander; **— some one for something** demander quelque chose à quelqu'un
ass âne *m.*
assure assurer

astonishment étonnement *m.*, surprise *f.;* **cry of —** cri de surprise *m.*
astray; go — s'égarer
at à, dans, chez; **— first** d'abord; **— last** enfin; **— least** au moins; **— once** tout de suite; **— home** chez soi
attend assister à
August août *m.*
Auteuil *suburb of Paris*
aunt tante *f.*
author auteur *m.*
autobus autobus *m.*
automobile, auto automobile *f.*, auto *f.*
autumn automne *m. or f.*
available disponible, libre
avenue avenue *f.*
avoid éviter
await attendre
awake, awaken *trans.* éveiller, réveiller; *intrans.* s'éveiller, se réveiller
aware; become — of s'apercevoir de 220

B

bachelor (*university*) bachelier *m.*
back; be — être de retour; **come —** revenir; **go —** rentrer, retourner; **on my way —** en revenant
bad mauvais; **that's too —** c'est dommage
badly mal
ball (*dance*) bal *m.*
bath bain *m.;* **— room** salle de bains *f.*
banquet banquet *m.*
battle bataille *f.*
basin bassin *m.*
be être, se trouver; y avoir; **— back** être de retour; **it may —** il se peut; **there must —** il doit y avoir; **there is** il y a; **I am to**

go je dois aller; **if I were you** à votre place, si j'étais vous
bear porter
beat battre 196
beautiful beau bel belle
because parce que; **— of** à cause de
become devenir 194; **what has — of him?** qu'est-il devenu?
bed lit *m.*
beer bière *f.*
before *adv.* (*time*) avant, auparavant; (*place*) devant
before *conj.* avant que
before *prep.* (*time*) avant; (*place*) devant; (*before infin.*) avant de
beg prier (de)
begin commencer (à *or* de), se mettre à 209; **— by** commencer par
behind derrière
believe croire 204
bell sonnette *f.;* **ring the —** sonner
belong appartenir 193, être à
Besançon *city in east central France*
beside à côté de, près de
besides d'ailleurs, et puis
best *adj.* le meilleur; *adv.* le mieux; **do one's —** faire son possible
better *adj.* meilleur; *adv.* mieux; **be — to** valoir mieux 227
between entre
big (*heavy*) gros(se); (*size*) grand
bill of fare carte *f.*
biography biographie *f.*
birthday anniversaire (de naissance) *m.*
bite mordre
black noir
blue bleu
board; on — à bord
boarding-house pension *f.*
boat bateau *m.;* (*liner*) paquebot *m.*
Bois de Boulogne *m. large park on the outskirts of Paris*

book livre *m.*
bore ennuyer
born né; **be —** naître 210
both (tous) les deux
bottle bouteille *f.*
boulevard boulevard *m.*
box boîte *f.*
boy garçon *m.;* (*errand boy in hotel*) chasseur *m.*
bread pain *m.*
'break' gaffe *f.;* **make a —** faire une gaffe
break casser, rompre; **— out** éclater
breakdown; have a — (*of auto*) avoir une panne
breakfast petit déjeuner *m.*
breakfast déjeuner
bridge pont *m.*
brief court; bref, brève
bring (*of things*) apporter; (*of persons*) amener; **— in** (*earn*) rapporter
broach aborder
brother frère *m.*
brown brun
building édifice *m.*
bureau; information — bureau de renseignements *m.*
burst éclater; **— out laughing** éclater de rire
business affaires *f. pl.*
busy occupé
but mais
butter beurre *m.*
buy acheter (from = à); **— a ticket** prendre un billet
by par, de

C

cablegram câblogramme *m.,* câble *m.*
café café *m.*
cake gâteau *m.*
call visite *f.;* **pay a —** faire une visite
call appeler; **— for** (*a person*) al-

ler chercher; aller prendre; — upon faire une visite à, aller (or venir) voir; — the roll faire l'appel; — up (*telephone*) téléphoner à, donner un coup de téléphone à
can pouvoir 225, savoir 226, *see Lesson XI.*
Canada Canada *m.*
Canadian canadien
candy bonbons *m. pl.*
cap casquette *f.*
capital (*city*) capitale *f.;* (*funds*) fonds *m. pl.*
car (*railroad*) voiture *f.,* wagon *m.;* (*auto*) voiture *f.*
card carte *f.;* postal — carte postale; student's — carte d'étudiant, carte d'immatriculation
care soin *m.*
care; — for (*like*) aimer; (*give care to*) soigner
carnation œillet *m.*
carry porter; — away emporter, enlever; — down descendre
cast lancer, jeter
castle château *m.*
catch attraper; — cold attraper un rhume, s'enrhumer
cause causer, faire, occasionner
celebrate célébrer, fêter
celebrity célébrité *f.*
cent sou *m.*
century siècle *m.*
certain certain
certainly certainement
certificate certificat *m.*
chair chaise *f.*
chalk craie *f.*
chance hasard *m.;* (*probability*) chance *f.;* by — par hasard
change changer; — one's mind changer d'avis
characteristic caractéristique
charlatan charlatan *m.*
charming charmant
chat causer
château château *m.*

chauffeur chauffeur *m.*
cheese fromage *m.*
chestnut-tree marronnier *m.*
child enfant *m.*
choose choisir
church église *f.*
cigar cigare *m.*
cigarette cigarette *f.*
circulate circuler
city ville *f.*
class classe *f.;* (*course*) cours *m.;* — room salle de classe *f.;* English — classe d'anglais; first — ticket, *see* ticket.
clean nettoyer
clear clair
clearly clairement
climb monter, grimper
cloak-room vestiaire *m.*
coach voiture *f.*
coat, overcoat (*men*) pardessus *m.;* (*women*) manteau *m.*
coffee café *m.;* have — prendre le café
cold froid; it is — il fait froid; I am — j'ai froid
cold (*in the head*) rhume *m.;* catch — attraper un rhume, s'enrhumer
colleague confrère *m.;* collègue *m.*
college student étudiant *m.*
Columbus Colomb, *discoverer of America*
come venir 194; — back revenir; — down descendre; — from (*originally*) provenir; — home rentrer; — in entrer, rentrer; — out sortir; — up monter; — with accompagner; — to get venir prendre
comedy comédie *f.*
comfortable (*things*) confortable; be — (*persons*) être bien
command commande *f.*
complain (of, about) se plaindre de 203
complete complet, complète
compose; be —d of se composer de

composition thème *m.*
compromise compromettre 209
condition état *m.*
conduct conduire 199
conductor receveur *m.*
confusion confusion *f.*, désordre *m.*
connection (*telephone*) communication *f.*
consent consentir (à) 188
console consoler
constantly constamment
construct construire 199
continual continuel(le)
continue continuer (à *or* de)
contrary; on the — au contraire
cook faire la cuisine
cooking cuisine *f.;* do — faire la cuisine
cool frais, fraîche; be — faire frais
correct corriger
cost coûter
could pouvoir 225
country (*political division*) pays *m.;* (*fatherland*) patrie *f.;* (*not city*) campagne *f.;* in the — à la campagne
course; of — naturellement, bien entendu
course (*at school*) cours *m.;* repeat a — refaire un cours; summer —s cours de vacances; take a — suivre un cours
cousin cousin *m.*, cousine *f.*
cover couvrir 192
crack fêler
cracker biscuit *m.*
cravat cravate *f.*
cream crème *f.;* vanilla — crème à la vanille
cross traverser
crossing traversée *f.*
crowd foule *f.*
crowded bondé
crush écraser
cry cri *m.*
cry, cry out crier; (*exclaim*) s'écrier; (*weep*) pleurer

cup tasse *f.;* the **Davis Cup** la Coupe Davis
curious curieux(se)
currant groseille *f.*
curtain rideau *m.*
cut couper; — short couper court à

D

dance danser
dancer cavalier *m.*, danseur *m.*, danseuse *f.*
dark sombre; (*of beer*) brun; be — faire nuit
daughter fille *f.*
dauphin dauphin *m.* (*Refers in Lesson XVI to the son of Louis XVI, supposed to have been killed in the Temple*)
day jour *m.*, journée *f.;* every — tous les jours; ten francs a — dix francs par jour
dead mort
deal; a great — beaucoup
dean doyen *m.*
dear cher, chère
death mort *f.*
decide décider de
delicious délicieux(se)
delight enchanter, ravir (with = de)
demand exiger, vouloir 229
demolish démolir
departure départ *m.*
depend dépendre
descend descendre
describe décrire 206
description description *f.*
desire désir *m.;* envie *f.;* have a — to avoir envie de
desire désirer
desk bureau *m.;* (*of teacher in classroom*) table *f.*, chaire *f.*
desperate désespéré
despise mépriser
dessert dessert *m.*

detail détail *m.*
diction diction *f.*
die mourir 191; **be dying** se mourir
difficult difficile
difficulty difficulté *f.*, mal *m.*, peine *f.*; **have — in** avoir beaucoup de peine (mal) à
dine dîner
dining-room salle à manger *f.*
dinner dîner *m.;* **at —** à dîner
diploma diplôme *m.*
direction direction *f.*, sens *m.*
discover découvrir 192
discredit discréditer
discuss discuter
dishes vaisselle *f. sing.*
disorder désordre *m.*
dispense with se passer de
distinguished distingué
disturb déranger
do faire 207; **— one's best** faire son possible; **how — you —?** comment allez-vous?
doctor médecin *m.;* (*title*) docteur *m.*
doctorate doctorat *m.*
dog chien *m.*
dollar dollar *m.*
door porte *f.*
doubt doute *m.;* **without —** sans doute
doubt douter (de)
doubtless sans doute
down en bas; **— stairs** en bas; **go —** descendre
dozen douzaine *f.*
drama drame *m.*
dress robe *f.*
drink boisson *f.*
drink boire 197
drive *intrans.* se promener (en auto *etc.*); *trans.* conduire (une auto)
drop *intrans.* tomber; *trans.* laisser tomber
dry sec, sèche
during pendant
dwell demeurer

E

each *adj.* chaque; *pron.* chacun; **— one** chacun; **— other** se, l'un l'autre, l'un à l'autre *etc.*
eager; be — to tenir à
eagerly impatiemment, avec impatience
early de bonne heure
earn gagner; **— one's pardon** se faire pardonner
ease aise *f.;* **ill at —** mal à l'aise
easily facilement
easy facile
eat manger
effort effort *m.*
egg œuf *m.*
eight huit
eighteen dix-huit
eighty quatre-vingts
either ou; (*after neg.*) non plus
elegant élégant
elevator ascenseur *m.*
eleven onze
embarrass embarrasser
embarrassment trouble *m.*, embarras *m.*
employer patron *m.*
end (*time*) fin *f.;* (*space*) bout *m.*, extrémité *f.;* **at the — of** au bout de, à la fin de
end finir, terminer; **— by** finir par
enemy ennemi *m.*
England Angleterre *f.*
English anglais
enjoy jouir de, goûter, savourer; **— oneself** s'amuser, se divertir
enormous énorme
enough assez
enter entrer (dans)
enthusiasm enthousiasme *m.*
entrance entrée *f.*
envelope enveloppe *f.*
especially surtout, spécialement
Europe Europe *f.*
even même
evening soir *m.*, soirée *f.;* **good —**

bonsoir *m.;* **in the —** le soir
ever jamais
every chaque, tout
everybody, every one tout le monde
everything tout *m.*
everywhere partout
evidently évidemment
exactly exactement, précisément
examination examen *m.;* **fail in an —** échouer à un examen; **pass an —** être reçu à un examen, réussir à un examen; **take an —** passer un examen
excellent excellent
except excepté
exclaim s'écrier
exclamation exclamation *f.*
excuse excuse *f.;* **make one's —** faire ses excuses
expect attendre
expensive coûteux(se), cher, chère
experience expérience *f.*
explain expliquer
exposition; World's — Exposition universelle
express (*train*) rapide *m.*
expressly (tout) exprès
extremely extrêmement
eye œil (*pl.* yeux) *m.*

F

fable fable *f.*
fail manquer (de); **— in an examination** échouer à un examen
fairly assez; **— well** assez bien
fall automne *m. or f.*
fall tomber
famous fameux(se)
far loin; **not —** pas loin
fast vite; **beat —** (*of heart*) battre fort
father père *m.,* papa *m.*
Faust Faust *m.*
favorable favorable
favorite préféré, favori, favorite

fear crainte *f.*
fear craindre (de) 203, avoir peur de
February février *m.*
feel sentir 188; (*of health*) se sentir
festival fête *f.*
fête fête *f.*
few (*not many*) peu de; **a —** *adj.* quelques; *pron.* quelques-uns
fewer moins
fifth cinquième
fifty cinquante
finally enfin
find trouver; **be found** se trouver
fine beau, bel, belle
finery; bit of — chiffon *m.*
finger doigt *m.*
finish finir, terminer; **— dining** finir de dîner
fireplace cheminée *f.*
firmly avec fermeté
first premier, première; **— class** (*of tickets*) première *f.;* **at —, in the — place** d'abord
five cinq
fix (*the eyes*) fixer
flatterer flatteur *m.,* flatteuse *f.*
flattering flatteur(se)
flavor parfum *m.*
flee *trans.* fuir 189; *intrans.* s'enfuir, fuir, se sauver
floor plancher *m.;* (*story*) étage *m.;* **fall on the —** tomber par terre
flower fleur *f.*
follow suivre 216
Fontainebleau *m. town south-east of Paris, famous for its château and its forest*
foot pied *m.*
for *prep.* pour; (*during*) pendant; (*in behalf of*) de la part de; (*since*) depuis; *conj.* car, parce que
forbid défendre (à quelqu'un de faire quelque chose)
force forcer (à), obliger (à)

foreigner étranger *m.*
forget oublier
former ancien(ne); *pron.* celui-là
fortunately heureusement
found fonder
fountain fontaine *f.*, Grandes Eaux *f. pl.*
fountain-pen stylo *m.*, stylographe *m.*
four quatre
fourteen quatorze
fourth quatrième
franc franc *m.*
France France *f.*
Francis François
free libre; (*without cost*) gratuit
freeze geler
French français; (*language*) français *m.*
Frenchman Français *m.*
fresh frais, fraîche
Friday vendredi *m.*
fried frit
friend ami *m.*, amie *f.*; a — of his, un de ses amis
from de
front; **in —, in — of**, devant; **in the — row**, au premier rang
full plein; (*of public conveyances*) complet
fun; **make — of** se moquer de
funny drôle; **what a — name!** quel drôle de nom!
furious furieux(se)
furnish meubler
furniture meubles *m. pl.*
future avenir *m.*; **in the —** à l'avenir, désormais

G

garden jardin *m.*
gardener jardinier *m.*
gateman contrôleur *m.*
gather cueillir 187
general général *m.*
generally généralement
gentleman monsieur *m.*
George Georges
German allemand
Germany Allemagne *f.*
get obtenir 193, prendre 212, se procurer; (*draw*) tirer; **come and —** venir chercher, venir prendre; **— along**, se tirer d'affaire; **— into** monter dans; **— late** se faire tard; **— out** *trans.* sortir; *intrans.* (*escape*) sortir; (*of a vehicle*) descendre; **— up** se lever; **— rid of** se débarrasser de; **— used to** se faire à, s'accoutumer à; **— a person on the 'phone** obtenir la communication; **— reserved seats** prendre des places en location
gift cadeau *m.*
girl jeune fille *f.*; **little —** petite fille, fillette *f.*
give donner; **— back** rendre; **— a lecture** faire une conférence
glad content, heureux(se)
glance regard *m.*
glass verre *m.*
gleam briller, étinceller
glimpse entrevoir 228
glory gloire *f.*
go aller 183; **— and get** aller chercher; **— astray** s'égarer; **— away** partir, s'en aller; **— back** rentrer, retourner; **— down** descendre; **— for a walk** aller faire une promenade, se promener; **— into** entrer dans; **— out** sortir; **— to sleep** s'endormir; **— to sleep again** se rendormir; **— through** parcourir, visiter; **— up** monter; **— with** accompagner, aller avec; **how goes it?** comment ça va?
gold or *m.*; *adj.* en or, d'or
good bon, bonne; **— evening** bonsoir
good-bye au revoir, adieu
good-looking beau, bel, belle
grandmother grand'mère *f.*
gray gris

great grand
green vert
ground terre *f.*
grove bosquet *m.*
grow; — old vieillir
guest invité *m.*, invitée *f.*
guide guide *m.;* — book guide *m.*
gust of wind coup de vent *m.*

H

half *adj.* demi; *adv.* à moitié; *n.* moitié *f.;* — hour demi-heure *f.;* — past one une heure et demie
hall salle *f.*
ham jambon *m.*
hand main *f.;* in the — à la main; on the other — par contre; in my —s entre mes mains
handsome beau, bel, belle
happen arriver, se passer
happy heureux(se), content
hard dur, difficile; — to please difficile; work — travailler dur (ferme)
hardly à peine, ne . . . guère
hat chapeau *m.*
have avoir 174; (*cause to*) faire 207; — a good time s'amuser bien; — just venir de + *infin.;* — to devoir 221, falloir 223, avoir à
Havre le Havre
he il, lui
head tête *f.*
health santé *f.*
hear entendre; — of entendre parler de
heart cœur *m.*
heat chauffer
Helen Hélène
hello bonjour *m.;* (*at telephone*) allô
help aider (à)
her la, lui, elle
her *posses. adj.* son, sa, ses
here; ici; — is voici

hers le sien *etc.*
hesitate hésiter
hide cacher (from = à)
high haut
him le, lui; —self lui-même
his son, sa, ses; *pron.* le sien *etc.*
history histoire *f.*
holiday fête *f.*
home; at — chez moi *etc.*, à la maison
hope espérer
hors-d'œuvre hors-d'œuvre *m.. invar.*
horse cheval *m.*
hot chaud; be — avoir chaud; (*of weather*) faire chaud
hotel hôtel *m.*
hour heure *f.;* half — demi-heure *f.*
house maison *f.;* at her — chez elle; boarding — pension *f.*
how (*in what manner?*) comment? (*exclamation*) comme, combien, que; — much, — many combien; — long combien de temps, depuis quand
however cependant; (*with adj. or adv.*) quelque + *adj. or adv.* que + *subj.*
Hugo, Victor (*1802–1885*), *French poet, novelist and dramatist*
humanity humanité *f.*
hundred cent; about a — une centaine; —s des centaines
hunger faim *f.*
hungry; be — avoir faim
hurry se dépêcher (de), se hâter (de); be in (such) a — être (si) pressé
hurt faire mal à

I

I je, moi
ice-box glacière *f.*
ice cream glaces *f. pl.;* (*one portion*) une glace

idea idée *f.*
if si
ill at ease mal à l'aise
immediately tout de suite
immense immense, énorme
immensely énormément
important important
impossible impossible
imprisonment détention *f.*, captivité *f.*
in *of place (specific location)* dans; *(less definite and figurative)* en; *of time (at the end of)* dans, au bout de; *(during the course of)* en
incident incident *m.*
inconvenience déranger
indeed en effet
indisposed souffrant
inform informer; **keep one —ed of** le tenir au courant de
information renseignements *m. pl.*; **— bureau** bureau de renseignements *m.*
inhabitant habitant *m.*
ink encre *f.*
inside à l'intérieur
insist upon *present and past indefinite of* vouloir 229, tenir à 193
instead of au lieu de
institute institut *m.*
intelligent intelligent
intend avoir l'intention de
interest intérêt *m.*
interest intéresser
interesting intéressant
intermission entr'acte *m.*
interrupt interrompre
interview; private — tête à tête *m. invar.*
into dans
introduce présenter
introduction introduction *f.*
invitation invitation *f.*; **recall an —** désinviter
invite inviter (à)
it il, elle, ce; le, la

J

Jane Jeanne
janitor concierge *m.*
jaw-bone mâchoire *f.*
Joan of Arc Jeanne d'Arc
John Jean
join accompagner; **will you — us?** voulez-vous être des nôtres?
journalist journaliste *m.*
July juillet *m.*
June juin *m.*
just juste, justement; **— as interesting** tout aussi intéressant; **— the same** tout de même, quand même; **have (had) —** venir de *with infin.* (venir *in present and imperfect only*); **I was — going there,** j'y allais justement

K

keep garder; **— from** empêcher de; **— waiting** faire attendre
kill tuer
kind bon, bonne; **be — enough to** avoir la bonté de; être assez bon pour, vouloir bien
kind sorte *f.*, espèce *f.*
kindness bonté *f.*
king roi *m.*
kitchen cuisine *f.*
knife couteau *m.*
know *(a fact)* savoir 226; *(be acquainted with)* connaître 201; **— how** savoir *(see Lesson XI)*
known, well- — connu

L

laboratory laboratoire *m.*
lamb agneau *m.*; **leg of —** gigot d'agneau *m.*
land débarquer
language langue *f.*
lap genoux *m. pl.*

large grand; (*bulky*) gros(se)
last dernier, dernière; passé; **at —** enfin; **— night** hier soir; **— Wednesday** mercredi dernier; **— week** la semaine dernière; **— year** l'année dernière, l'année passée
last durer
late tard; (*behind time*) en retard; **it is getting —** il se fait tard
Latin latin
latter celui-ci, ce dernier
laugh rire 214; **— at** rire de
laughing; burst out — éclater de rire
laughter rires *m. pl.*
lawsuit procès *m.*
lawyer avocat *m.*
lay poser, mettre
leaf feuille *f.*
learn apprendre (à) 212
lease bail *m.*
least *adj.* le moindre; *adv.* le moins; **at —** au moins
leave (*go away from*) *trans.* quitter, *intrans.* partir 188, s'en aller 183; (*go out of*) sortir 188; **— behind** laisser
lecture conférence *f.;* **— room** salle de conférences *f.;* **give a —** faire une conférence
left gauche
leg jambe *f.;* **— of lamb** gigot d'agneau *m.*
lend prêter
less moins
lesson leçon *f.*
lest *conj.* de peur que; *prep.* de peur de
let laisser, permettre (de) 209
letter lettre *f.;* **— of introduction** lettre d'introduction
library bibliothèque *f.*
lie mentir 188
life vie *f.*
light léger, légère
like aimer; désirer
likeable sympathique

line ligne *f.;* **stand in —** faire (la) queue
listen (to) écouter
literature littérature *f.*
literary littéraire
little petit; *adv.* peu; **as — noise as possible** le moins de bruit possible
live vivre 218; (*dwell in*) demeurer à *or* dans, habiter
living vivant
lobby foyer *m.*
London Londres *m.*
long *adv.* longtemps; **a — time** longtemps; **as — as** tant que; **how long?** depuis quand? combien de temps? **no —er** ne ... plus
look regarder; **— at** regarder, examiner; **— after** s'occuper de; **— for** chercher; **— me up** venir me voir
lose perdre; **— one's way** s'égarer, se tromper de chemin
lot; a —, —s of beaucoup de, des quantités de
love aimer
lower baisser
luck chance *f.*
lunch déjeuner *m.;* (*of picnics*) lunch *m.*, goûter *m.*
lunch déjeuner
Luxembourg *see French-English vocabulary*
lycée lycée *m.*

M

mad enragé
magnificent magnifique
maid bonne *f.*
mail mettre à la poste
maintain maintenir 193
make faire 207; **— again** refaire; **— the acquaintance of** faire la connaissance de; **— fun of** se moquer de; **— + *adj.*** rendre

maliciously malicieusement, méchamment

man homme *m.*; **young —** jeune homme (*pl.* jeunes gens)

mansion hôtel *m.*

many beaucoup; **as — as** autant que; **so —** tant

Marais (Le) *a quarter of Paris, once aristocratic, now popular*

mark marquer

marmalade marmelade *f.*

Marseilles Marseille *f. French port on the Mediterranean*

marshal maréchal *m.*

Mary Marie

master maître *m.*

master-piece chef-d'œuvre *m.* (*pl.* chefs-d'œuvre)

match (*sport*) match *m., pl.* matches

mathematics mathématiques *f. pl.*

May mai *m.*

may pouvoir 225; **it — be** il se peut

me moi, me

meal repas *m.*

mean méchant

meat viande *f.*

meet (*by chance*) rencontrer, trouver; (*by appointment*) retrouver, aller trouver, venir trouver; (*make the acquaintance of*) faire la connaissance de; **come (go) to —** venir (aller) à la rencontre de

memory souvenir *m.*

menu menu *m.*

Meudon *town between Paris and Versailles*

Mexico Mexique *m.*

middle milieu *m.*; **in the — of** au milieu de

midnight minuit *m.*

might pouvoir 225

million million *m.*

mind esprit *m.*; **change one's —** changer d'avis

mine le mien, *etc.*

minute minute *f.*

miser avare *m.*

miserable misérable

Miss Mademoiselle, Mlle *f.*

miss, be missing manquer; **I — him** il me manque

mistaken; be — se tromper

mistress maîtresse *f.*

moment moment *m.*; **at any —** d'un moment à l'autre

Monday lundi *m.*; **—s** le lundi

monastery monastère *m.*

money argent *m.*

money-lender usurier *m.*

month mois *m.*

monthly par mois, mensuellement

more plus, davantage (*see page 62 note 1*); **not any —** ne ... plus

morning matin *m.*; matinée *f.*; **yesterday —** hier matin

most le plus; **(the) — of** la plupart des (*takes plural verb*)

mother mère *f.*, maman *f.*

motive motif *m.*

Mr. Monsieur, M.

Mrs. Madame, Mme

much, very — beaucoup; **as —** autant; **how —** combien; **so —** tant; **too —** trop

museum musée *m.*; **the Army Museum** le Musée de l'Armée

music musique *f.*

must falloir 223, devoir 221 (*see Lesson XI*); **there — be,** il doit y avoir

my mon, ma, mes; **—self** moi-même

N

name nom *m.*; **his — is** il s'appelle

name nommer; **be —ed** s'appeler, se nommer

Napoleon I *emperor of France 1804–1815;* **Napoleon III** *1852–1870*

national national

naturally naturellement

near *adj.* proche; *adv.* près; *prep.* près de

nearly presque
necessary nécessaire; **be —** être nécessaire, falloir 223
necktie cravate *f.*
need besoin *m.*
need, have — of, be in — of avoir besoin de, il me (lui, *etc.*) faut + *noun or pron.*
neither ni *with* ne
never jamais; (*with verb*) ne ... jamais
new nouveau, nouvel, nouvelle; **(brand) —** neuf, neuve
New England la Nouvelle Angleterre
news nouvelles *f. pl.;* **piece of —** une nouvelle
newspaper journal *m.*
next prochain; **— day** le lendemain; **— week** la semaine prochaine; **— year** l'année prochaine
nice gentil(le), bon(ne); **it is — here** on est bien ici, il fait bon ici; **it is — of you (to)** c'est gentil de votre part (de), vous êtes bien gentil (de)
nicely gentiment
night nuit *f.;* (*evening*) soir *m.;* **last —** hier soir
nine neuf
nineteen dix-neuf
no non; *adj.* aucun, pas de, pas un; **— one** personne *m. with* ne
noble noble, beau, bel, belle
noise bruit *m.;* **the least possible —** le moins de bruit possible
noisy bruyant
none (*not any*) pas de; (*not one*) aucun, pas un
nor ni *with* ne
Norman normand
not ne ... pas; **— at all** pas du tout
note noter
nothing rien; (*with verb*) ne ... rien
notice remarquer, s'apercevoir de 220

novel roman *m.*
now maintenant
number (*quantity*) nombre *m.;* (*of a house*) numéro *m.*
nut noix *f.,* noisette *f.*

O

object objet *m.*
obliged obligé de
obtain obtenir 193
occasion occasion *f.*
occasionally de temps en temps
occupy occuper
occur se passer, arriver
o'clock heure *f.;* **one —** une heure
October octobre *m.*
Odéon *m. theatre in Paris*
of de
offer offrir 192
office bureau *m.,* cabinet de travail *m.*
often souvent
oh oh
old vieux, vieil, vieille; ancien(ne); (*in expressions of age*) âgé; **be ten years —** avoir dix ans, être âgé de dix ans; **grow —** vieillir
on sur; (*with pres. part.*) en
once une fois; (*formerly*) autrefois; **at —** tout de suite; **— a week** une fois par semaine
one un, une; *indef. pron.* on
oneself soi
only seulement, ne ... que
open ouvert
open ouvrir 192; **— on** donner sur
opening ouverture *f.;* **— of classes** ouverture des cours
opera opéra *m.*
or ou
orchestra orchestre *m.;* **— seat** fauteuil d'orchestre *m.*
order; in — that *conj.* pour que, afin que; **in — to** pour, afin de
order commander
orient oneself s'orienter

other autre; —s d'autres; **the —s** les autres

ought devoir 221 *in condl. or condl. perf.*

our notre, nos; **—s** le nôtre; **—selves** nous-mêmes

overcoat pardessus *m.*

overcome surmonter, vaincre 217

overheated surchauffé

owe devoir 221

own propre *before noun*

P

pack; **— a trunk** faire une malle

page page *f.*

painting peinture *f.*

palace palais *m.*

papa papa *m.*

paper papier *m.; (newspaper)* journal *m.;* **writing —** papier à lettre

pardon pardon *m.;* **earn one's —** se faire pardonner

pardon pardonner

parent parent *m.*

Paris Paris *m.*

Parisian parisien(ne)

park parc *m.*

partner (*at dance*) cavalier *m.,* danseuse *f.*

pass passer; **— an examination** être reçu (réussir) à un examen

passage (*selection*) morceau *m.,* passage *m.*

passenger voyageur *m.,* passager *m.*

past passé *m.*

patience patience *f.*

patient client *m.,* malade *m.*

pay, pay for payer; **— a visit** faire une visite

pen plume *f.*

pencil crayon *m.*

pension pension *f.*

people (*individuals*) des gens *m. pl.,* des personnes *f. pl.;* (*as a mass*) du monde *m.;* (*nation*) peuple *m.;* (*one, they*) on; (*lower classes*) peuple *m.;* **young —** jeunes gens *m. pl.*

perceive remarquer, apercevoir 220; (*mentally*) s'apercevoir de, remarquer

percent pour-cent *m.*

perfect parfait

perfect perfectionner

perfectly parfaitement

performance représentation *f.,* spectacle *m.*

perhaps peut-être

permit permettre 209

person personne *f.*

Philistine Philistin *m.*

philosopher philosophe *m.*

pick cueillir 187

picnic pique-nique *m.;* **go on a —, have a —** faire un pique-nique

picture tableau *m.,* peinture *f.*

piece morceau *m.*

pity plaindre 203; **it is a —** c'est dommage

place endroit *m.,* lieu *m.;* (*position*) place *f.;* (*seat*) place *f.;* **in the first —** d'abord; **in your —** à votre place; **take —** avoir lieu

place mettre 209, placer

plan plan *m.,* projet *m.*

platform estrade *f.;* (**— and desk of professor in classroom**) chaire *f.*

play (*theatre*) pièce *f.*

play jouer; **— tennis** jouer au tennis

pleasant agréable, bon(ne)

please plaire à 211; **if you —** s'il vous plaît

pleasure plaisir *m.*

pocket poche *f.*

point; **— out** indiquer; **— to** montrer du doigt

pond étang *m.*

poor pauvre

poorly mal

porter (*at station*) facteur *m.*

possible possible
postal postal; — **card** carte postale *f.*
poster affiche *f.*
post-office bureau de poste *m.*
postpone remettre 209
potato pomme (de terre) *f.*
pound livre *f.*
practical pratique
practice (*of lawyer*) étude *f.*
prefer préférer, aimer mieux
prepare préparer
presence présence *f.*
present cadeau *m.*
present présenter
pretty joli
prevent empêcher
preventive préventif(ve)
prince prince *m.*
principal (*of lycée*) proviseur *m.*; (*of girl's lycée*) directrice *f.*
prison prison *f.*
prize prix *m.*
proclaim proclamer
produce produire 199, causer; (*a play*) représenter
professor professeur *m.* (*referring to man or woman*)
program programme *m.*
promise promettre 209
propose proposer, offrir 192
proposition proposition *f.*
provided that pourvu que
put mettre 209; — **on** mettre, (*of shoes*) mettre, chausser; — **out** (*inconvenience*) déranger; **be — out with** en vouloir à, être fâché avec *or* contre

Q

quarter quart *m.*; (*section of city*) quartier *m.*; — **of an hour** un quart d'heure; **Latin —** Quartier Latin
queen reine *f.*
question question *f.*

quietly doucement, tranquillement, sans faire de bruit
quite (*entirely*) tout, tout à fait; (*rather*) assez

R

radio T.S.F. (= téléphonie sans fil) *f.*, radio *f.*
rain pluie *f.*; **in the —** sous la pluie
rain pleuvoir 224; — **in torrents** pleuvoir à verse
raise lever
rapidly rapidement
rather (*preferably*) plutôt; (*somewhat*) assez; — **than** plutôt que; **I should —** j'aimerais mieux
reach parvenir (à) 194, arriver à
read lire 208
reading-room salle de lecture *f.*
ready prêt
realize comprendre 212
really vraiment, en effet, réellement
reason raison *f.*
recall rappeler, se rappeler (*see page 95 note 1*); — **an invitation to** désinviter
receive recevoir 220; (*welcome*) recevoir, accueillir 187
receiver (*of telephone*) récepteur *m.*
recently récemment, l'autre jour
recognize reconnaître 201
recommend recommander
red rouge
refuse refuser
register (*at a university*) s'inscrire 206, prendre ses inscriptions
regret regretter
reign régner
remain rester
remember se souvenir de 194, se rappeler (*see page 95 note 1*); — **me to** rappelez-moi au bon souvenir de
rent louer

repeat répéter; (*a course*) refaire 207
reply répondre
representative représentant *m.*
republic république *f.*
reputation réputation *f.*
request prier, charger
reserve réserver
reserved *see* seat
residence résidence *f.*, demeure *f.*
rest (*remainder*) reste *m.;* the — of you vous autres
restaurant restaurant *m.*
retort réplique *f.;* a good —! bien répliqué!
return (*come back*) revenir 194; (*go back*) retourner; (*go, return or come back home*) rentrer; (*give back*) rendre
rich riche
rid; get — of se débarrasser de
ride promenade *f.* (en auto, à bicyclette, *etc.*) ; take a — faire une promenade
right droit *m.*, raison *f.;* all — bien, volontiers; be — avoir raison; — away immédiatement, tout de suite
ring bague *f.*
ring, — the bell sonner; hear a bell —, entendre la sonnerie
rise monter, s'élever; (*get up*) se lever
rival rival *m.*
Riviera (la) *name given to the Mediterranean coast between Marseilles and Spezia*
roast rôti *m.*
roll; call the — faire l'appel
room pièce *f.*, salon *m.*, salle *f.;* bed — chambre *f.;* furnished — chambre meublée; lecture — salle de conférences; — with bath chambre avec bain
rose rose *f.*
round rond
row rang *m.;* in the front — au premier rang

rubbers caoutchoucs *m. pl.*
run courir 186

S

sake, for the — of à cause de
salad salade *f.*
salon salon *m.*
same même
sardine sardine *f.*
satisfied satisfait, content; be — with se contenter de
say dire 205; I —! dites donc!
scarf écharpe *f.*
school école *f.*
scientist savant *m.*
seasick; be — avoir le mal de mer
seasickness mal de mer *m.*
season saison *f.*
seat place *f.*, place assise *f.;* orchestra — fauteuil d'orchestre *m.;* vacant — place libre; get reserved —s prendre des places en location
seat; — oneself s'asseoir 222; be —ed être assis
second second, deuxième
see voir 228; — again revoir
seem sembler
Seine (la) *river of France*
seize saisir
seldom; it is — that il est rare que
sell vendre
send envoyer 184; — for envoyer chercher, faire venir
sense sens *m.*
sentence phrase *f.*
September septembre *m.*
serious sérieux (se)
seriously sérieusement
serve servir 188
service service *m.*
set the table mettre le couvert
seven sept
seventeen dix-sept
seventh septième
several plusieurs

share part *f.*
sharp (*of time*) précis; **at 5 o'clock** — à 5 heures précises
she elle
shop boutique *f.*, magasin *m.*; — **window** devanture *f.*, vitrine *f.*
short court; **cut** — couper court à
shout crier
show montrer
shrewd malin, fin
sick malade; **get** — tomber malade
side côté *m.*; **on all** —s de tous côtés; **on both** — des deux côtés
sign affiche *f.*, écriteau *m.*, pancarte *f.*
silence silence *m.*; **in** — en silence
silent silencieux (se); **be** — se taire 211; garder le silence, rester silencieux
similar semblable
simple simple
since (*time*) *conj.* depuis que; *prep.* depuis
sincerely sincèrement; — **yours** bien à vous; cordiale poignée de main
single seul
sir monsieur, M. *m.*
sister sœur *f.*
sit (down) s'asseoir 222; — **at table** se mettre (s'asseoir) à table; **be** —**ing** être assis
situated situé
six six
sixty soixante
sleep dormir 188; **go to** — s'endormir
sleepy; be — avoir sommeil
slice tranche *f.*
slight moindre; —est le moindre
slow; be — (*of a watch*) retarder
small petit
smell sentir 188; — **good** sentir bon
smile sourire 214
smoke fumer
snow neige *f.*
so (*before adj. or adv.*) si, tellement; (= *it*) le; (*therefore*) ainsi, donc, par conséquent; (*loose connective beginning a sentence*) ainsi, alors; — **many,** — **much** tant; — **that** *conj.* (*purpose*) afin que, pour que, de sorte que *with subj.*; (*result*) de sorte que *with indic.*; *prep.* afin de, pour *with infin.*
sob sangloter
society société *f.*, beau monde *m.*
solution solution *f.*
some *partitive* de, en; (*a few*) *adj.* quelques; *pron.* quelques-uns; — **one** quelqu'un
something quelque chose *f.*
sometimes quelquefois
son fils *m.*
soon bientôt, tôt; **as** — **as** aussitôt que, dès que; **as** — **as possible** le plus tôt possible
Sorbonne (la) *see French-English vocabulary*
sorry; be — regretter (de), être fâché (de)
soup potage *m.*
South America Amérique du Sud *f.*
space espace *m.*
Spain Espagne *f.*
Spanish espagnol
speak parler; — **to** parler à, adresser la parole à
spectacle spectacle *m.*
spend (*money*) dépenser; (*time*) passer
spite; in — **of** malgré
spoil gâter
square carré
stadium stade *m.*
stairs escalier *m.*; **go up** — monter
stand (up) se trouver, être debout; — **in line** faire (la) queue
standing; be — être debout; se trouver
state état *m.*; **the United** —s les Etats-Unis
stateroom cabine *f.*
station (*railway*) gare *f.*; (*sub-*

way) station *f.;* **St. Lazare —** la Gare St.-Lazare
stay séjour *m.*
stay rester
steak bifteck *m.*, entrecôte *m.*
steamer paquebot *m.*, vapeur *m.*
still toujours, encore
stingy avare
stop *trans.* arrêter; *intrans.* s'arrêter; (*of auto or train*) s'arrêter, stopper
store magasin *m.*
story histoire *f.;* quite a — toute une histoire
stream of water jet d'eau *m.*
street rue *f.*
strict sévère, strict
stroll (along) flâner
student étudiant *m.*, élève *m.;* college — étudiant *m.;* —'s card *see* card; new — nouveau *m.*, nouvelle élève *f.*
study étude *f.*
study étudier
subject sujet *m.*
subside se calmer, s'apaiser
subway métro *m.* (*abbrev. of* chemin de fer métropolitain); — train une rame du métro.
succeed réussir (à)
such tel, telle, pareil(le); — a un tel
suddenly tout à coup, soudain
suffer souffrir 192
suggest suggérer
suit costume *m.*, complet *m.*
suit convenir 194, plaire 211
suitcase valise *f.*
summer été *m.;* — courses cours de vacances *m. pl.*
Sunday dimanche *m.*
superb superbe
suppose supposer; — we go ... si nous allions ... voulez-vous aller . .
sure sûr, certain
surprise surprise *f.*
surprise étonner, surprendre 212

surround entourer
Switzerland Suisse *f.*
syrup sirop *m.*
system système *m.*

T

table table *f.;* at — à table; set the — mettre le couvert
table-cloth nappe *f.*
take prendre 212; (*accompany*) mener, conduire 199; (*carry*) porter; (*require*) falloir (*see* § 80); (*a course*) suivre; — advantage of profiter de; — an examination passer un examen; — charge of se charger de; — from (*a person*) prendre à; — from (*pick up*) prendre dans (sur, *etc.*); — one's seat prendre sa place; — place avoir lieu; — up again reprendre; — a walk (ride) faire une promenade
talentless sans talent
talk parler; (*chat*) causer
talker causeur *m.*
tall grand
Tartuffe (le) *play by Molière*
task tâche *f.*
taste goûter
taxi taxi *m.*
tea thé *m.;* take — prendre le thé; — room salon de thé *m.*
teach apprendre
teacher professeur *m.*
tear down démolir, abattre 196
telephone téléphone *m.*
telephone téléphoner, donner un coup de téléphone à
tell dire 205; (*relate*) raconter
temple temple *m.*
tempt tenter
ten dix
tennis tennis *m.;* play — jouer au tennis
terrace terrasse *f.*
terrible terrible, affreux(se)
text texte *m.*

than que; *(before numerals)* de; *(before infin.)* que de

thank remercier (**for** = de); **— you** merci; **no — you** (non) merci

thanks to grâce à

that *adj.* ce, cet, cette, ces; *indef. pron.* cela, ce; *rel. pron.* qui, que; *conj.* que

the le, la, les

theatre théâtre *m.*

their leur; **—s** le leur

them les, leur; eux, elles

then alors; *(next)* ensuite, puis

there là, y *before verb;* **— is (are)** il y a; *(pointing out)* voilà; **— must be** il doit y avoir

therefore donc, par conséquent

these *adj.* ces; *pron.* ceux-ci, celles-ci

thesis thèse *f.*

they ils, elles; on; eux, elles

thing chose *f.*

think penser, croire 204; **— of** *(have one's thoughts on)* penser à; *(have an opinion of)* penser de

third tiers *m.; adj.* troisième

thirsty; be — avoir soif

thirty trente; **about —** une trentaine

this *adj.* ce, cet, cette, ces; *pron.* celui-ci, celle-ci; **— is** c'est, voici

those *adj.* ces; *pron.* ceux-là, celles-là

thousand mille; *(in dates)* mil; **—s** des milliers *m.*

three trois

throw (away) jeter

Thursday jeudi *m.*

ticket billet *m.; (railway etc.)* billet *m.; (theatre)* place *f.;* **first class —** billet de première classe, première *f.;* **second class —** seconde *f.;* **— window** guichet *m.*

time temps *m.; (hour)* heure *f.; (repetition)* fois *f.;* **another —** une autre fois; **at a better —** plus à propos, à un meilleur moment; **a long —** longtemps; **every — that** toutes les fois que; **in —** à temps; **on —** à l'heure; **have a good —** s'amuser (bien)

timidly timidement

tip pourboire *m.*

tired fatigué

tiring fatigant

to à; *(with cities)* à; *(with fem. sing. names of countries)* en; *(with others)* à; *(in order to)* pour, afin de; *(at the house of)* chez

toast toast *m.,* pain grillé *m.*

today aujourd'hui

together ensemble

tomb tombeau *m.*

tomorrow demain; **— evening** demain soir; **until —** à demain

tonight ce soir

too *(also)* aussi; **—, — many, — much** trop

top sommet *m.; (of tree, etc.)* cime *f.*

Topaze comedy by Marcel Pagnol

touch toucher

Touraine Touraine *f.*

tourist touriste *m.*

towards vers

town ville *f.;* **in —** en ville

train train *m.;* **subway —** rame du métro *f.*

tramway tramway *m.*

translate traduire 199

traveler voyageur *m.*

treatment traitement *m.*

tree arbre *m.*

trip voyage *m.*

triumph triomphe *m.*

true vrai

trunk malle *f.*

try essayer (de), tâcher (de), chercher (à)

Tuesday mardi *m.*

tumult tumulte *m.*

turn *intr.* se tourner; **— around** se retourner

twenty vingt
two deux
typical typique

U

ugly laid
umbrella parapluie *m.*
uncle oncle *m.*
under sous
understand comprendre 212
unfortunately malheureusement
United States Etats-Unis *m. pl.*
university université *f.*
unless *conj.* à moins que *with subjunctive; prep.* à moins de
until *conj.* jusqu'à ce que (que alone, after attendre) *with subjunctive; prep.* jusqu'à
upon sur
uproar vacarme *m.*
upset bouleversé
up to jusqu'à
urge engager (à)
us nous
use se servir de 188, employer; get —d to se faire à, s'accoutumer à
usher ouvreuse *f.*
usually d'ordinaire, généralement

V

vacant libre; — seat place libre *f.*
vacation vacances *f. pl.*
vaccine vaccin *m.*
valise valise *f.*
vanilla vanille *f.;* — cream crème à la vanille *f.*
vegetable légume *m.*
very très, bien; *adj.* même (*placed after noun*)
view vue *f.*
visit visite *f.;* pay a — faire une visite à
visit (*persons*) faire une visite à; (*things*) visiter
visitor visiteur *m.*
volume volume *m.*

W

wait (for) attendre; keep —ing faire attendre
waiter garçon *m.*
walk promenade *f.*
walk aller à pied, marcher; take (go for) a — se promener, faire une promenade
want vouloir 229, désirer
warm chaud; be — (*of persons*) avoir chaud; (*of weather*) faire chaud
wash laver
waste perdre
watch montre *f.*
watch (*look at*) regarder
water eau *f.;* charged — eau gazeuse, eau de Seltz; running — eau courante
way (*road*) route *f.*, chemin *m.;* (*means*) moyen *m.;* by the — à propos; on the — en chemin; on my — back en revenant; any — quand même, en tout cas
we nous
wear porter
weather temps *m.;* fair — le beau temps; be fine — faire beau
Wednesday mercredi *m.*
week semaine *f.*, huit jours; next — la semaine prochaine; once a — une fois par semaine; two —s quinze jours
weep pleurer
welcome accueillir 187
well bien; —! eh bien!, (*surprise*) tiens!
well-known connu
what *interrog. adj.* quel; *interrog. pron.* que? quoi?; (*asking for a definition*) qu'est-ce que c'est que . . . ?; *rel. pron.* ce qui, ce que; *exclam.* quoi! comment! — a quel; — is his name? comment s'appelle-t-il?
whatever tout ce qui, tout ce que; quoi que + *subjunctive;* quel que

+ *subjunctive* (*see* § 154, 4)
when, whenever quand, lorsque; (*interrog.*) quand?
where où
whether si
which *adj.* quel; *pron.* qui, que, lequel; — **one** lequel
while (*time*) pendant que; en *with present participle;* (*although*) quoique *with subjunctive;* tout en *with present participle;* (*whereas*) tandis que
white blanc, blanche
who qui
whoever quiconque, celui qui, qui que + *subjunctive* (*see* § 154, 4)
whole tout, entier, entière
whom *interrog.* qui; *rel.* que, lequel
whose *interrog.* à qui; *rel.* dont, duquel
why pourquoi; *exclam.* mais; *conj.* mais; — **not?** pourquoi pas?
widow veuve *f.*
will, be —**ing** vouloir (bien)
willingly volontiers
wind vent *m.;* **gust of** — coup de vent *m.*
window fenêtre *f.;* (*of a shop*) devanture *f.*, vitrine *f.*
wine vin *m.*
wish désirer, *condl. of* vouloir 229
wit esprit *m.*

with avec, chez
without *conj.* sans que; *prep.* sans
woman femme *f.*
wonder se demander
word mot *m.;* (*spoken*) parole *f.*
work travail *m.;* (*of author*) œuvre *f.*
work travailler
worse *adj.* pire, plus mauvais
worth; be — valoir 227
wrap manteau *m.*
write écrire 206
writer écrivain *m.*
writing-paper papier à lettre *m.*
wrong; be — avoir tort

Y

year an *m.;* année *f.;* **last** — l'année dernière; **next** — l'année prochaine
yellow jaune; **turn** — jaunir
yes oui; (*after negative assertion*) si; — **I do** mais si
yet encore
yesterday hier
you tu, te, toi, vous; *indef.* on
young jeune; — **people** jeunes gens *m. pl.*
your votre, vos; —**self** vous-même; —**s** le vôtre

INDEX

Unless preceded by *p.* (page) all numbers refer to paragraphs.

à, before infinitive, 161, 3
  adjec. or noun + à before infinitive, 162
  adjec. + à + infin., 162, 164
  with names of countries, 7, 2
  with names of cities, 9
adjectives
  agreement of, 19, 20
  as adverb, 95
  comparison of, 27, 29
  demonstrative, 84
  double forms in masc. sing., 16, 4
  feminine of, 15, 16
  in after a superlative, 28
  indef. adjec., 136–149
  interrogative, 134, 135
  plural of, 17, 18
  position of, 21–24
  position of pred. adjec. in exclamations, 26
  possessive, 110–113
  present participle as, 160
  redundant **ne** after a comparative, 27 note; 67
  superlative of, 28
  with double meaning, 25
  + à + infinitive, 162, 164
  + de + infinitive, 163
adverbs
  adjec. used as, 95
  comparison of, 96
  formation from adjectives, 94
  irregular comparison of, 98
  adverbs of quantity with partitive, 12, 2c
  superlative of, 97
age, expressions of, 123

agent of passive, 48
après with perfect infinitive, 168
après que with past anterior, 79
articles
  forms of def. and indef., 1
  combination with de and à, 1
  agreement of, 2
  use of def. art., 3, 4
  with gen. nouns, 4, 1; 11
  with titles, 4, 2
  with countries, 4, 3
  with nouns of wt. and measure, 4, 4
  with days of week, 4, 5
  with names of languages, 4, 6
  with names of cities, 9
  replacing poss. adj., 113
  with partitive, 12
  omission of def. art., 4, 2a; 5
  after de, 5
  after en, 5, 7
  in partitive, 12, 2
  omission of indef. art., 6
  before pred. noun, 6
assez, pour + infin. after, 166
aussitôt que with future or future perfect, 38
  with past anterior, 79
aucun, negative, 59, 64
  as indefinite, 138
autre, 143, 148
  difference between **un autre** and **encore un**, 143 a
auxiliaries, avoir and être, 44–48
avoidance of subjunctive, 157

bien, adverb of quantity, 12 c

cardinal numbers, table of, 99
  pronunciation of, 100
  taking s, 101
  mil and mille, 102
ce, demonstrative pron., 87, 2
  demonstrative adjec., 84–86
  as subject of être, 68–70
  rel. pron., 91, 127
ceci, 87, 89
cela, 87, 89
celui, etc., as demonstrative pron., 87, 88
  rel. pron., 128
cent, multiples of taking s, 101
certain, 139
cities, *to, at, in* with cities, 9
collectives, 107
commencer par, 167
comparison of adjec., 27, 29
  of adverbs, 96
conditional perfect, 71
conditional sentences, 73
conditional tense, 71
conjunctive pronouns, 52–54
countries, *to, in, into* with names of countries, 7
  from with names of countries, 8
  gender of names of countries, 7 note

dans, with names of countries, 7, 3
date, expressions of, 102, 106, 122
de, adjec. or noun + de before infinitive, 163
  after verbal expressions and adjectival phrases, 12, 3c
  before agent with passive, 48
  combined with def. art., 1, 2
  from with names of countries, 8
  from with names of cities, 9
  infinitive followed by, 161, 2
  with partitive, 12
definite article, *see* articles
demeurer, vivre, habiter, *p. 113*
demonstrative adjec., 84
  agreement of, 85
  with —ci and —là, 86

demonstrative pronoun
  ceci and cela, 87, 89
  ce and il, 68–70
  ce + rel. pron., 91, 127
  forms of, 87
  use of, 88
depuis, 36, 75, 3
devoir, special uses, 74
disjunctive pronouns, 52, 53, 55
dont, use of, 126

empêcher, with redundant ne, 151, note 3
en, with partitive, 13, 14
  with names of countries, 7, 1
  as a pron., 57
  non-agreement of past. part. after, 51
  with present participle, 165
entendre with an infin., 83 note
et used in numbers, 100, 4
être as auxiliary, 45–48
  agreement of past. part. after, 50–51

faire, special uses of, 83
falloir, special uses of, 80
finir par, 167
fractions, 108
future perfect, 37, 38
future tense, 37, 38
  after quand, lorsque, aussitôt que, 38

guère, position of in negations, 61

habiter, vivre, demeurer, *p. 113*

il as subject of être, 68–70
imperfect indicative, 75
  translating *would*, 72, 3
imperfect subjunctive
  substitutes for, 157
  after the conditional, 152 note 4
indefinite adjectives, 136–149
indefinite article, *see* articles
indefinite pronouns, 137–149

infinitive
  verbs followed by à, 161, 3
  verbs followed by de, 161, 2
  after other prepositions, 165–168
  après + perfect infinitive, 168
  as a noun, 169
  for a subordinate clause, 157
  noun or adjec. + à + infinitive, 162
  noun or adjec. + de + infinitive, 163
  par + infinitive, 167
  pour + infinitive, 166
  without following prep., 161, 1
interrogative adjec., 134–135
interrogative pronoun, 130–133
interrogative word order, 30–34

jamais, position of in negation, 61
  meaning *ever,* 59 note

laisser with an infinitive, 83 note
lequel, etc., as interrogative, 131
  as relative, 124
lorsque with future or future perfect, 38

même as an adverb, 142 note
  as indef. pron., 142
mil, 102
mille, 102
moi replacing me, 54, 3a

ne, redundant ne, 27 note, 67, 151 note, 155 note
  in a negation, 59, 60
  ne ... que, position of in a negation, 63
  used without pas, 66
negation
  list of negatives, 59
  ne used without pas, 66
  omission of ne and verb, 65
  position of, 60–64
  redundant ne, *see* ne
n'importe + interrogatives, 149
ni ... ni in partitive construction, 12, 3a

noun clause, subjunctive in, 151
noun + à + infin., 162
  + de + infin., 163
  plural of, 40
  plural of compound nouns, 42
numbers, *see* cardinal, collective, ordinal
numerals, *see* cardinal, collective, ordinal

on, 56, 141
  as substitute for passive, 49
once, 109
order, word order of pronoun objects, 54
  interrogative word order, 30–34
ordinal numbers, 104
  position and agreement, 105
  use of, 106

par before expressions of time, 4 4a
  before agent in passive, 48
  replacing à, 83 note
  after **commencer** and **finir**, 167
participle, *see* past and present
partitive construction, 10–14
pas, position of in negation, 61
  pas un as indefinite, 138
passive voice, 48
  agent with, 48
  substitutes for, 49
past anterior, 79
past definite, 77
past indefinite, 76
past participle, agreement of, 50, 51
personal pronouns
  conjunctive, 52, 54
  disjunctive, 52, 55
  order of conjunctives, 54
personne, position of in negation, 62
  meaning *person,* 59 note
peur, de — que, redundant ne with, 155, 3 note
plupart with de + article, 12, 2c

pluperfect tense, 78
plus, position of in negation, **61**
point, position of in negation, **61**
possessive adjectives, table of, 110
 replaced by def. art., 113
 used to translate *own,* 111, 2
 use of, 111, 112
possessive pronouns, table of, 114
 agreement of, 115
 mine, etc. after être, 116
 a friend of mine, etc., 117
pour + infinitive, 166
 assez, trop + **pour** + infinitive, 166, 3
pouvoir, special uses of, 81
prepositions
 à + infinitive, 161, 162
 adjec. + à + infinitive, 164
 après + perfect infinitive, 168
 de after **quelque chose** and **rien,** 144
 de with partitive, 12
 de + infinitive, 161, 163
 par + infinitive, 167
 pour after **assez** and **trop,** 166
 pour + infinitive, 166
 with names of countries, **7, 8**
 with names of cities, 9
present participle, 159, 160
present tense, 35, 36
 with **depuis,** 36
pronouns, *see* personal, possessive, demonstrative, relative, interrogative
 word order of, 54

quand, with future or future perfect, 38
 with past anterior, **79**
quatre-vingt taking s, 101
quel as inter. adj., 135
quelconque, 145
quelque as indefinite pron., 140
quelque chose followed by **de,** 144
quiconque, 145

rappeler, se — and **se souvenir,** *p. 95*

redundant **ne,** *see* **ne**
reflexive verbs, auxiliary of, **45**
 for passive, 49, 2
 agreement of past part. after, **51**
relative pronouns, 124–129
 compound relatives, 127, **128**
 où, 129
 preceded by **ce,** 91
rien, as subject of a verb, **64**
 followed by **de,** 144
 position of in negation, **61**
 used alone, 65

savoir, special uses of, 82
sembler with indic. or subj., 151, note
should and *would,* translated by **devoir,** 72, 1; 74
 as conditional, as habitual act, as volition, 71, 72, 73
si in conditional sentences, **73**
 meaning *whether,* 73, 1
soi, 56
souvenir, se — and **se rappeler,** *p. 95*
subjunctive mood
 avoidance of, 157
 in adjective clause, 154
  after a general negation, 154, 3
  antecedent qualified by superlative, 154, 2
  indefinite antecedent, 154, 1
  with compound rel., 154, 4
 in adverbial clauses, 155
 in noun clauses, 151
 in principal clauses, 156
 replaced by other constructions, 157
 sequence of tenses, 152, 153, 158
 significance of, 150
 substitutes for, 157
 with redundant **ne,** 151 note, 155 note

tel, use of, 146
tenses, *see* present, imperfect, etc.
 sequence of in subjunctive, **152, 153, 158**

than, 27, 96, 1
  before an infinitive, 27, 1
time, expressions of, 118–121
toi replacing **te,** 54, 3a
tout, 147
trop, pour + infinitive after, 166

l'un . . . l'autre, 148

verbs, auxiliary of, 44–46
  agreement of past part. after, 50, 51
voir with an infinitive, 83 note
vouloir compared with the future, 39
  compared with the conditional, 72, 2
vivre, demeurer, habiter, *p. 113*

what, translation of, **127, 132, 135**
whatever followed by subjunctive, 154, 4
whether translated by **si,** 73, 1
whoever followed by subjunctive, 154, 4
whose as a relative, 126
  as an interrogative, 133
word order, interrogative, 30–34
  of pronoun objects, 54
would and *should,* 72
  would translated by imperfect, 72, 3
  translated by **vouloir,** 72, 2

y as pronominal adverb, 58

BRUNO

La France à Travers les
Siècles
by Gifford
Macmillan

L'Ile Dernière 40 mi west of
grand Ile

along the Gulf-shore
~~Possoto wharf~~